PENG

IF IT'S MONDAY I<s> MUST BE MAD</s>

Srinath Perur's writing—essays, reportage, travelogues, translations—has appeared in various publications including *India Today*, the *Guardian*, *Fountain Ink*, *Granta*, *n+1*, *Hakai* and the *Outlook Traveller*.

Perur is the English translator of Vivek Shanbhag's Kannada novella *Ghachar Ghochar*. He lives in Bengaluru when he is not travelling.

If It's Monday It Must Be Madurai

A CONDUCTED TOUR OF INDIA

SRINATH PERUR

PENGUIN BOOKS

An imprint of Penguin Random House

PENGUIN BOOKS

USA | Canada | UK | Ireland | Australia
New Zealand | India | South Africa | China | Singapore

Penguin Books is part of the Penguin Random House group of companies
whose addresses can be found at global.penguinrandomhouse.com

Published by Penguin Random House India Pvt. Ltd
4th Floor, Capital Tower 1, MG Road,
Gurugram 122 002, Haryana, India

Penguin
Random House
India

First published in Viking by Penguin Books India 2013
Published in Penguin Books by Penguin Random House India 2018

Copyright © Srinath Perur 2013

All photographs, unless otherwise mentioned, are by the author.

ISBN 9780143417774

Typeset in Sabon Roman by SÜRYA, New Delhi
Printed at Repro India Limited

www.penguin.co.in

Contents

Contents

INTRODUCTION

The official at Immigration, Mr Pandey, looked glumly at me as I told him why I was going on a conducted tour to Uzbekistan. 'If you're a writer,' he said, unconvinced, 'then why are you travelling with a group?' Serious travellers, and certainly travel writers, look upon the conducted tour as the lowliest form of travel. Even travelling with a friend or two can invite contempt. Jonathan Raban, for instance, warns anyone considering travelling with company: 'You're never going to see anything; you're never going to meet anybody; you're never going to hear anything. Nothing is going to happen to you.' The remonstrance is all the more applicable to writers: according to Paul Theroux, 'In the best travel books the word *alone* is implied on every exciting page.' I was trying to write a travel book entirely through conducted tours, a book in which I'd *never* be travelling alone. Mr Pandey's was only the latest voice in a chorus of sceptics, but he'd caught me off guard. I mumbled something about travel being cheaper this way, and he let me pass. But it was a rattled writer who rejoined his thirty-three travel companions.

I'd managed to steer clear of conducted tours until early 2011, when a magazine assignment took me on a week-long bus-tour of Tamil Nadu. How bad could it

1

be, I'd asked myself before going. I had my answer before the first day was up: the tour was wrist-slittingly dull, the boredom so comprehensive that it occasionally transmuted itself into mild hysteria to redeem itself. I was with a group of retirees, and with faithful monotony we went from temple to temple seeking priority darshan. My fellow travellers were set in their ways, and there were no conversations to be had, only discourses to flee from. It didn't help, either, that I'd had to surrender all sense of volition: I went where the guide asked me to go, stayed there exactly as long as I was told to.

Even as I longed to break free, I began to notice that a conducted tour by definition offers something that solitary travel cannot: other people, and the opportunity to know them. There's close and sustained contact with one's fellow tourists; they stand out against the backdrop of new places; the exertions of travel can bring to the surface aspects of character that are otherwise hidden; being away from the responsibilities of work and family, with all travel arrangements taken care of, people tend to relax, grow expansive and reveal themselves for who they are (or at least who they think they are).

My next assignment turned out to be a conducted tour as well, this time a trip across Europe in a bus full of fellow Indians. We ate Indian food throughout, watched Hindi films on the bus, played *antakshari*, and in between only fleetingly ventured into Europe. We'd quickly take a photograph, tick the place off our lengthy itinerary, and return to the mobile little India our group constituted. If it had to be done in such a spectacularly passive fashion, then why travel at all?

These tours often stand for far more than the travel itself. A strong element of middle-class aspiration is at work, especially in overseas tours. Conducted tours allow for the conquest of the exalted 'foreign' without much effort or discomfort. This is travel as a symbol of leisure and economic sufficiency, and the conducted tour is now a rite of passage among the middle class. For those who have retired and seen to it that their children are settled, or are otherwise considered to have 'finished off their responsibilities', the conducted tour is the new *vanaprasthashrama*—with the real work of life done, one can turn one's attention to frills such as travel. Across all age groups, travel signals success and affluence, and is displayed to one's peers through endless slide-shows and albums of photographs. Just as Indians in previous decades posed for photographs with their telephones and TVs, we now picture ourselves against the Eiffel Tower or the London Eye, or at least the gopuram of the Madurai Meenakshi temple.

For those who are passionate about travel, it is rendered far more affordable with a conducted tour. This is particularly true of foreign travel, which can prove ruinous if done independently on the Indian rupee. For those who live with an extended family, the conducted tour may temporarily offer freedoms not easily available at home: spending time in the company of one's spouse on one's own terms; being able to dress as one wants. For some it is also about socializing (as with my uncle, an inveterate conducted tourist, who goes with the same tour company every time because he knows he'll be travelling with 'people like us'). For youngsters, especially girls with overprotective elders at home, an organized tour may be the only way to receive permission to travel. For many, the wide world of airports, officious Immigration officers, unfamiliar food, and foreign customs is simply too much to navigate, and they take conducted tours precisely because nothing is going to happen to them.

It may be that we are cautiously coming upon individualism, or that many more now have a disposable income—whatever the reasons, Indians are increasingly looking to travel, and their chosen way of doing so is the conducted tour. There has simultaneously been an emphasis on developing tourism, and the last decade has seen an explosion in the variety of tours on offer in India—tours targeted at the young, or foreign tourists, or farmers, or women, or the elderly. Destinations can range from villages in India to almost any place in the world. Travel themes—in addition to the usual sightseeing and pilgrimage—now include music, adventure, ecology, food, sex, photography, and much more. If you can think of a reason to travel, there's probably a tour company that offers it in a convenient package. The kinds of tours being offered and the people going on them capture something particular about these times. Thus the idea of a book about India and Indians written through the medium of conducted tours.

For the purposes of this book, a conducted tour is a travel experience with a fixed itinerary, orchestrated by someone else, and undertaken in a group. I tried to pick tours that between them covered a variety of themes, destinations, modes of transport, and fellow tourists. As

I went on more tours, I found I was also unknowingly testing the limits of what this format of travel had to offer: the last couple of tours, such as the pilgrimage to Pandharpur, or the Shodh Yatra that takes people on a walking tour of villages in search of traditional knowledge, were nothing like the Tamil Nadu and Europe tours I had started with. The ten tours written about in this book range in duration from three hours to three weeks, in cost from a few hundred rupees to over a lakh. They were all undertaken in the company of different groups in the years 2011 and 2012. Two of the tours are to places outside India, but in the company of Indians; a couple are with foreigners in India; the rest with Indians in India. Many of my fellow travellers appear here under names that are not their own.

Travelling for this book turned out to be more fun and educative than I had expected. For the first time in my life I rode a camel, drew water from a well, slept under a truck, cleaned my teeth with a neem twig, went on a substantial pilgrimage, and danced to an item song. I rediscovered music, took a (not entirely planned) dip in the Kerala backwaters, visited a slum, and went to parts of India I had always wanted to see. Among the hundreds of people I ran into were farmers, renunciates, medicine-men, musicians and sex workers. If travel is about new experiences, places and people, about inward shifts as well as geographical displacement, then it turns out that travel is after all possible through conducted tours. And should Mr Pandey happen to read this book, I trust he will agree that it is not entirely outrageous for a writer to want to travel with a group.

1
THE GRACE OF GOD

Our tour bus

This is my first time on a conducted tour: eight days in a Tamil Nadu Tourism bus, moving south from Chennai in short hops along the coast to Kanyakumari, and back via Madurai and Trichy. Our tour guide is the industrious Mr N, who will prove ever-willing to provide unscheduled stops at places of religious significance.

I am on assignment for *Outlook Traveller* magazine along with photographer Jyothy Karat. She and I are by far the youngest of the twenty-one tourists on board. The rest are between fifty and sixty-five years old, many just-retired with 'settled' children. The bulk of our group is Telugu speaking—a few couples plus eight or ten members from a single family. There is an immediate division along linguistic lines with all the Telugu speakers forming a solid group. The outliers are Jyothy and I, a Bengali couple and an NRI woman who looks remarkably like Johnny Lever.

The men on the tour have worked in banks and public sector undertakings, one has been a headmaster. The women are mostly housewives. All this is revealed in a 'self-introduction' session organized by Mr N after we leave Chennai. We take turns to lurch up to the mike at the front of the coach to state—Mr N is always exact in his directions—'name, place, what you are doing, and designation'. The men, to a man, speak for their wives. The Bengali gent delineates his identity in three crisp sentences: 'I am from Calcutta. I am a Bengali. I am a retired government servant.' Ms Lever says, 'I've left my husband and come to tour India.' The other women burst into applause, as eloquent a self-introduction as any. They also proceed to ignore Ms Lever for the rest of the tour.

Mr N has been a tour guide for close to twenty years, and he knows his flock eerily well. He's brought along a stool that acts as a much-needed additional step while boarding the bus. He declares ad hoc restroom breaks that always have grateful takers. If he announces a medical shop, there are always people who've run out of their pills. It had struck me as odd that he specifically asked us to mention *designation* while introducing ourselves, but a day into the tour I'm beginning to see how much it matters. The headmaster is not simply a teacher, the Regional Manager did not just work in a bank. The official persona still lingers about the men, and travel takes the aspect of an inspection tour. 'How was the food?' one man asks me after lunch. I tell him I enjoyed it; what did he think of it? He grimaces and shakes his head: 'Not up to the mark.' Every aspect of the tour is up for comparison and assessment over the next week: food, the coach, rooms, the driving, sunsets, temples, even the gods.

In the bus I sit at a window seat near the back. The Regional Manager takes the aisle seat in front of me, reclines his backrest, and asks through the gap, 'What do you write about?' I tell him. 'Economics is more interesting,' he says, and embarks on an epic monologue. I learn, among other things, that the national savings rate is down from 23 per cent to 21 per cent and that the high point of RM's professional life involved seeing the Allahabad GM pulled up for dozing off in a training session. I make strategic seating choices for the rest of the trip, but am cornered in various other places. One morning after breakfast RM comes up to me and points at Jyothy, who is taking pictures in the distance. 'I have thought of a poetic name for your friend,' he says. 'She is Lens Lass.'

Lens Lass is less than half the age of the next youngest person on the tour (myself excepted), and realizes right on Day 1 that this tour may not have much to offer by way of fun. On the first evening of the tour we go boating in the mangroves of Pitchavaram, down the coast from Pondy. Seven of us in one rowboat, the ride is proving sedate, even somnolent, when the headmaster cries out to the boatman, 'Slow! Slow!' LL confesses she is feeling trapped. It doesn't help that Ms Lever is developing a motherly crush on her, and even attempts to create a rift between us. LL is advised to be wary of me: 'He appears to be a good person, but in this world you never know.'

Throw a stone in Tamil Nadu and chances are it'll be one chipped off an old temple. Our tour itinerary tries to squeeze in as many of those as possible and our typical day is a blur of temples. In addition, Mr N stops at temples that are not on the itinerary with the preamble: 'Who wants a bonus point?' For the record, the under-fifty lot never once raise their hands, but the bus stops anyway. In addition to Mr N's bonus points, there is a map-cum-booklet about Tamil Nadu temples being passed around which results in requests for detours and halts that Mr N often grants.

I enjoy the odd visit to a temple, but this rushing from one temple to another is a bit much for me, and it's taken me by surprise since this was supposed to be a general tour of Tamil Nadu. In addition, I'm accustomed to travelling with far more freedom, an idea that doesn't exist on a tour like this with Mr N telling us where to leave our footwear, where to queue up for special darshan, which shrines to skip, and exactly how long to take before returning to the bus. This lack of agency combined with the fact that serial temple visiting is not my thing at all quickly makes me miserable. The day passes in long, dispirited intervals with occasional near-hallucinatory episodes during which everything suddenly seems absurdly comical.

In temples the dutiful LL prefers to take photographs in the outer halls and corridors rather than pay her respects along with the others. This causes Ms Lever no small amount of worry for LL's soul. At the Meenakshi temple in Madurai, she takes ten rupees from LL to make a proxy offering. At Suchindram she tells LL, 'Because you didn't come in I went down on my knees and prayed for you.' She also starts carrying an empty Tic Tac box that she fills with sacred ash to be applied on LL's forehead. LL is much taller than Ms Lever, and this renders frontal attack impossible. Ms Lever therefore chooses ambush, and for a week the temples of Tamil Nadu are filled with squeals and clouds of ash that settle to reveal a daubed and distraught Lens Lass.

Also having trouble with temples is the Bengali gent. 'They're all out to make money,' he says, every time he sees a board announcing ticket rates for expedited darshan. 'Does God love me more if I pay him?' At Rameswaram we are waiting together while the rest of the bus has water poured on them from twenty-two different wells. He can barely conceal his disgust as a chubby priest passes by. 'Look at that health,' he says. 'It's from all that ghee bought with people's money.' Most of my conversations with him happen at the entrance to temples. 'I am a tourist, not a pilgrim,' is his refrain as he refuses to enter and stands outside like a third *dwarapalaka*. It is on one of these occasions that I discover what he probably reveres. He grows animated when I mention Bengal's contribution to Indian public life in the days before Independence. 'Has there been another saint like Bibekanando?' he asks, with debate-hall flourish. 'Another poet like Tagore? Another freedom fighter like Bose?'

The present is, alas, less glorious. In addition to temples, the Bengali gent is also having trouble with the food. On

Day 1, he seems pleased as he calls home and reports in a ringing voice what he ate as part of a South Indian breakfast, and later in the day, a South Indian lunch. By breakfast, Day 3, he wants bread and butter, which is not part of the tour's menu. The restaurant says they don't have bread, and it is only after the Bengalis leave that the European couple nearby get their toast. He is also unhappy that the group eats only at restaurants that are either 'pure' or 'classic' vegetarian. We are about to enter one such place for lunch when he points at the restaurant next door with a board listing Chettinad meat preparations. 'Why can't we go there?' he asks me. I tell him he should just eat there if he feels like it, but he wants to get his money's worth from the tour, even if it means enforced vegetarianism.

It's 'national integration day' according to Mr N, a day on which we visit in succession the Vaitheeswaran temple, the dargah at Nagore, and the church at Velankanni, all shrines believed to work wonders for one's health. A good number among us are overweight, and as we go wheezing, gasping, shuffling, waddling down the long corridors at Vaitheeswaran temple, it seems evident that our health issues and after-breakfast pill-popping can be attributed to heaped plates and a general lack of exercise. In any case there's a cute tonic ceremony to be performed here: small packets of salt, pepper and jaggery are being sold, and one circles them ritually around one's head before emptying them. Previously, Mr N tells us, the contents would be cast into the temple tank, but as the temple's reputation grew the water ended up such a sticky mess that there are now separate tubs for the purpose. A dip in the tank is supposed to cure almost any disease, though I wonder how it's faring now with the reduced condiment levels.

According to Mr N the temple is particularly renowned for its ability to cure abdominal ailments. It certainly worked in the case of a friend of mine who, as a child, had been missing school often owing to an unbearable pain in his stomach. Doctors had been of no use, so his worried parents took him to Vaitheeswaran Koil and had his head shaved. My friend then decided it was easier to go to school than to subject himself to escalating forms of alternative treatment. The stomach ache disappeared, and a family that swears by Vaitheeswaran Koil was born. I hope there's more in it for the woman rolling on the ground, outstretched hands joined in supplication, struggling to finish a lap of the considerable temple perimeter. A grim matronly figure, either mother or mother-in-law I surmise, gives her a hefty shove now and then as if she were a gas cylinder. Nearby, at Velankanni, we see further self-mortification as pilgrims (though none from our coach) walk nearly a kilometre on their knees to the site of a Marian apparition.

At the Nagore dargah Mr N asks me not to enter the innermost part of the shrine. 'They'll think you're a foreigner and ask you for money,' he says, looking at my jeans and ponytail. But everyone else is passing through without trouble, so I go in nevertheless. Mr N is right, as always. A boy notices me and tells a scholarly looking old man in Tamil, 'Make him sit.' The old man looks up from the floor and authoritatively pats the ground next to him, but I walk away.

The health quotient aboard the coach plummets as the tour progresses. Leg pain is endemic. Vomit-streaked windows and a new-found asceticism at buffet tables hint at gastric strife. There are multiple contenders for sleeping on the last seat of the bus while the able-bodied are out. On the penultimate day, in Trichy, Mr N tells us there are 400 steps to the Rockfort temple, and those of us who are unsure about the ascent can remain in the bus. More than half the group do not budge from their seats.

There is also an accident on the bus. Some people have shrewdly been buying five-litre containers of water to refill smaller bottles, and one such container falls on someone's head from the luggage rack. There is blood, a trip to hospital, stitches, a precautionary scan. For this to happen after visiting a couple of dozen temples, after covering multiple bases by going to three shrines of different religions that deal specifically with bodily well-being, might easily make one wonder if anyone up there is listening.

Divine deafness apart, it can be questioned if even the general psycho-spiritual effects of pilgrimage are preserved in what essentially amounts to devotional pub-hopping: roaring from temple town to temple town in a comfortable bus, buying fifty-rupee tickets to beat the queues, and paying quick obeisance at a couple of the more important shrines in the temple complex. I can see how pilgrimage might work in other circumstances: the effort of long travel can break the rut of the mundane; time spent in such travel can be calming or introspective; one's sense of empathy can be jogged by the opportunity to practise charity and the feeling of belonging to a wider, interconnected community can be reinforced; shrines can uplift with their use of space, architecture and iconography; a journey of faith can have a joyous culmination in a temple. But here, there simply isn't time for any of that. The group is only being passively herded about, its palms coming together reflexively before everything it is shown.

In Madurai the group joins palms before a scale model of the temple complex. In Rameswaram, it does so in front of an empty stone platform on which Gandhi's ashes were briefly placed before being dispersed in the sea. At Chidambaram there is the *rahasya*—Shiva's embodiment as space. Mr N doesn't think much of it. He tells us: 'The men have to take off their shirts and banians before going in. You have to wait in front of a yellow curtain. They will open it after some time and there will be nothing behind it. If you want to see this you can pay fifty rupees and go.' A little later the group joins palms before nothing at all and rushes back to the bus.

One of the men in the group shoos away a beggar outside a temple. He tells me, somewhat sheepishly, 'They will actually have more money than us.' The area just outside every temple teems with beggars, and our group displays an entire catalogue of responses over the length of the tour: the stone-faced head-shaking while avoiding eye contact; the annoyed clucking that makes out the beggar to be unspeakably rude for impinging upon one's conscience; the production of osculatory noises to show that one is fundamentally sympathetic, but unwilling to shell out owing to philosophical considerations; the feigning of total blindness and deafness; a sort of low-grade kabaddi directed at escaping multiple little hands that want to touch one's feet or tug at one's clothes. Some capitulate on a case-by-case basis, favouring the more severely deformed. I randomly give away any coins I might have, but there seem to be no completely guilt-free routes of escape.

The Regional Manager tells me that in the end it is poor people who are responsible for being poor. There are schemes that allow them to rise from poverty, and he has himself been in charge of disbursing agricultural loans. But those who take these loans seldom use them fruitfully. They drink it away or spend the money on a daughter's wedding. These loans are often waived and are a drain on the taxpayer. The poor will rise by participating in the economy. Those with money will consume, production will rise accordingly, and opportunities will be created. But many of the poor are simply not interested or capable of participating in the economy, and the nation suffers. I ask him if this is not simplistic—what about cultural factors that prevent people from changing their modes of livelihood overnight, or the marginalization of people when governments align themselves with the interests of those who are already wealthy. For example, I ask him, what is a farmer to do when his land is acquired for a large project of some sort and he is resettled unfairly or not at all? According to RM, this sort of thing happens quite rarely. These people are very shrewd, he says, and many of these cases actually involve someone playing the media or the government for some easy money.

In the space of a few encounters, RM has revealed himself to be a Hindu nostalgist. He is genuinely sad that there are practices and traditions of great value that are being ignored today. Chanting Om, for example, will even dissolve small brain tumours. He also hints that pretty much all religion, culture and civilization in the world had a Hindu point of origin. 'We have to think,' he tells me, 'why Christ sounds so much like Krishna.' He points out similarities between Latin and Sanskrit— the words for father and mother in the languages are respectively *pater* and *pitr*, *mater* and *matr*. I manage to interrupt with something about the languages having a common origin, but he cuts me off with a disgusted look: 'We should study everything properly, not simply say something.' His cornering of me turns out not to be casual. 'You are a writer,' he tells me. 'You should inform people about these things. We should keep young people in the grip of our culture so that they can never leave.'

RM is also conflicted in all sorts of ways. 'We have lost our culture in India,' he tells me, 'but these days the Indians are following according to the Vedas in the US.' It turns out his children live in the US, his grandchild is a US citizen, and even as he says 'We must make our nation and our country proud,' he is wearing a neatly pressed 'New York City' T-shirt.

Our group spends every night in a different Hotel Tamil Nadu. Finding oneself in a new room every night quickly becomes disorienting. The rooms themselves are quite comfortable, but each one has its own idiosyncrasies. The TV remote in Trichy can only change channels in descending order, and in what is possibly a life-changing insight I learn I'm only interested in a channel after it has blinked by. Thanjavur has that rare thing—a palace turned into a budget hotel. The palace part is expressed in bathrooms so large that not just bathroom singing, but bathroom dancing and even bathroom middle-distance running present themselves as viable diversions. My own eye-stinging, slip-sliding debut in these activities occurs when the shower tap comes off and skitters away while I am soaped from head to toe. In Kanyakumari the shower taps are firm enough, but they call for the rotational finesse of a safe-cracker if they are to yield water that isn't too hot or too cold. A midnight swarm of mosquitoes descends in another room. Elsewhere, there is a temperamental ceiling fan that starts with a violent jerk only when its regulator is positioned in a secret, narrow band. In one bathroom, a wash basin tap spins droplessly before becoming a water cannon. The cumulative effect is a constant hum of mild dread that makes it impossible to be completely at ease even in a perfectly comfortable room.

Mr N is quite the tyrant when it comes to keeping the time. This is understandable when it comes to reporting to the bus in the morning, or with instructions of the 'be back in twenty minutes' sort, but he also dictates at what time we are to have dinner from the common buffet at the Hotels Tamil Nadu. One evening I'm losing an argument with a shower when there is pandemonium in my room beyond—the bell buzzes, the phone rings, there is loud banging on the door. I rush out fearing the worst, but it is only Mr N telling me I'm ten minutes late for dinner.

The only other slackers are the Bengali couple. But they are hardened veterans of conducted tourism who have seen off many a Mr N. I tell them I'm from Bangalore and they go, 'Ah, BangaloreMysoreOoty. We've seen it.' They have the air of conquest that habitués of conducted tours seem to acquire: 'We've done the North East. We've finished Rajasthan.' Only Himachal Pradesh seems to have put up any resistance: 'You can't do it in one tour. It took us two tours to complete HP.'

Kodaikanal, Day 6, is the only day without temples. Mr N has to explain that 'we are going to enjoy the climate and atmosphere'. We gaze listlessly from a couple of viewing points, visit a shopping centre, and we have finished Kodaikanal. We must return to the hotel by six lest the cold get to anyone and worsen the health situation. Lens Lass and I cannot take it any more. (My notes for the day read: 'Breakdown from sheer boredom.') We plot a temporary escape. We will go into town in the evening, check email, have a beer and eat at a restaurant that is not Hotel Tamil Nadu. Ms Lever has evidently been eavesdropping. She makes barbed comments about bottles, tells LL in a betrayed tone, 'You think I don't know anything, but I know exactly who you are.' The next morning at breakfast, perhaps in apology, Ms Lever places a marigold plucked from the hotel's garden next to a speechless LL's camera.

RM has also been tuning in, judging by the way he enters conversations midstream with complete context.

It is clear that Lens Lass and I are the subject of much curiosity on the bus. Much of this curiosity seems to be born of a moral horror at the idea of a man and a woman travelling like this on work. At one point Lens Lass and I have been chatting about relationships while RM is two rows ahead in a fully reclined seat. There is little salacious content in our conversation, but at the next available opportunity RM decides to lecture LL about the wretched plight of single mothers he has seen in the US. It quickly becomes clear that RM believes single mothers are single mothers because they don't know who the father of their child is. I am awed that he is able to imagine a life of such staggering promiscuity. On the last day of the tour, LL tells one of the women that we are staying the night in Chennai and leaving for Bangalore in the morning. She asks LL, 'Whose house are you staying at in Chennai?' LL says we will stay at a hotel, and the woman is visibly shocked. (But we have been staying at hotels all along. Perhaps the shock is due to LL being unchaperoned after the tour ends.)

On Day 1 Mr N says, 'The success of our tour depends on the cooperation of four things: the coach, the coach pilot, myself and the respected tourist.' These elements have cooperated and the tour ends on the evening of Day 7 in Trichy. The next day is to be spent on the road to Chennai (though it'll turn out Mr N can't resist a couple of bonus points en route). Mr N gives a short valedictory address beginning, 'By the grace of God, we have completed our tour successfully.'

That evening in Kodaikanal, each time LL and I ask for the Internet place we're told 'Keep going up', and the road only seems to get steeper. When we get there the power goes out, and I chat with the owner for a while. It turns out it is mostly the expensive star hotels that have a restaurant-with-bar, but there's always the government-run Hotel Tamil Nadu. We're back where we started. But those couple of hours out in the bracing cold, with no set time to return, with no fixed path to take, and not a temple in sight, remain my most pleasant memory of the tour.

2
SAARE JAHAAN SE ACHHA

A tour group in Drubba, Germany, waits for a cuckoo clock to chime

The Victoria-Jungfrau Grand Hotel at Interlaken has in its 150-year history hosted guests such as Mark Twain and the Emperor of Brazil (there used to be one, apparently). But it has only ever honoured two people by naming suites after them. One is Louis XVI. The other is Yash Chopra. Outside the hotel on the town's main street, the Höheweg, is a plaque dated April 2011 that marks the appointment of Chopra as an ambassador of Interlaken for featuring the area in his films and bringing in large numbers of Indian tourists. I get a sense of just how many at Jungfraujoch—'The Top of Europe'—where the Bollywood Restaurant serves Indian meals at an altitude of almost 3500 metres. A board lists no fewer than sixteen Indian tour groups expected for lunch. These are all bus tours of Europe that have happened to cross paths here today. Which means there must be hundreds of buses filled with sightseeing Indians making their way across Europe on any given summer day.

We are forty-four people on one of those buses: couples ranging from middle-aged to retired; children accompanied by grandparents; two middle-aged women who are childhood friends. We are from all across India: Calcutta, Mumbai, Nagpur, Bangalore, Trivandrum. Tilting the balance towards the south is what comes to be known as the Chennai-Arcot gang: a group of eighteen composed of the directors of a Chennai chit fund and their families.

Our tour manager, a tall, moon-faced, bespectacled Parsi man in a black suit, has been in the business for twenty-eight years. His job on a tour like this is to be friend, guide, disciplinarian and shopping consultant to the tourists, while simultaneously doing the organizational heavy lifting of a military general. The tour itinerary is tight—in fifteen days our bus has to make its way from London to Milan through Holland, Belgium, France, Switzerland, Germany and Austria, while packing in the flurry of sights promised in the brochure. The constraints are several. Indian food has to be arranged all along, which means being present at certain restaurants at certain times. And a conducted tour, especially one with several senior citizens, marches on its bladder, calling for frequent halts. Then, the bus drivers in Europe cannot be driven too hard since an automated system prevents the bus from starting if it is not stationary for a specified period every few hours. In addition, our group goes on to experience lost luggage, traffic snarls and a bus breakdown. It helps that the tour manager knows his way around Europe better than most European bus drivers and can suggest shortcuts that don't even appear on the driver's GPS. I sit next to him for part of the tour and am amazed by the amount of logistical jugglery that goes into getting us through the itinerary: the calling in advance to set up meals and confirm accommodation; the changing of SIM cards every time we cross a national boundary (and in Europe, you can't sit in a bus for an hour without finding yourself in a different country); the improvising of the itinerary based on weather, time, tourist traffic at destinations, and mandatory driver rest stops.

The tour manager knows just how good he is at his job. Early on, he announces, 'You are lucky I am your tour manager,' and continues to remind us of this at regular intervals. On a day when we're delayed first by traffic and then by our bus breaking down, I tell him it's not our day today but he smiles the smile of a man who comes into his own during a crisis and tells me, 'Don't worry, my friend. You are with me.' It's all well even when he speaks glowingly about himself in the third person, but I start to worry when one morning he begins saying to anyone who comes to him with a problem, 'Don't worry, I am your Shah Rukh Khan.' Thankfully, this only proves to be a lead-in to the film he's going to play for us later on the bus: the Shah Rukh Khan starrer

Main Hoon Na. But I can't look at him for the rest of the trip without being reminded of his heroic self-image.

Right outside Gatwick airport, Shah Rukh Khan, endowed with a powerful voice that is high-pitched, nasal and yet, by some quirk of voice-box construction, rasping, shouts: 'Don't just rush into the bus like in India.' On board he alerts us to common pitfalls: eating on buses is not allowed and makes us liable for fining if seen by the police; in the hotel rooms, we will have to pay for anything we eat or drink from the mini-bar; in hotel bathrooms, the shower curtains go inside the bathtub rather than outside, ignorance about which has led to overenthusiastic bathers being fined in the past. He emphasizes again and again that this is not India, that you can't do something wrong and get away with it. As he puts it, 'There are two words you won't find in Europe: "mercy" and "free".'

Perhaps it bears reminding that we're in Europe, because it isn't evident. Certainly not in the company we keep— all Indian. Nor in our first destination, on the evening of our arrival in London—the plush and somewhat hotel-like Swaminarayan Temple. Nor in the food: on the flight we had square idlis with hummus chutney for breakfast, chhole masala and kheer for lunch, and now, hungry in London, I nip over to a shop next to the Swaminarayan Temple and find it stocked with Indian sweets and savouries. The first food to pass my lips in Europe: samosas. Then we head to an Indian restaurant called Apni Rasoi for dinner, which is a buffet of naan, paneer, rice, dal, curd, papad, pickle. I ask one of the southern contingent how he liked the food, and he beams: 'As long as there is curd all food is good only.'

The only ones with a clear sense of having left home seem to be the Chennai-Arcot gang, who are wearing Arctic-level warm clothing on this pleasantly cool summer evening: thick jackets and sweaters over sarees, ear warmers, cotton stuffed in ears to keep the cold out, and in a couple of cases, even woollen gloves.

We have only a single, incredibly full day in London. We set out for a quick bus tour in the morning. Behind me in the bus are a middle-aged couple from Kerala—the female half seems to know everything about London. She completes SRK's sentences like an overeager schoolgirl and giggles sometimes at his pronunciation. 'Glovesester Road' announces SRK. She hisses 'Gluster' and struggles to contain her laughter. We have a quick 'photo stop' at Kensington Palace, where there's an orgy of reciprocal picture-taking. On to Madam Tussaud's for more photographs, this time posing with waxworks of Bollywood stars put there for the benefit of Indian tourists. Then to the Tower of London, where all we're really interested in is the Kohinoor, which we generally agree is smaller than we expected and set in a crown of appallingly chintzy velvet. Despite all the rushing about, London comes across as enchanting. There's a definite sense of continuity with the past—the clopping horses near the palace, the distinctive black cabs in whose boots we're told it is customary to keep a little hay in solidarity with their ancestors, the horse carriages.

London is also expensive. One of the women in the Chennai-Arcot gang, Lakshmi, asks for my help in finding a restroom for her elderly mother. When we get to one, a board reads '50p'. Lakshmi looks at her mother and says, wide-eyed, 'Amma! Forty rupees, Amma!' Her mother decides she'll just hold it in until something more reasonable turns up.

In the evening we are to leave from Harwich on a giant ferry bound for Holland. The bus will travel with us in the belly of the ship. SRK collects all our passports, gets them stamped and returns to the bus. He then attempts to call out names to return the passports, but South Indian names are impossible for him. He calls out the easiest part of the name—sometimes the middle name, sometimes the rarely used expansion of an initial, and sometimes strangled sounds that correspond to no one's name on the bus. We play pass-the-passport for a few minutes after which SRK distributes card-keys to our cabins on the ferry, again by trying to call out names. Cabins have been assigned to couples by matching names on the passports—which are a mess of maiden names, father's names, family names, and middle names. Further, many of the South Indian names are common—one woman's maiden name might be the same as a stranger's father's name—and as a result of all this, bizarrely mismatched couples are created and announced to coy laughter. In one family's case, husband, wife and child have all been separated. SRK gives up and asks us to work it out among ourselves.

Thinking back on the tour, I have only fragmented memories. My notes give me the chronology, but the second I look away, Continental Europe shuffles itself into an assortment of scenes, snapshots, glimpses. We are mostly in our little India—on the bus or in an Indian restaurant, and we dip into Europe seemingly at random. Early on in the tour, SRK tells us that we are to think of the entire tour as a movie trailer. 'Get a feel for the place now,' he says, 'and come back later if you like it.'

The experiential parts of the itinerary are the cable car rides, the brief glacier walks, trains that go up scenic mountainsides, the amusement park rides on land and snow. The distinctive aspects of Europe—its art, architecture and culture—are relegated to quick 'orientation' tours that involve walking around a place with monuments of interest being pointed out. But the great cities manage to assert some of their personalities even in the limited time we have: half-day bus tours in London and Rome; boat rides in Amsterdam and Paris.

In Florence, SRK takes us to the main square—the Piazza de la Signorina—and points out Michelangelo's David and a cluster of statues. He shows us the road to the Duomo and the Ponte Vecchio, and we are free to walk around for about an hour. One of the men on the tour who has vaguely heard about Florence's reputation for art and architecture, tells me later, 'I am very disappointed with Florence. I thought there will be much more.' But, there is! It's just that much of it is indoors and not amenable to being seen within an hour. We have passed by the Uffizi, one of the world's important art museums, without even realizing it; we haven't had the time to ascend the Duomo or any other structure that provides a wide view of the city; even the David we have seen is the weather-beaten replica in the square. It's the same story in Innsbruck and Brussels, where a quick walk round the old city square allows us to tick off the place. A perfunctory tour of Europe is what the group seem to want, and it is what we get. We drive nearly 500 kilometres out of our way to touch Germany, but we only visit a cuckoo clock factory and briefly walk around the centre of Heidelberg.

Perhaps the only ones who are upset by this aspect of our tour are the two women childhood friends from Chennai. One of them has retired, and with both their children in college in the US, they've decided to take this tour together. (One of them has never travelled abroad before, so the tour is also partly a way to get a UK visa stamp in her passport in the hope that it will pave the way for a US visa to visit her son.) Our tour itinerary lists the Louvre and the Vatican, and they've come with visions of the Mona Lisa and the Sistine Chapel. But, no. All we're getting of the Louvre is: 'Can you see that pyramid through the gate? That's the Louvre.' And in the Vatican, all we visit is the Basilica. The childhood friends feel short-changed, and even more so when they realize from talking to others that they've paid more than most people for the tour. In the coming days they often sum up their general feelings with the bitterly-delivered words, 'It's a rip-off.'

Most of our group, though, isn't really bothered with cultural exploration, and SRK explains to me that it is with these people in mind that the tour is designed. There are other tours for those who want to actually enter museums and monuments. He still enjoys holding forth on local culture though, usually in a slightly hectoring tone, making broad generalizations about the people and their way of living. The group pays little attention, with people occasionally dozing off. He tells me with the air of a martyr, 'I know they are sleeping, but I must provide information.'

Why are we in Europe if we're so uninterested? The best I can surmise, we are on this tour not for discovery or exploration, but because it is a symbol of leisure and economic sufficiency. A trip such as this signals to others— and ourselves—that we are the kind of people who go to Europe on vacation. It has become a rite of passage for the middle-aged middle class, and like other rites of passage, it must be ruthlessly documented. The purpose of this tour is to generate evidence that we have been to Europe.

It is the iconic monuments—the Eiffel Tower, the Leaning Tower of Pisa, the Colosseum—that give us the greatest joy since they offer the most compelling evidence of where we have been. We go not so much to see them as to confirm their existence, to reassure ourselves that we are after all in the place we aspired to be. We see nothing in Europe. We come here with pictures in our heads, and we leave with our heads in those pictures.

When the Eiffel Tower comes into view for the first time, the whole bus whoops. SRK smiles benevolently and says, 'Tomorrow we go up.' An ever-pragmatic elder from the Chennai-Arcot gang asks hopefully, 'Lift is there?' We don't go up all the way, but the view is after all secondary; the essential thing is to get one's picture with the tower in the background. At Pisa, we note that the Tower of Pisa indeed leans, but we are mildly surprised that it is shorter than it looks in pictures. Here it is customary to take clever pictures in which one appears to be supporting the tower. In Switzerland, we note that the countryside looks fully as pretty as in a Yash Chopra film, and now we have a chance to appear in it as well. The obsessive taking of pictures is facilitated by what are known as photo stops. In Rome we don't enter the Colosseum or even approach the actual structure. The bus stops on an elevated road nearby from where the structure can be neatly framed in the background. Everyone quickly takes pictures of one another with the Colosseum as backdrop and we move on.

The near-maniacal compulsion to take photographs shows itself most clearly at the clock factory in Drubba, Germany, where a large cuckoo clock ejects two stiffly dancing wooden couples every half hour. As the moment draws closer, the tour groups stand grimly poised with

Photo Stop, Pisa

their cameras: it is more important to record than to see. Some have brought along camcorders for occasions like this one. One of the men in our group has a camcorder attached to one eye so often that a ten-year-old boy in our group starts referring to him as Video Uncle. He films so prolifically that on the rare occasion that he doesn't—usually when he wants his photograph taken with foreign cars or people—his spine is still arched back, his gait still dainty. When he's recording he turns in slow circles and talks to his camera in the present-continuous drone of a sports commentator, though the only thing I can recall him saying, over and over, is, '*Yeh jagah bahut achchi hai.* This place is very good.' In a parking lot somewhere we come across a camper van, and Video Uncle begins filming through the windows until someone tells him it's rude because there are people living inside.

If I can speculate about the others and why they're here, so can they about me. My presence on the tour is a mystery in the beginning because I don't fit the profile of the others—middle-aged or retired, travelling with wives and families. Initially, people think I'm with the tour company. I get asked questions about our itinerary; someone asks me for help with their luggage. When it becomes clear that I'm in no way SRK's right-hand man, the rumour spreads—I never manage to find out how—that I'm a music composer for Kannada films. I strenuously deny this whenever anyone asks, but the idea persists. Further, one of the tour members has misheard my first name and disseminated it among the group as Sreesanth. In addition, SRK insists on bellowing out my father's first name from my passport whenever he has to hand over room keys or entrance tickets. For no fault of mine I end up as a shadowy character. One of the group members decides to get to the bottom of it all. He confronts me with my two prevalent names and asks me which one is right. I tell him it's neither, and he sulks, thinking I'm playing a trick on him. We're halfway through the tour before my name, my vocation, and the fact that I'm here on assignment for a magazine become clear. One of the childhood friends tells me, 'I wondered what you were doing here. My son would never come on a tour like this.' Even then, towards the end of the tour an old man accosts me with, 'So, I hear you're a film director?'

After hearing about the breadth of my creative activities, a woman on the tour wants me to talk to her husband. Their daughter (who's not on the tour) wants to study art, but her father insists she become a doctor or engineer, and this has become a source of conflict at home. Maybe, she says, I could talk to her husband and reassure him that art needn't be a dead end. I try bringing it up with him, but he's not interested in any wisdom I may be able to dispense.

Lakshmi, outgoing by nature, is the de facto leader of the Chennai-Arcot gang. An added qualification is that she works in a nursery school, and after years of herding children, her voice is now capable of such extremes of volume and pitch that it can reach all corners of a vast European square to summon the eighteen members of the Chennai-Arcot gang. Lakshmi is around forty, and having married early, she has a son who's now in college. She's here with her mother and brother, and this distance from her own household seems to have taken her back in time. She develops a childlike crush on the only unaccompanied male in the group. I find her popping up next to me at meals, on chairlifts, at photo stops. She's one of those effervescent people who are fun to be around, so her company is never unwelcome (except for the time she inveigles me into joining a game of antakshari). At Jungfraujoch, walking out onto a viewing terrace puts one in the middle of a spectacular snowscape. I'm taking in the view when Lakshmi walks up, slips frantically on the ice, and steadies herself on my arm. It's like a scene from a Tamil film, down to the cry of 'Ae! Lakshmi!' from her mother who, it turns out, is glaring at her from the entrance to the terrace. On the flight back from Milan, Lakshmi looks for me on the plane and slips into the vacant seat next to mine to give me a bar of chocolate and say goodbye, and for a moment I'm infected too by the distant pang of something last felt on a playground bench.

Lakshmi is tasked by some of the others on the tour with finding out details of my personal life. She asks so bluntly at first that I refuse to talk about it. When she persists over a few days, I relent and answer her questions. Everything I tell her is common knowledge by the next morning, and people make winking references to ordinary aspects of my life just because they've managed to find out.

In the meantime, Europe passes us by.

While we may be eating Indian food, watching Hindi films on the bus and travelling with people like us, we are not entirely insulated from Europe. Our ways and mindsets are constantly being probed by the foreign land we find ourselves in.

Over two days spanning Amsterdam and Paris we have what amounts to a crash course in losing our prudishness. It begins when SRK, who likes to give a frank account of local people and their way of life, starts introducing us to the red-light district in Amsterdam. As we drive past the area he says, 'This is the first place where a man could window-shop for a woman.' The woman behind me—Mrs Gluster—emits a hiss of disapproval that intensifies when SRK clarifies: 'Of course, these days we have bisexual and all that.' He continues, 'It is not a proper place at all. It is hard to even talk about it.' Mr Gluster mutters: 'Then why don't you stop?' SRK goes on: 'It is so depressing to go inside. You even find women of seventy-five and eighty doing business.' The Glusters are by now groaning loudly. SRK: 'These people are so crazy when it comes to sex, they even have a museum for it.' And it is not just the people it would seem—the animals here behave like animals too. A little later we are at a farm to see how cheese is made. I am standing next to two boys and their mother, looking at cattle feeding in a barn, when a bull begins exploring his amatory options. The mother quickly herds the boys away.

The Lido cabaret in Paris stages a variety show capable of dazzling the most jaded eye. To mention just one spectacle of many, the Indian-themed part of the show—

likely a nod to the conducted tours in attendance—begins with a large stone temple with carvings and figurines that rises from a perfectly flat stage after which the sculptures of dancing girls on the sides of the temple come alive and begin performing. SRK has asked us to dress as smartly as we can, and a couple of the men in our group have worn formal shirts or jackets. Still, looking around the sea of tables with men in dinner jackets and women in dresses, with liveried waiters in attendance, there's no denying that the Indian tour groups add a cheerfully discordant note to the room. We have women in saris, sneakers and windcheaters; men in shiny shirts. In a particularly noticeable triumph of function over form, a man from another Indian tour group walks in wearing a monkey-cap.

For dinner we have Indian food prepared by the French chefs at the Lido. The first course is a shallow bowl containing two samosas garnished with a slice of lime. The samosas prove excellent, but it is the eating that poses a problem, since cutlery has been laid out as at a formal dinner. Two of the retired men, obviously well-versed in the ways of the West, gather their cutlery outside-in and struggle gamely with knife and fork. A woman sitting near me mashes the samosas with her fingers, hails a waiter, and asks for ketchup. Others adopt every other style in between. SRK has warned us about the show: 'There will be topless women. It is French culture and we can try to appreciate it.' We all sit there placidly—children with parents and grandparents, husbands with wives—and watch near-nude women perform high kicks in unison. Only the samosa masher, still displaying a robust lack of affectation, turns occasionally to see exactly where her husband's eyes are focused. I later ask Mr Gluster, who was so flustered in Amsterdam by SRK's mere mention of sex, if he enjoyed the show. He's impressed that there was no hooting. He tells me suavely, 'If a function like this happens in our place, they'll all simply create a hullabaloo.' The childhood friends ask Lakshmi's mother what she thought of it all. 'At least the girls were thin,' the old woman replies in Tamil, sounding relieved. 'Otherwise it would have looked terrible.'

There's safety in numbers, and we tend to cluster when faced with anything unfamiliar. One hotel has a revolving door, and two elderly men who have been waiting apprehensively dart in behind me as I enter. With three of us crammed in a single lobe, the door jams for a while before starting again and flinging us out. When one of the group members risks a coin in a coffee machine, a few others will stand around and watch with interest. Faced with the novelties of right-side traffic and unfamiliar pedestrian crossings that change from country to country, we simply amble across roads in a sprawling migratory herd causing SRK to come shouting, 'This is not India! You cannot cross wherever you want!'

We carry a rhythm of doing things that seems to be at odds with the orderliness of Europe. In line for coffee at the breakfast buffet, we are supposed to pick up, in turn, a cup, a saucer, a spoon, and little tubules of sugar before actually getting to the coffee. I have to make an effort not to first fill coffee in a cup and then go back for the rest—the order in which I'd make coffee at home. This temptation is not mine alone, and these queues end up degenerating into huddles. Extend this behaviour to the whole buffet, and to groups of Chinese and Eastern European tourists who are no doubt following their own cultural choreographies, and there is plenty of dining-hall chaos to be seen.

One evening in Chamonix, after an early dinner, about a dozen of us go out for a stroll. Lakshmi is being chatty as always, when a tipsy Punjabi doctor interrupts her: 'Lakshmi, I can't make out if you are speaking Madrasi bhasha or English.' It's true that she speaks English with unabashed Tamil cadences. She tells him, 'Doctor-saab, you also have a Punjabi accent.' Which is true, too. He says, in earnest, 'Punjabi excent is the best English excent.' And there begins, in France, that discussion which seems unavoidable among any diverse group of Indians: North Indians vs. South Indians. It's the North Indian who prevails here, simply by virtue of being drunk and voluble. He summarizes: 'North people are idiots, but they know how to enjoy. South people have more money, but they don't want to spend.' He grabs my arm and says, 'Tell me—am I right or wrong?' It's possible he's right, I say, trying to be polite. Maybe it has something to do with the north historically having known more war and strife; maybe this somehow led to a keener appreciation for all things festive. The idea stirs the doctor deeply. Tears well up in his eyes. 'My family lost everything during Partition,' he says. He tells us he's angry with Gandhi for pandering to Pakistan. He's bitter that most Hindus from Pakistan came to India, but relatively few Muslims from India crossed over. And, he concludes, it is to compensate for all this anguish that North Indians try to enjoy life.

The next morning we take an enormous cable car up to the skiing area of Glacier 3000. We troop into an enclosed box so large that it holds our entire tour group, another Indian tour group, and several European skiers. As the car pushes off, there's a loud shout of '*Ganapati bappa . . . MORYA!*' The Europeans look shaken. It's the other tour group, entirely Hindi-speaking and louder in every sense than ours: some are wearing cowboy hats and leather jackets; one man is wearing pink jeans. (And once we reach the top, they will take posing for pictures to new heights: swaggering Dev Anand-like while a wife or friend shoots a video; borrowing a bottle of champagne from the bar for photographs in which they pretend to be living it up.) In one corner of the cable car, Mrs Gluster (who's from Kerala) hisses to a few of us, 'The North–South divide is so clear!' The Punjabi doctor listens wordlessly.

Our group becomes slightly withdrawn inside the cable car, as if our experience of being in Europe is somehow diminished by the very presence of the other group. SRK too seems to feel a sense of competition with the other tour manager. Midway through the ride, he points out the window of the car and shouts over the chatter to address both groups: 'You see those orange balls along the cable? Can anyone tell me what they are for?' No answer. 'Anybody?' he yells, looking meaningfully at the other tour guide. Nothing there. After revelling for a while in the overall ignorance, he tells the whole car that the balls are meant to divert birds. Our group breaks out in applause. SRK has asserted himself over the other tour manager, and by proxy so have we over the other group.

At some of the hotels we stay in, I get the sense that Indians may be more of an economic opportunity than welcomed guests, and that this might be the price we pay for past transgressions, for being too unconcerned about being in a foreign land. In Switzerland, the chalet we stay in gives a sheet of printed instructions specifically for Indians. One line, highlighted, underlined, and in bold, hints at a history of housekeeping disasters: 'Thank you for taking your shower or have your bath in the shower or in the bathtub and not on the floor. The wet carpet room will be charged 300 CHF.' SRK tells me of things done to bidets that are best not gone into, and of hotels that have sent back crime-scene pictures after rooms have been vacated by Indian tour groups.

I sit with SRK in the bus for much of the tour, and his considered opinion is that Indians stand out as yahoos in Europe. He asks me: Why do they have to shout all the time? Why do they have to belch so loudly? Why do they always hoot when they yawn? Why are they incapable of crossing the road at the correct place? He's nostalgic for the time when a conducted tour of Europe was an exclusive thing: 'Ten years back the kind of people coming were better. They had to be rich then. Now even villagers are coming.'

Even the relatively sophisticated get into some awkward situations. On the cogwheel train up to Jungfraujoch, one of the childhood friends is taken unwell. She is brought to the bench facing the one I'm sitting on, and she lies down moaning and writhing. Someone massages her legs and undoes a button on her trousers, at which point I put some distance between the scene and myself and go sit next to SRK.

One of the women comes over to SRK and asks if the train can somehow be stopped. What's wrong with her, he asks. She needs to use a toilet urgently and there isn't one on the train. 'She has to wait till the next station,' SRK says. That's only about fifteen to twenty minutes. Or forever, if you're in her position. After a brief struggle she decides she can't hold it any longer, and gasps a request for a plastic cover. The other childhood friend goes around collecting paper-bags and plastic covers. The stricken one rushes to the modest privacy of the space near the door of the compartment. Everyone else looks hard out of the windows.

'Aamras,' SRK says, his cheeks drooping in disgust. I look at him, uncomprehending. He reminds me that the previous day's meal included aamras. 'I have been watching how much people eat,' he says, nodding contemptuously towards the door. He pats his stomach: 'Aamras creates pressure. Altitude creates pressure.' He lengthens the word to 'pray-shir' which makes it sound like a distinctly malevolent force.

'What should I do with this?' The childhood friend looks relieved, and is toting a plastic bag with more nested bags inside. SRK looks away. 'Throw it in a dustbin at the station.'

Others have overindulged in the aamras too. At Jungfraujoch, Video Uncle's shooting schedule is disrupted by him having to heave violently. The oldest member of our group is a frail man of around seventy, who along with his wife has been sent on the tour by their son. They've been having a hard time keeping up with the group, and are often the last to return to the bus. Today, he hasn't eaten because of an upset stomach and is shivering in the cold. Someone takes him to the restroom and warms his hands with the blow-dryer. I support him while he walks. He points at his stomach and flicks his wrist: 'Completely out.' His wife has remained in the hotel room today since she's unwell: 'My family also out.' He looks miserable as he tells me, 'Our time is bad.'

The elephant in our tour bus is the weak Indian currency. Our money counts for nothing here. Every time we step out to buy something or do something, we are preoccupied with not spending money, or if it is absolutely necessary, with spending as little as possible. We turn into one of Madame Tussaud's waxworks in front of menus and price-boards, furiously performing mental multiplication by sixty-five or seventy, arriving at answers we seldom like. A vending machine swallows my fifty euro cent coin and I'm stung that thirty-odd rupees can simply vanish like that.

In Paris, I look at the laundry rate-list in the hotel room and grow faint—every article of clothing I possess cost me less to buy in India than it would cost to wash here. I may have copped a feel of luxury by coming with a conducted tour, but it's clearly not going to hold up. After champagne and a fancy meal at the Lido show, I return to my room and get busy with laundry at the wash-basin. Before leaving for the next day's sightseeing, I'm worried that the drying clothes will be discovered. More specifically, I have an image in my mind of a French maid entering the room and having her delicate sensibilities offended at finding it festooned with

Indian food stall at Rhine Falls, Schaffhausen, Switzerland

underwear. (My terror at the prospect of such exposure may have something to do with frequent boyhood viewing of a certain class of infotainment, and the ensuing reverence for the institution of the innocent and pliable French maid.) The do-not-disturb door hanger has text on both sides in French. I have a hunch as to which side says 'Stay out', but I'm taking no chances. I run down to the lobby, where there are a few Internet terminals, and use an online translator to verify that I've got the right side. I return in the evening and am shocked to see that the bed has been made. Such betrayal! The next morning, just before I leave the room, there's a knock on the door with a woman's voice attached. It's probably the maid—I open the door with apprehension. She's nothing like my mental image of a French maid. She's dark-skinned and matronly, probably an immigrant from somewhere in North Africa. Through signs, I communicate that I'm about to leave, and she can do the room later. Her French is halting (not that I'd understand it), and it's possible she has trouble reading the door hanger. In any case, I needn't have worried about what she'd think—we both know there's no such thing as economic égalité in the world, and her lined face suggests she has seen far worse than a hotel room with a few drying clothes.

The cost of living takes a toll on how we travel. I can't imagine a trip like this one happening in India without tea and coffee being consumed at every opportunity, but here we are more circumspect. Food, on the rare occasion when we have to fend for ourselves, proves expensive. There are seven tour groups staying at the hotel in Paris, and some of them are on their own for the day's lunch. The breakfast buffet is ransacked and there's nothing left by 7.30 a.m. Water is something else we're not keen on paying for when a half-litre bottle costs upwards of Rs 100. SRK tells us we can drink tap water in Europe, so we fill bottles in our hotel rooms and carry them with us, looking for refill opportunities. In Antwerp, when the bus stops for fuel, half the group lines up for the single toilet inside the petrol pump's store with bottle in hand. Worse than paying for water, everyone agrees, is paying for access to toilets. Turnstile hacking becomes a group activity—some try to sidle through, kids duck across. Some highway stores charge for using toilets, but give vouchers that can be redeemed against purchases. A couple of group members hit upon the idea of standing by the cash counter and selling the vouchers to those who are making purchases. After a long series of paid toilets, SRK says the magic words 'free toilet' and the bus erupts in cheers. One of the childhood friends tells me about saving money at both ends: 'So much I'm having to sacrifice. No tea, no coffee. Even water I'm only drinking sip-sip.'

Some far-sighted members of our group have brought provisions from home, and despite it being an offence to eat in European buses, Good Day biscuits and Haldiram's packets do the rounds. We get to know our fellow travellers. For some, travel is about things completely removed from the place we're in. It's touching to learn that this tour is the first time Mr and Mrs Gluster are travelling together in their two decades of marriage. They had a son who was born with a severe disability that required one of them to always be with him; he died some time ago and now they are beginning to venture forth. There's a Muslim couple from Calcutta on the tour, and the wife often wears tight sweaters, jeans and boots. Her husband tells me theirs is a conservative family and there's no way she can dress like this at home. She gets a chance to try different clothes when they travel. They don't even take the clothes back home. As he puts it, 'This is all use-and-throw.'

The group bonds quickly. Birthdays are celebrated, mutual acquaintances are discovered, shopping is presented for approval, women gang up to bargain for handbags. Within a few days, the rear half of the bus begins to play antakshari, and they keep at it for the rest of the tour. I've endured many sessions of antakshari in my life, but I've never heard this particular song sung in any of them: *Sa* comes up, there's a moment's pause, and as if they all have the same thing on their minds, everyone bursts into 'Saare jahaan se achha'.

3
DESERT KNOWLEDGE CAMEL COLLEGE

At the base of Jaisalmer Fort

For all their stalwart ship-of-the-desert virtues, it must be said that camels are not the most reassuring of rides. Not, at least, to the novice. The simple part is hitching oneself astride a seated camel. Then it gets on to its feet in a clamber of knees and spindly limbs, a process that first threatens to send one toppling onto the camel's neck and then, at one stage or the other, in every other direction. It is no more reassuring when the camel begins to walk. Its padded feet, highly spoken of in school biology textbooks as an adaptation for desert life, turn out to be not all that padded. Each step comes like a kick in the backside. The camel's gait, graceful enough to watch against dunes and sunsets, translates for the rider into a series of wild involuntary hip-thrusts, each one followed by an unsettling jolt. Add to this the fact that one is a fair way above the ground, that there is only the merest of knobs to hold on to (at least on the saddles that we have), that as a result of another of their adaptations to desert life camels can walk unperturbed through viciously thorny shrubs that require evasive leg-raising by the riders while barely hanging on, that they tend to sputter alarmingly, nod violently to shake off flies, and on occasion let out a loud strangulated moo that would do a Hollywood dinosaur proud, and you have the sort of ride that, at least to someone who has just clambered atop a camel for the first time, feels distinctly life-threatening.

It is always a relief in these circumstances not to be the most cowardly of a group, to have at least one other person who panics before oneself. In the case of this particular camel safari from Jaisalmer, the face-saver is Biswajit, a Bengali man of around thirty who lives in Delhi. He wears a beard and large thick-rimmed spectacles that stamp his face with a look of fierce serious-mindedness. This makes it all the more diverting to hear him cry out every time his camel shows signs of life. At one halt near the end of the safari, his camel, shifting its weight from leg to leg, begins, nostrils trembling, to sniff the backside of the camel in front. Biswajit, fearing the camel will throw him off, cries out, falsetto, to the man holding his camel's reins: '*Bhaiyya! Bhaiyya! Yeh kya kar raha hai? Yeh gira dega!* What is he doing? He'll throw me off!' He continues to improvise on those lyrics, a strange whimpering opera, until the camel driver grins and tugs the camel away.

Biswajit's younger brother, Shantanu, is his opposite: clean-shaven, languid and intrepid. When ticks from the camel bite his ankle, he casually hoists his foot to the saddle and scratches. (I wouldn't dream of such acrobatics. My legs clasp the camel's side, and though I'm sure there's some sort of graceful roll-with-it technique that makes the rider one with the animal and all that, I'm not about to experiment.) My camel Bablu is tied to Shantanu's camel Captain. The ropes are with Dwarkadhish, a man probably in his thirties or forties, but rendered agelessly wizened by the desert. Immediately after Biswajit's panic attack, Shantanu in a naked act of sibling one-upmanship decides he wants to see how fast the camels can go. He twists his torso around and puts the suggestion to me. Having just smiled superiorly at Biswajit's predicament, I have no choice but to agree.

'*Yaar*,' Shantanu calls out to Dwarkadhish. '*Yaar, thoda ise bhagao*. Mate, make this run.' D speeds up, tugging at the ropes. I'm hanging on with some difficulty when I hear Shantanu say, '*Yeh kya hai? Theek se bhagao yaar.* What's this? Make it run properly.' D breaks into a trot. Another gear change and Dwarkadhish is running hard, tilting into the sand, camel ropes tied around his waist.

Even while bouncing and bucking like a rodeo contestant I'm wondering why Dwarkadhish's plight feels vaguely familiar. We eventually stop to let the others catch up; Dwarkadhish tries to regain his breath. It comes to me: I'm thinking of the scene from *Do Bigha*

Zameen in which a ricksha puller is induced to go faster and faster by a man who is racing a woman in another ricksha. The ricksha puller, Shambhu, looks increasingly ecstatic as his fare is revised upwards by the laughing man. He manages even to overtake a horse carriage, but then his ricksha's wheel comes off and he's injured in the resulting tumble. Of course, Shantanu and I have done nothing so obviously crude, but we *are* soon to give Dwarkadhish his tip.

A camel safari is the thing to do in Jaisalmer, the centrepiece around which most tourists plan their visit. Less than an hour's drive away are the shifting dunes at Sam and Khuri that, relatively free of the scrub that punctuates the Thar's sands, promise the picture-perfect desert experience. Agents dealing in camel safaris are packed in and around the tourist hub of Jaisalmer Fort. You can tell just how central camel safaris are to tourism here by the fact that board after board outside these shops announces a 'non-touristic' camel safari.

Jaisalmer Fort stands atop the Trikuta hill, the sandstone apparently having accreted from and risen above the flat desert sands. It was built in the twelfth century by the Bhati Rajput ruler Maharawal Jaisal, after whom the fort and the surrounding city take their name. The new fort was to be a more secure capital, and was severely tested over the next couple of centuries. Alauddin Khilji's long siege of the fort in the late thirteenth century culminated in its population being almost wiped out: the women threw themselves onto pyres and the men fought to the death. The abandoned fort was resettled by surviving Bhatis. The story repeated itself a century later, followed by a string of attacks of smaller magnitude. Jaisalmer Fort has known much pain—but also prosperity. After submitting to the emperor Akbar, and with subsequent alliances with the Mughals, Jaisalmer entered a period of peace. It was an important staging post for trade between India and central Asia and beyond. Duties on camel caravans made it a rich state; merchants and craftsmen from Gujarat and other parts of Rajasthan settled here. The city grew beyond the fort walls and spread out. Signs of this prosperous period still remain in the intricately carved multi-storeyed sandstone havelis of merchants and courtiers, their interiors studded with coloured glass and mirrors. In the nineteenth century, maritime trade began to dominate and Jaisalmer's importance and income declined. Today, a couple of thousand people live in the huddled houses and labyrinthine lanes of Jaisalmer Fort. Old houses and havelis have been converted into hotels and restaurants. Smaller homes have sprung concrete extensions to old sandstone to serve as guest houses. Overflowing holes in walls sell essentials for the international tourist: toilet paper, rolling paper, imported cigarettes and chocolates, mineral water, soft-drinks, tissues, hand sanitizers. Others sell camel-hide leather goods. Men in vivid turbans sit around playing *Kesariya Balam* on mournful cousins of the sarangi.

On the wide and winding approach to the fort, you will be accosted by men who offer you their services as guides. Once a fee has been arrived at, they will name the fort's massive gates, take you to the elaborate Jain temple, the palace and the Lakshminath temple, show you a few remaining cannons and the many stone cannon-balls that lie on ramparts like outsize marbles, and point out places from where warriors poured hot oil on those trying to storm the fort. If you are Bengali—and many Indian tourists here are—you can get a Bengali-speaking guide. The fort has been a magnet for Bengalis ever since Satyajit Ray made *Sonar Kella*, a film in which the prospect of treasure and the ensuing nefariousness have various oddball characters dashing from Calcutta to Jaisalmer Fort by a combination of train, car and, of course, camel. The treasure turns out to be non-existent— and the film ends with a pile of rubble inside the fort.

The last gate of the fort opens into a square. Autorickshas and vehicles can drive up to here, and prospective guides hang around to attach themselves to alighting tourists. The air is thick with unfulfilled waiting. I'm at one of the chai stalls here when the sullen torpor of the afternoon curdles into aggression. Some of the locals are slapping and shoving two smartly dressed young men out of the fort. I ask someone what happened. Must be Indian tourists who misbehaved with a foreign girl, I'm told. One guide marks me as his own even after I've refused his services. If I change my mind, I'm ordered to go to his house and find him. Later in my stay, another guide makes me write my phone number in his diary despite my telling him it's my last day in Jaisalmer. He calls the next day and hangs up abruptly when I tell him I've left Jaisalmer.

At one of those chai shops I overhear a middle-aged

man from Uttar Pradesh raving to his guide about the lunch his family has just eaten. He simultaneously sports two hairstyles, an office-ready trim in the front and a discreet tuft at the back of his head. The meal was cooked and served by a *budhiya* who lives alone. She must be at least eighty, he says. The guide, all smiles (it was his recommendation that they eat there), says she may be even older. The tufted man had remarked to the budhiya about how clean she had kept her house. She'd said, 'I'm a Brahmin. It's my dharma.' This line is quoted repeatedly in between praises of her cooking, her enterprise, her attention to cleanliness, and the love with which she serves meals.

Later that night I'm walking around the lanes inside the fort, trying to decide where to eat, when I see a frail old woman sitting at the entrance to a narrow stairwell. 'Vyas Meal Service' reads a sign by the door. A neighbour sees me pause and eggs me on—the old woman's a *bechaari*, she lives alone, cooks to earn her living. The morning's overheard recommendation makes the choice for me. I abandon the cross-cultural allure of the Ristorante Italiano Om right opposite and follow the old woman up the stairs.

The house is as clean as promised—a single room with a bed at one end, a kitchen corner into which a gas-stove, tin boxes and steel vessels are all packed in. Elsewhere about the room are a TV and a phone. She's already made *ker-sangri* (a curry of wild beans and berries that is the signature dish of these parts) for someone who's requested a packed dinner. She's prepared a little more than necessary for the order, so she suggests I have it with my meal instead of the regular curry she'd make. We talk while she makes rice, rotis and dal. She's widowed, but not entirely alone: her daughter lives in town, but outside the fort, and visits daily; a neighbour drops in while I'm there to give her some prasad; a boy looks in to ask if she needs anything from the shop. She mentions family in Mumbai, a grandson who died some years ago as a young man. 'He would have had kids by now,' she says. The tufted man from earlier in the day turns up. He's asked for ker-sangri and puris to eat on the train he's about to catch. My jeans and my unambiguous pony-tail mark me out as closer to the foreign tourists than to him. '*Aap bhi idhar khaate ho?* You also eat here?' he asks.

The food is wonderful—fresh, flavourful and satisfying. As I eat, the old woman and I chat. She's garrulous on the subject of her family, asks me about mine. She tells me about how things have changed in Jaisalmer. Most significantly for women, they earlier had to trek down the Trikuta hill to the Gadisagar lake to fetch water. Now, you just have to turn a tap. The actual cooking she does with practised fluidity, but it's not easy for her to move about. While she squats near the gas-stove in a corner of the room, she asks me to pass her a few things, to pick up a wooden rest to sit on. I've been calling her 'maaji' all this while; I ask her what her name is. 'What is it to you?' she asks, suddenly angry. She tells me about the wretchedness of having to welcome strangers into her house despite her being from a Brahmin house, about how she only tolerates it because she doesn't want to depend on anyone else. Had her husband been alive. . . .

She sheds a tear or two. I am effusive in apology and tell her I regard her as I do my grandmother, that I only asked because I like hearing names from an older time. She takes a while to be mollified. 'It's not your fault,' she says, now stoic. 'It's these times we live in.' She tells me of a young Indian couple who had once come there to eat and she, to make conversation, asked where they were from. The man had snapped at her: 'What is it to you?' That's why, she says, she said the same thing to me. Maybe it's her way of keeping up with the times. She repeatedly asks me not to feel bad and eventually does tell me her name. (I won't commit her name to print, but these being the times we live in, her name shows up at several places on the all-knowing Internet—in restaurant reviews and tourist testimonials. There's something about the casualness with which foreign tourists refer to her by her first name that makes me wonder if I just caught her on a bad day.) I wash my plate over her protestations, replace my wooden seat. She shows me a menu card. The pricing is consistent with that of the restaurants around. It has my standard thali at Rs 120, but she points out that the ker-sangri was special. I pay her Rs 150 and leave in the wake of her blessings.

I'm to spend a few more days in Jaisalmer and I've told the old woman I'll be back for her cooking. But I've seen the effort it takes her—physical as well as emotional—and I'm reluctant to trouble her. Anyway, from what I understand she isn't in any dire need of money, and cooks for tourists more to preserve her sense of independence. I end up not going back (though I can't help feeling guilty about that too). It's similar to my long-standing dilemma about cycle-rickshas: should I, still able-bodied, allow myself to be physically ferried about by another person? Or does my squeamishness only deny someone much-needed income from work that they after all volunteered for? Once in Jabalpur, having adopted the latter view, I found myself being hauled up a slope with vein-popping effort by an elderly cycle-ricksha driver. Alarmed, I asked if I should get off and walk up, but this only injured his professional pride and he barked at me to stay where I was. Maybe he, the old woman and Dwarkadhish are, in a way, attenuated versions of the ricksha puller from *Do Bigha Zameen*. Shambhu had moved from his village to the city desperate to raise the money that would allow him to reclaim his patch of land from a zamindar. His ricksha-pulling was voluntary as well as a consequence of his helplessness.

If there is any such helplessness in Jaisalmer Fort, it may be the obligation to benefit from tourism at all costs. There are other places in India—old Varanasi, Fort Kochi, Srinagar—where one brushes constantly against the tourist economy. But it is possible to imagine these places as functioning human settlements in the absence of tourism. This is much harder to do in the case of Jaisalmer Fort. Perhaps it is the fort's walls that mark the area within as a purely tourist zone, and oblige the people corralled within to be connected to tourism in some way. It is not clear that tourism can support everyone here, but it is too good an opportunity to let go of, and people persist. The tourist is a commodity to be possessive about, and the result is a strangely intrusive and self-interested friendliness. Everywhere in the fort one senses the caginess that comes from your neighbours and relatives also being your business competitors. Some are more successful than others in making a go of it, and it is perhaps the rest who wait around—surly, entitled, and in their own way, helpless.

The fort itself isn't doing so well. Changing climate is one reason: the fort was constructed in much drier climes and Jaisalmer, in the last few decades, has been receiving anomalously sharp showers that tend to turn to slush the heat-insulating mud used for roofing. It also hasn't helped that the fort received a violent jolt during the 2001 earthquake epicentred in Bhuj in neighbouring Gujarat. Then there's the fact that the fort has been besieged by tourists. Old structures have been ruthlessly modified to accommodate them. It's quite common to see a curtained window in a fort wall or turret, indicating there is a hotel room with a sought-after view on the other side. The availability of on-tap water, so essential for tourism, may literally be sinking the fort. Drainage is poor, and water from the restaurants and guest houses is seeping into the soil below the fort's foundations. A few turrets have already collapsed.

Attempts have been made by conservation groups and the government to relocate the inhabitants of the fort, or at least to prevent tourists from staying within the fort. But as the old woman tells me, many of the fort's inhabitants have been living here for generations and can't be expected to move now. Keeping tourists out would mean the loss of sustenance and the writing off of considerable investment. So, the tourist economy here is composed of various categories of parties whose interests are all at war in involved ways: establishments that are either licensed or unlicensed; that lie within, alongside or outside the fort perimeter; that are in self-owned premises or rented. Add to all this the occasional PIL and the pressure from conservation groups and the government, and it's hardly surprising that vibes of rancorous intrigue pervade the fort. As it stands, the fort is on the World Monuments Watch list, and the Lonely Planet travel guide has stopped listing guest houses and restaurants inside the fort in an attempt to encourage responsible tourism.

Irresponsibly, I'm staying at one of the many guest houses propped against the innermost wall of the fort. The place is the second edition of a popular guest house, operating under the same name with a suffixed 'Annexe'. It's run by Raja, a stout sleepy-looking man in his early twenties, perennially found lying under a blanket on a sofa in the tiny reception area. There are four rooms on the first floor to accommodate a range of budget backpackers. The view from the landing is of the terraces of Jaisalmer at the foot of Trikuta Hill, the spillover from the fort—Jaisalmer Annexe?—that is now the main town. In the distance is an expanse of rocky desert with intermittent shrubs and cellular towers. My room is tiny, mostly occupied by the bed. In the bathroom, flushing makes the water in the toilet well up alarmingly before it subsides, bringing to mind the picture of my ejecta painfully making their way through the foundations of the fort, causing it to slump a little more with each flush.

Every guide, hotel owner and bystander is an insistent agent for camel safaris. Most tourists to Jaisalmer will want to do one, and it's a high-margin business with a decent finder's fee. So, in the cramped confines of the fort, the business acquires a cut-throat aspect. There are accounts of how tourists have been lured by cheap rooms, then turned out when they booked a safari elsewhere. Anyway, Raja is too savvy to badger me about a safari. (It's not for nothing that his guest house was in the Lonely Planet guide when it still listed places inside the fort.) He is off-handed about it, telling me as I'm leaving or entering, 'If you want to go on a camel safari, just let me know.' After all, I'm under his roof. Where else would I go?

Raja knocks on my door one afternoon. 'We need to talk about something. Come down,' he says. A few young men are sitting in the cramped reception area. They want Raja to accompany them to an overnight party at a farmhouse, but Raja can't leave his guest house unattended. They've been discussing the situation for a while and they've decided to ask me to join them. (It's Holi, nearing the end of the tourist season, and I'm the only one staying here at the moment.) One of them, bright pink in the Holi aftermath, is giggling uncontrollably. I ask what they plan to do at the farmhouse. 'Nothing like that,' Raja tells me. 'We're all Brahmins. We don't do anything like that. We'll just cook, eat, listen to music and go to sleep.'

'I wouldn't mind even if you did anything like that,' I tell Raja, and one of his friends perks up noticeably. 'If you want something, we'll get it for you,' one of them says. I'd join them, but I've come here straight from other travels and I'm looking forward to some rest, to catching up on reading and writing. I tell Raja to go ahead and not worry about me. He appoints me manager for the night. He points upstairs and tells me the rates for each of the rooms. The 300-rupee room he'd shown me is now 500. I ask him why. 'Foreigner rate,' he says. If I fill up the guest house, he'll knock a day's rent off my bill. But no one turns up in the night.

When I finally bring up the camel safari, Raja gives me a range of options. The most basic plan is a half-day safari that involves taking a jeep to the dunes, followed by a camel ride, sunset, and dinner to the accompaniment of local music and dance. Next comes the overnight safari that involves visiting a village and a gypsy settlement, camping in the desert, and returning in the morning. The others are extensions of this one: stay two nights in the desert, or spend up to two weeks going all the way to Bikaner by camel. 'Indians only take the half-day safari,' Raja tells me. This is apparently due to the discomfort of sleeping in the open combined with concerns for their safety. But they come to see the desert and ride a camel, so the optimal intersection of adventure, safety and comfort turns out inevitably to be the half-day safari. Raja seems taken aback when I tell him I want to do the overnight one. He has developed his own logistical chain for the safari—jeep, drivers, camel owners, helpers—and he uses them only for guests staying with him. He'll organize an overnight safari for me, but it'll be expensive since I'm going alone. I ask him if he will recommend a safari organizer in the fort so I can go with a group. He refuses. 'I can't take responsibility for you,' he tells me. He warns me that I might end up alone in the middle of the desert with an unscrupulous bunch of people. Better, he says, to pay a little more and be safe. I tell him I'll think about it.

There are plenty of camel safari shops in town. I go to one that always seems to have tourists about it—Ganesh Travels. The board hanging outside lists the services offered along with a charmingly modest self-endorsement: 'Probably the best in town.' The proprietor's card reads Sebastian Vyas. The surname is common enough here—it's a Brahmin gotra that makes up much of Jaisalmer Fort, including Raja and the old woman—but how did he come to be named Sebastian? He tells me his name really is Subhash, but he goes by Sebastian so foreigners don't have trouble pronouncing it. He comes from a village about an hour's drive away, Barna, where the film *Rudaali* was shot. That's where we'll be going. He has an overnight safari leaving in the afternoon. I can leave my bags with him if I want. (Most safari operators offer a free cloak-room and a shower the next day so that a backpacker can come to Jaisalmer, do a camel safari and leave without having to book a room.) I pay Sebastian less than a third the price Raja quoted.

I rush back to the guest house and ask Raja if I can leave my luggage there while I go on the safari. I'll stay there for a day or two after I return. He refuses. He's grim-faced about the fact that I've gone to someone else for the safari. It's better for everyone, he says, if I pay half the day's room-rent and depart with my luggage.

Banished, and with time to kill, I stack my luggage in Sebastian's storeroom and go down for lunch to Jaisalmer Annexe, where it's possible to get a good, cheap thali without any tourist overheads. I return and wait in the lane outside Sebastian's office for my safari-mates to show up. We're seven people in all. There are the brothers Biswajit and Shantanu, and the former's girlfriend, a large dreadlocked baby-faced woman named Rina. The other three are Americans in their twenties—two women and an anguished-looking man who is so depleted from a stomach bug that he barely speaks through the safari.

We walk to the base of the hill and get into a jeep. I'm in front with a carton of eggs on my lap. A guide who's to be dropped off to tend to another group squeezes in next to me. 'My name Mister Khan,' he introduces himself. Mister Khan is one of the more experienced guides around. He's spent all his life among camels, he says. His long-lashed, kajal-lined eyes have even come to look like a camel's. His English sounds surprisingly polished but the accent is unplaceable. The words are English, but he puts them together in a way that's all his own. This must come from learning the language from an assortment of foreigners who speak English influenced by their own tongues. The result is a delightful and uniquely expressive English. One of the American girls tells Mister Khan his English is very good and asks if he learnt it at school. 'No school,' he says. 'Desert knowledge camel college.'

The road wends its grey way through the afternoon glare. There are occasional patches of sand, but more often it's grit with small rocks strewn about. Shrubs and the odd tree grow at intervals, apparently considerate enough to avoid crowding, but actually survivors of a nasty contest for limited resources. Settlements here are small and well-spaced out too, or there wouldn't be enough water and land to go around for cultivation and grazing. In the last few years, windmills have been taking up large tracts of desert land, causing camel-owners to form an association to protect their animals' grazing lands. The *Times of India*, Jaipur, reports this under the headline *Thar camels riding into the sunset?* and goes on to suggest that camels are 'staring balefully at a bleak future'. Windmills have also been accused of marring those very sunsets for those on a camel safari, particularly around the Sam dunes. The *ToI* headline: *Wind turbines sounding the death-knell for tourism in Jaisalmer?*

About half an hour out of Jaisalmer, we drive off the road for the village visit. It's the village the jeep driver lives in. He tells us to click away as much as we want. Cameras emerge; their owners crouch near children. Women are in demand, especially if they happen to be carrying pots. Someone picks up a frightened baby goat and poses for a picture. The stricken American gets out of the jeep and sinks to his haunches, his face buried in his folded arms. He stays there a long time.

Many houses here are finished with smooth mud plaster. This I'm told is the traditional way of building houses here—walls of uneven sandstone plastered with mud, and roofed with timber, reed matting and a thick layer of mud. The houses stay cool in summer, but need to be replastered every year. So, in keeping with the times, those who can afford it have started using cement.

The jeep halts by the road near a 'gypsy village'. To our right is a gently sloping mound with a ramshackle cluster of shanties at the top. As soon as we stop, about a dozen children in grimy clothes come tearing down the mound and surround our jeep. They want chocolate, biscuits, cigarettes, pens, ten rupees. A few women follow them down, trying to sell overpriced trinkets. The kids are eager to sing and dance in return for money; they ask us to take their pictures. None of us buys anything or asks the kids to perform. Everyone here is so willing to give us what we want that we must deny wanting those things. The pandering is so knowing that it presents to us a caricature of ourselves. Do we want to see their homes, asks the driver. We don't. The jeep tears itself away from a throng of children as we leave. Only Rina has managed to comport herself with some grace. A girl has tugged at her shawl and asked for it. Instead of recoiling, Rina has proposed an exchange and now sits in the jeep wrapped in a blinding pink chunni.

We alight at the edge of Barna. While we wait for our camels, Biswajit is expansive on the subject of developing village tourism in India. According to him, tourists are wasting their time going to tourist destinations. Real India is in the villages, but there's no information about how to get there. Biswajit wants to write a guidebook to address the problem. He's already involved, in a way, with tourism—he's part of a global network that connects travellers to people who are willing to offer them a spare bed for no charge. He's come to Jaisalmer because it's close enough from Delhi for a quick getaway with his girlfriend who's visiting him (and the desert does seem to meet his standards of authenticity). His brother Shantanu works in an IT company and has sneaked away for a couple of days to come here after telling his boss he's unwell. He likes to travel, but finds it hard to get away.

Though not quite in the way Biswajit means, the camel safari *is* a limited form of village tourism. People here have traditionally been farmers, growing bajra and jowar, and using camels as their main ploughing animal. The camel safari for tourists began—according to the precise Sebastian Vyas—in 1982. It has become a lucrative business in the years since, providing employment to several villages around dunes and, of course, to the agents in Jaisalmer.

Our camels

We are a camelcade of seven, an animal per tourist. While we play at being intrepid adventurers, there's an accompanying staff of around ten to keep us safe and in comfort. We start out in the early evening, the camels led by men on foot. The boys run alongside, picking up footwear or water bottles as they are jolted off. We spot a fox and a couple of deer along the way. As we move beyond the village the scrub becomes sparser and the dunes begin. I would have more to say about the ride, but my camel Bablu is so reckless going downhill that hanging on in terror is all I seem to remember.

We reach camp in less than an hour. There's a jeep waiting there for us. A heap of mattresses, quilts and cots lies in the sand. On one side of our campsite are dunes. On the other side is some vegetation, essential for firewood and as cover for when nature calls.

The stricken American has been so far past caring that he's been leaning all the way back on his camel, eyes closed, torso to the sky, clutching the ropes behind him that hold fast the saddle: a pretty good approximation to the camel pose in yoga. Once we reach camp, he staggers off the camel and I hear him speak for the first time. He asks the man leading his camel: 'Do you guys eat camels?' He receives no reply. He collapses to the ground and lies motionless on his back. A cot is set up for him and he goes to sleep.

The camels, relieved of their saddles, root around in the shrubs for a snack. The cooks have already got started. There's chai, and we're soon stuffing ourselves with an assortment of fried snacks while we wait for the sun to set. We talk. The stricken American and the two girls he's accompanying are returning to the US from South Korea, where they've been teaching English. Rina is Russian and is in India through her association with a well-known spiritual organization (or cult, if you are so inclined). She's here on a five-year student visa to learn Hindi and Sanskrit at Mathura, but she's given that up and has instead been working in Goa as a guide for Russian tourists. She says she's been trying not to trill her Rs so much because it gives away her nationality. 'It's not good to be Rrrusian in Goa,' she explains. There's a sudden cry from the stricken American.

One of the camels is standing beside his cot, its tail waving over him. He springs up with a nimbleness I had not suspected him to be capable of. He's brushing something off his clothes and the cot—it's the shit of the desert. With the entire Thar at its disposal, the camel has chosen to go right over him. The boys lead the camel away. After the general mirth has subsided we wonder if this is the camel's response to his question. But he's too far gone to worry about it and goes right back to sleep.

The sunset is probably pretty. It's hard to tell because, duty-bound, we're rushing about to take pictures while it lasts. Two fires are lit, one for cooking and one for us to sit around. Coolers come out of the jeep—beer for sale. There's desultory conversation, experiments with low-light photography. The couple cuddles. Some of us go off in the non-dune direction to gather bramble and wood for the fire. One of the American girls pushes the wood around randomly, a clumsy imitation of what our minders are doing to feed the flame. I rearrange the wood and blow into it to get it going again. 'He's the fire whisperer,' she says. Dinner makes its appearance—chapati, dal and a potato-tomato curry, spiceless in deference to sensitive palates and stomachs. One of us asks the boy who's serving—he must be around ten—why he doesn't eat with us. He's been to the same school as Mister Khan: 'First guest then best.'

I wander off to relieve myself and my eyes get used to the dark. Seen from the top of a dune, the desert is crowded with twinkling points of flames from other groups like ours. There's some faint music to be heard from the safaris who get in dancers and singers for evening performances. In the distance is a thin horizon of sodium light. I wonder if it's the border with Pakistan, only a few kilometres away.

There are enough cots to go around, but they're not part of the package. My safari-mates are not too happy about having to pay, but they're even unhappier at the prospect of desert insects crawling over them. The staff rides off on the camels to sleep in the village, leaving behind only one minder. He and I sleep on mattresses laid on the sand. In the morning it turns out we're the

Our campsite in the desert waits for us

only two who've had a decent night's sleep. The desert cold has pierced through even the thick quilts and kept the rest awake. 'That's why we sleep on the sand,' the minder says. 'It's warmer.'

The kids, the camel drivers and the cooks are back in the morning. For breakfast there's tea, biscuit-sized slices of bread, crimson mixed-fruit jam, banana and boiled egg. I go to the 'kitchen' while tea is being prepared in the morning. The boys are lounging about smoking bidis, talking about Rina. The first-guest-then-best boy is referring to her as '*jadhi gori*, fat foreigner'. One of the cooks is staring at her in the daylight with frank curiosity, as if she were an animal in a zoo. He's puzzled about her dreadlocks and asks the other cook: '*Yeh baal asli hai?* Is this hair real?'

Part two of our camel ride is about to begin. How long do we want to ride, one of the camel drivers asks. We riders exchange awkward glances. I'd be happy to get into a jeep right now, as would at least some of the others. We've exchanged notes in the morning and discovered an outbreak of extremely sore waists, hamstrings and backsides. (Hip of the desert?) But we've paid up for this and there's no way we're backing out. 'Half an hour,' someone mumbles. So we hop on to our camels for a ride as perilous and more painful than the previous evening's. This is the stretch in which Shantanu gets Dwarkadhish to lead our camels in a sprint, and for a while it's me who's looking balefully at a bleak future, hearing death-knells in the hectic tinkling of Bablu's bell. I'm grateful to dismount when we finally reach a tarred road. The jeep to Jaisalmer is to meet us here. Shantanu and I have a whispered discussion about how much to tip

Dwarkadhish. What's the going rate for asking a man to run along with your camel so you can safely have your thrills without learning to ride? A hundred rupees.

I ask the jeep driver how much someone like Dwarkadhish makes from this work. Not much, he says. The amount varies depending on the safari shop, but most of it goes to the outfit in Jaisalmer; some is spent on transport and food, on paying the cooks and helpers. The camel and its owner receive, by his estimate, something like Rs 150 for an overnight safari. But this is fair enough, he says, because the locals would get nothing if agents didn't send tourists from Jaisalmer.

Whatever the logistics of getting there, there's no denying the timeless charm of the desert. Late at night, after the campfire has burnt itself out and the others have gone to sleep, I walk off into the dunes and sit for a while in the cool sand. In the far distance is the barking of dogs, the faint tinkle of camel bells. The almost full moon lights up the rippled swells—a grand, rolling landscape in shades of chalk and grey-blue. My mind subsides and all I am is *there*, alone and replete.

It only lasts a couple of minutes. I become knowing once again and find myself exhilarated, pleased with where I am. I instinctively reach for my phone. I can't see any towers, but it shows a signal. I send a message halfway round the world to someone I'm missing. I call a friend in Mumbai with whom I used to go on night treks in the Sahyadris, to brag about my location. With the fire out, our camp is invisible in the night. As I retrace my footprints, I rue spoiling the moment by getting my phone involved. It's not me, I console myself. It's these times we live in.

4
FOREIGN CULTURE

Making our way through the backwaters

The tourists up and about at 7 a.m. in Fort Kochi are those who've signed up for one of the organized day-trips: a trek, or an elephant safari, or, as in our case, a backwaters cruise. We meet our van—a Tempo Traveller—outside the agent's office and get a guided tour of Fort Kochi's homestays and guest houses as the other cruise-goers are picked up. Soon we're around twenty people, ranging from young backpackers to middle-aged couples, mostly from Europe or the United

States. For at least the first hour, as we drive out of Kochi to the place where we are to get into the boats, all I can hear around me are American voices—at a volume not as if we were scrunched up in a van, but scattered across a vast prairie.

'How's the place you're staying at,' a woman in front yells to her seat-mate. 'It's okay but not so clean?' the other hollers back. At the back of the van there's outrage about how expensive homestays are in Fort Kochi, and some bragging about bargaining to bring down prices from one single-digit dollar to another. Travel schedules are broadcast: 'Delhi, Jaipur, Ajanta, Ellora, Goa—we got sick—Hampi, Kerala. We didn't play it very well.' There are childlike affirmations of individuality: 'I was reading this really thick book? I threw it away after I finished?' From another part of the van: 'This is my camera bag? I never go anywhere without it?' A woman sitting across the aisle from me complains about the heat or germs or both: 'I never drink juice or Diet Coke when I'm home . . . but here!' She shakes her head at the ravages of third-world travel.

The non-first-world axis on the tour is made up of me and my two companions. I'm the sole Indian on this tour; Pao is from Mexico; Ana is Argentine, but lives in Mexico City. Ana and Pao are not happy campers in present company. For one, they are both accustomed to hard travel, and clearly feel that going on a conducted tour is beneath their dignity. There is considerable rolling of eyes on their part accompanied by rapidly spoken Spanish sentences in which I occasionally hear the phrase *super turistico*. Then there's the inescapable fact that we're amidst US citizens, something guaranteed to summon up a latent resentment in most Central and South Americans.

When asked where they're from, most US tourists say, 'America.' Now, if the asker is from Mexico or Argentina, she's from America as well, and doesn't take kindly to the appropriation of an entire continent. (This appropriation hasn't always been notional either. Pao has told me earlier about how in the nineteenth century the United States invaded Mexico and forced it to sell around half the country's land at a pittance, a move that still rankles.) There are other nationalities in the van— there is a French couple conversing in sibilants, a perennially smiling man who I later learn is from the UK—but Ana and Pao are put off in general and make no effort to mingle with the other tourists for the rest of the day. And since this tour was my idea, I feel obliged to stick with them.

In any case, Ana and Pao have enough conversational fodder to sustain them for a while. They're old friends meeting after some months and have a lot to catch up on. Ana is also more voluble than usual because she's emerging from almost complete isolation. Since coming to India she's done *two* vipassana courses in quick succession—twenty days without speaking. Now she's taken up a room close to Cherai beach with the intention of spending her time swimming and meditating. She's been forced to persist with her silence because she speaks no Malayalam or English, and no one at Cherai speaks Spanish. Even ordering food is such a hit-and-miss activity that she's given up and taken to eating mostly fruit. She's even lost her name. She's really Analia, but her landlord calls her Anamika.

All this is good for her meditation, but her desire to swim is complicated by the men of Cherai, who gather in droves to see her emerge from the sea. She has mastered the English phrase 'You are alone?' from it having been said to her so many times, and one day, she is shocked to find a boy of only twelve or so pester her for a kiss. I get to see some of this first-hand when Pao and I visit her at Cherai a couple of days before our backwaters cruise. Since she has company, Ana suggests we go for a swim. I get out of the water first and am approached by two college-going boys. 'Which country?' one of them asks. 'India,' I say. He repeats 'India' several times with mounting incredulity. Pointing to the water: 'Which country those girls?' 'South America.' To date, no one has looked at me with more reverence and awe than this boy. 'Sir,' he says, extending his hand, 'please tell us your secret.' The boys have been trying to chat up foreign women for a while, but have been constantly ignored. 'I think so foreigners don't like us,' he says. He just wants to make friends, learn about their culture, but they simply won't respond. If that's all he wants, I tell him, he could start by approaching families or older people instead of young women who are alone. He's been noticing Ana at the beach for a while now. What's the name of the fair one, he wants to know. I refuse to tell him. 'Okay, tell us your name at least.' I tell him. Am I on Facebook? I am. And then, craftily, 'Are they your friends on Facebook?' I tell him he shouldn't trouble people when it's clear they're not interested. 'We're asking you because you're also Indian,' he says and changes tack: 'Sir, what is your idea of foreign culture? Good or bad?' What does he mean by foreign culture? I ask—but he won't say. I try pointing out that everyone he sees here is on vacation, and that their lives may be very different back home. But his mind is made up: 'We like foreign culture. I want to marry a foreigner and go there.'

Kerala and its backwaters have been welcoming foreign culture for a long, long time. A couple of kilometres inland from Cherai, recent excavations at Pattanam village may have uncovered the site of the ancient port of Muziris. Known as Muchiripattanam in Tamil Sangam texts, it makes an appearance in the encyclopaedia of Pliny the Elder, and the Tabula Peutingeriana, a map of the global road network in Roman times. In the last couple of centuries BCE, goods from Europe sailed across the Mediterranean to Egypt, then travelled overland and down the Nile to Red Sea ports from where ships sailed to India. Amphoras of wine, olive oil and fish paste were sent to Muziris (among other things, surely), and the ships returned loaded with black pepper, for which, the Sangam text *Akananuru* makes it clear, the Yavanas paid in gold. Muziris was located inland by the river Periyar, making it necessary for ships to offload their cargo into smaller vessels. Pepper, the bulk of the return cargo, was brought from Kuttanadu in canoes through the backwaters.

A little to the north of Cherai, at Azhikode near Kodangallur, the apostle Thomas is supposed to have landed in 52 CE, bringing Christianity to India. Today there stands here a gaudily festive shrine. Its centrepiece is a bone from the apostle's right arm, kept inside a chamber with sliding glass doors that are opened by turning a miniature helm-wheel. For some reason, beside the chamber with the bone relic is the bright-pink model of an enormously enlarged human heart with pronounced blood vessels and a somewhat futile aspiration to anatomical correctness.

Mural at the Marthoma shrine, Azhikode, depicting the arrival of the apostle Thomas

It is said—in the passive voice of unverifiable history—
that Thomas was brought here by a Jewish merchant,
one of the Malabar Jews supposed to have been here
from an even earlier time. 'Some say from the time of
King Solomon,' says the booklet handed to me at the
nearby Chennamangalam synagogue (recently restored
by the Kerala tourism department, and possessor of the
oldest Hebrew text in India—a tombstone outside the
building inscribed with the date 1269 reads 'Sara, the
daughter of Israel'). Just down the road from Thomas's
shrine is the Cheraman Juma Masjid, supposed to be the
oldest mosque in India, built in the seventh century,
during the lifetime of the Prophet. And of course, there
are seriously old Hindu temples in the vicinity. The area
is a gold mine of history and culture (it is said), and the
Kerala government is just about beginning a massive
Muziris Heritage Project aimed at conserving sites and
attracting tourists.

On the bus to nearby North Paravur, where the trees
have been bandaged in red cloth by a communist party—
a kind of casual communism seems to be the opium of
the masses here—I ask the man sitting next to me about
the posters I keep seeing for the Muziris heritage festival.
He turns out to be one of the organizers. It's the first
edition of the festival and the idea is to keep this one
local before opening it up to tourists. There's going to be
dance, music, even a dog show. Later in the year will be
the first Kochi-Muziris Biennale, an international art
festival. Ultimately, the government plans to start an
academic institution to support the project and, according
to Kerala Tourism's website, 'more than 25 museums to

appreciate the Muziris Heritage'. But called to inaugurate a seminar as part of the festival, the former chairman of the Indian Council for Historical Research, M.G.S. Narayanan cautioned against hasty commercialization. *The Hindu* of 6 February 2012 reports him as saying that more evidence is required before the site can be declared to be Muziris, making him at least the second doubting Thomas in the vicinity.

In 1341 the Periyar changed course after a massive flood and Muziris fell off the map. Nearby Kochi had meanwhile risen to prominence as a port. It was again the lure of spices that brought Vasco da Gama to these parts in 1498 by a direct sea route. European navies could now fight it out along the coast. Fort Kochi, taken successively by the Portuguese, the Dutch and the British, was awash in foreign culture, and even today feels distinctly European.

Rivers rush down from the Western Ghats; the Arabian Sea heaves with the tides. In the middle is a lush zone of indecision between land and water, an intricate system of islands, marshes, lagoons, lakes, and canals that extends along half the state's coastline: the Kerala backwaters. Some of the water is fresh, some brackish. Some channels are man-made, others natural. Just one of the main channels, National Waterway 3, is 205 kilometres long. Of the five lakes, the largest, Lake Vembanad, is a wetland system that covers over 2000 square kilometres. Some three dozen rivers pour into this area. From the times of Muziris, and probably earlier, these waters have been used for cultivation and transport. In recent decades, they have also become Kerala's foremost tourist attraction.

Thatched barges—*kattuvalam*—traditionally used to transport rice along the backwaters are now converted into motorized living quarters for groups of tourists, complete with toilets, bedrooms, kitchens and verandas (made habitable at night by the aggressive deployment of mosquito coils). The most expensive of these boats are veritable palaces, complete with air-conditioning and doting staff. Those who do not opt to stay on one of these barges—for lack of money or time—have other avenues to explore the backwaters.

Ours is a day-long backwaters cruise. About an hour after we've left Fort Kochi, the van pulls over near a bridge, and our guide for the day materializes. Rejith is a large, fiercely dark-skinned man with a thick moustache. He's built along classical lines, possessing the sort of heftiness that is admired in South India as 'good personality'. He's not so much pot-bellied as barrel-stomached: his middle is a taut sloping orb that suggests balance, stability and content. He wears a precision-ironed light blue shirt, sleeves rolled casually to mid-forearm. On his left wrist is a sturdy watch with a loose gold-plated bracelet. His *mundu* is daintily aproned-up above his knees. His English is patchy and fashioned entirely from Malayalam syllables. He delivers his commentary in an indistinct take-it-or-leave-it mumble that makes it evident that he's not in the least awed by his international audience. Despite living in a place where the winds of other cultures have blown forcefully and for

as long as anyone can remember, Rejith seems so
completely of this land, so at ease with his place in it,
that I can't help being a little envious.

My own cultural roots can be said to run wider than
they run deep. It's tempting to see here the foreign hand
of our late colonizers, in whose wake I wore a tie to
school and spoke exclusively in English there. Early on, I
found I could lose myself in books, and these books were
almost always set in the UK or the US. For a few hours a
day, I'd travel to imaginary worlds that had little
resemblance to what was around me. It may be that this
early practice has served me well: these days, I manage to
travel physically as well, and find myself vaguely at home
no matter where I am. But it is also true that I am at least
something of a tourist everywhere; there is no place
where I feel entirely at home, as I imagine Rejith does
here.

This particular tour, from the terse overview Rejith
gives us, will involve a small boat, a big boat, a spice
tour, lunch, and rope-making. We walk down for a few
minutes till we're under the bridge. 'Now we will go in
three boat,' Rejith says. There is some confusion in the
group about what kind of boat this might be, but it's
resolved quickly enough when we see three small boats
waiting for us. We clamber in clutching our bags and
cameras, six to eight of us in each boat. Rejith doesn't
enter any of the boats. He will join us later.

The boatman lowers a long pole into the water, thrusts,
and pulls it out hand-over-hand. This silent slow-mo
pistoning pushes us along almost without our noticing it.
Soon we've left the wide channel we started in and are in

a labyrinth of narrow waterways. Sections of it are tunnels of green—tangled vegetation gripping the banks and together with trees forming a canopy. Palms curve photogenically over the water; in the middle-distance are brazenly green patches of paddy. The morning sun ducks in between glowing yellow leaves. The mood is mellow aboard our boat. Pictures are taken with almost meditative composure. Hands are lowered over the side of the boat to dreamily trail the water. The assorted chirping of birds is in the air. A cow lows in the distance. A mighty moo in our midst rocks the boat.

It's Ana. I later learn that she and her brother used to imitate animal and bird calls when they were children. Maybe she's missing home, maybe it's the strain of all that muteness and isolation. Whatever it is, she seems quite pleased with her effort. There are more distant moos, immediately reprised. Ana, Pao and I are sitting near the back of the boat, and it's obvious from the intensity with which the others don't turn around that their idea of a good time on the backwaters doesn't include animal calls. Had Ana received the slightest acknowledgement—a look, a smile, a nod—she probably would have stopped here. But the stiffened backs and the attempt to pretend the three of us don't exist only spur her on. She barks back at a dog. She caws after a crow. More cows. She expands her repertoire to other birds. She traps air between her upper cheeks and gums, and grimaces to issue a croak. I start out being mortified by the sounds, but by the time the boat stops at a largish patch of land, Pao and I are laughing and even joining in.

Rejith is waiting to take us around a spice garden.

How did he get here before us? 'Motorbike,' he grins. As if he could be expected to plash about in boats for no good reason. He walks us around, pointing out paddy fields, coconut and areca nut trees. He stops by a shrub that's about his height with fruit the colour and shape of small unripe mangoes, and tells us the fruit is poisonous. 'Only three use for this,' he says and counts them off on his fingers: 'Insecticide. Pesticide. Suicide.' His delivery is so deadpan that it takes a while for people to start tittering. Rejith goes on: 'Locally we call it mango. Because if man eat, then man go.'

The next half hour is spent among spices. This place could be a botanical museum. It's an indicator of just how fertile this area is that every step yields something to taste or smell. Rejith points to a pepper vine and plucks some green peppercorns that he gives us to eat. Glances of appreciation and surprise are exchanged: it tastes just like pepper! There's clove, cardamom and nutmeg. Chillies are plucked and handed out for tasting, with a few proudly spice-tolerant foreigners taking cautious nibbles. Rejith scratches a tree and invites us to smell the wound. Cinnamon! Everyone leans on the tree, rubbing noses while trying to get in a good sniff. There are wide-eyed meaningful looks flying around that seem to silently say, 'It's true! Spices grow in Kerala!' There's a coffee plant, a spice called coffee pepper; there's basil and Thai basil; there's that leaf that one is always fishing out of biriyanis. Pao, Ana and I are clearly being given a cold, or at least cool, shoulder by the rest of the group. No one turns to us with those looks of excitement. I once notice from the corner of my eye that the woman to my right doesn't pass me a leaf that's been handed out for sniffing and instead lets it fall to the ground. The three of us are by now a solid subversive bloc within the group. We display exaggerated enthusiasm for a while, smelling deeply and nodding and mmm-ing loudly. But there's a man in his fifties, wearing a sleeveless Tiger Beer vest, who is doing the tasting-smelling-exclaiming routine with such gusto that he outstrips even our acting.

Spices are available for sale under a nearby awning. Primed by all the sniffing and tasting the group huddles around buying packets of pepper, cardamom, clove and cinnamon that are then stowed into backpacks. For a moment it feels like nothing has changed over the last five hundred years. But historically, what the West gave us in the gustatory arena might be more significant than what they took. The discovery of direct sea routes from Europe put India a hop away from the just-discovered continent of America. A number of plant species endemic to Central America were transported to India by the Europeans with the intention of cultivating them in similar latitudes. The chilli came via the Portuguese and was quickly absorbed into Indian cooking. Tapioca, now a staple in Kerala, came from South America, as did one of the prominent cash crops here, the cashew. Also, fruits such as the papaya, *sitaphal*, pineapple and *chiku*. Add to the list maize, potato, sweet potato, groundnut, tomato and *rajma*, and one has to wonder whether the advent of the European spice trade didn't ultimately have a greater effect on food in India than in Europe.

Rejith points to a pot tied to a palm tree and explains that it's a kind of local beer. Pao wants to know if she can get a taste, but the toddy tapper isn't around. As consolation Rejith brings down grapefruit from a tree using a hooked pole, peels them deftly with a borrowed Swiss knife, and distributes sour chunks among us. All through this activity he maintains an economy of movement that would seem lethargic if it weren't so obviously effective. 'Now we see rope-making,' he says and leads us to a nearby house where in the yard an old woman is walking backwards, feeding coir with both hands from a bundle around her waist to two lengthening sections of rope. The other ends are hitched to an electric wheel that does the twisting. Straggly coir enters one side of her lightly closed palms and rope issues from the other. We gather around to take pictures of this Spiderman act. Tiger Beer is ecstatic, grinning wildly and shaking his head in disbelief. He decides to video the whole process and positions himself some distance in front of the wheel. He's so engrossed, one eye to the viewfinder, the other pinched shut, that he fails to notice that the woman is backing into him. There's a flurry of whirring rope and wild stumbling and they both narrowly escape a fall. She has to start over with the rope.

Back to the boats. It's noon and sticky and hot, the sun an enveloping glare. The magic of the morning's boat-ride is hard to recall. We return to the bridge from where we started, and as we walk to the van, Pao notices a shop in front of which a few men in lungis are partaking of a white liquid. 'What's that?' she asks. I tell her it's a toddy shop—where the stuff in the pots that we saw tied to the trees ends up. Pao turns and makes straight for the shop. This creates a flutter among the men lounging outside.

They call out to Rejith in panic, who comes running and steers her away. It's not customary for women to enter these places, he tells us. If we want toddy he'll buy some for us. He returns shortly with a litre of toddy in a water bottle that we've emptied for the purpose.

The toddy is cool and tastes like a zesty buttermilk. Some of the others in the group have been looking at the bottle with curiosity, but are wary of consuming it. 'Is that the stuff he was telling us about?' a woman asks me. 'Yes. Try some.' I proffer the bottle. She looks aghast: 'No, thank you.' Tiger Beer has bounded up in the meanwhile: 'May I try some?' I hand him the bottle. He takes a swig and is reliably rapturous. 'Not bad at all! I must say it's not bad at all!' He's from the UK and his tasting demeanour suggests he's some sort of connoisseur. 'Maybe . . .' he grimaces in concentration. 'Maybe they could add something to it. Fruit. Or yes—spices! It could make a really good drink.'

We're to take the van to a place about ten minutes from here where we'll get into a bigger boat. I've been making good progress with the toddy. Pao has been taking the occasional sip, but Ana isn't interested. I ask her to try some, but Pao nudges me: 'It's better she doesn't drink. She can get a little wild.' It seems wise not to instigate her. I gulp down the rest of the bottle.

The toddy in my empty stomach is already making me glow. The first casualty is my spirit of journalistic enquiry. I will return from the cruise without knowing the name of a single place we've been to. At an unknown location we enter a boat that may or may not be a rice barge. But it certainly has a natural majesty to it. As with a bird's nest, the demands of living in this region are addressed with skill and instinctive grace using material from around here. The boat even *looks* like a giant bird's nest. Its length is covered by a patterned canopy of bamboo and palm-leaf matting. Large semicircular gaps in the sides provide views. There's space enough for cane chairs for twenty of us and a toilet at the back that flushes into the water. At the front is a proudly upturned prow from where the boatman drives the boat by grounding his pole and taking a few heaving steps towards the stern.

In what is possibly a rice barge, on what is possibly a lake

We're headed for lunch to a small palm-thicketed island that's barely a couple of hundred metres away. It's terribly sultry. Pao fans herself with the palm of her hand and jokes, 'We should just jump off the boat and swim.'

I laugh and nod before I realize she isn't joking. She and Ana have got up from their chairs and are scouting for a suitable place from where to abandon ship. I drag them back. It's not clean, I tell them. Who know how many such boats flush into the water every day? Or what else gets thrown into the water? They reluctantly give up the idea as we approach the shore.

The antithesis of the boat in terms of design is the single structure that stands on the island—a squat tin-roofed room built for backwater tourists to have lunch. There's an attempt to keep the view uninterrupted by constructing the walls almost entirely of metal grille, which has the unfortunate effect of making the room feel like a cage in a zoo. There's beer for sale here, but not toddy. I take Rejith aside and ask him if some can be arranged. Notes change hands and the boatman sets out by himself to fetch two litres. Lunch is rice, sambar, avial, beans toran, and curd, served on a plantain leaf. Rejith goes around as each item is served mumbling 'Spicy' or 'No spicy'. The scene unfolding in front of me in jump-cuts is surreal: people sitting in a cage, eating off plantain leaves with spoons, with bottles of beer on the side.

The toddy has a reckless edge to it. When Ana and Pao declare after lunch that they're going to swim, I see no reason to dissuade them. How dirty can the water be after all? What can a few boats flushing their toilets into this expanse of water do? Anyway it's all natural. I look on approvingly. Pao's changed into her swimsuit. Ana's wearing outsize trunks that look strangely familiar until I realize they're mine and must have been taken from my bag. They slip and slide through the slush at the edge of the island and into the water, laughing and hooting. They call to me to join them. Why not. I strip down to my briefs and plunge in. The water's perfect—still and cosy, an amniotic bliss. We splash about until Rejith comes to the shore and calls out to us to get into the boat. The others are inside, waiting somewhat sternly.

The boat sets off gently into wider waters. A couple of hours here and we will return to the van and then Fort Kochi. It's quiet on board—people are lost in their thoughts or books or music players. The three of us, sitting at the back with Rejith, are still giddy from the swim. The stillness on the boat feels oppressive by comparison. Pao asks Rejith, a little concerned, 'Is everyone always so quiet on these tours?' 'Yes,' says Rejith. Then, in the manner of one sharing an insight gained through long experience: 'They are hearing to the nature and birds.' A few have dozed off. I ask why there are no other Indians on the tour. He says Indians tend to prefer shorter tours. Many Indian tourists here are from the North, and they have different tastes: 'North Indians want motor boat. Speed.' Accordingly, Kerala Tourism operates motorized boats for their custom. I offer Rejith some toddy, but he refuses. 'Don't you drink?' I ask, and wound his pride. 'Treatment,' he tells me, stiffly. 'Some Ayurvedic medicine I am having. Otherwise two litres daily after boat goes back.'

It somehow makes sense to me that Indians opt for a shorter or faster tour. Maybe Pao, Ana and I are in the same boat as the rest of the Indians? It's all nice and pretty here, but we don't seem to treat these surroundings with the hushed reverence of the rest of the group.

Perhaps the backwaters are so sought after among foreign tourists because they bring together in profusion the elements of a tropical idyll—sun, water, palms—but if you're already from a sunny country that's no stranger to palms, maybe you can only gaze at them for so long. If you asked someone who actually lives in these parts, say the aspiring émigré from Cherai, to take a day-long backwaters cruise, he might just jump off after a while and swim home.

Pao and Ana settle down in the open space behind the canopy. I go and sit beside Tiger Beer. 'Isn't it beautiful,' he grins, looking out at the view. He'd have stayed here longer if he'd known. He's in India only for a week— Goa and Kerala. But he'll be back sometime for a longer visit. 'My sister lives in Goa you know,' he tells me. 'So you came to see her?' 'No, we're estranged.' Silence. 'I came here for a very specific purpose,' he says after a while, still beaming. 'My niece died in England. There's a beach in Goa where she liked to practise yoga, so I came to scatter her ashes there.' Such human drama in that terse outline of lives lived between continents. Who knows what their story is.

And who knows what they're all thinking about, dreaming about, all these foreigners behind their sunglasses, floating in the middle of what I guess is a large lake. In the distance is land, marked by arrays of palms peeking over one another like meerkats in a wildlife documentary. Where are we? I mean to ask Rejith later but I forget. I know we're somewhere in the Kerala backwaters and I know the toddy's wearing off and dragging me to sleep, but beyond that I haven't a clue in the wide world.

5
MEMORIAL TO THE VICTIMS OF REPRESSION

A dancer about to be showered with soums

About halfway into the three-hour flight from Delhi to Tashkent, I fear the plane will begin to spin anticlockwise and spiral down. This is because almost every passenger from the right and middle sections of the plane has risen and crowded into the left aisle, with some actually crouched above those sitting in the leftmost seats of the Uzbekistan Airways A310. This exodus, in many cases with point-and-shoot in hand, is the result of people on the left calling out to their friends in other parts of the plane to come see the snow-capped mountain range visible on their side. The call's reach is particularly devastating because, with only a few exceptions, the aircraft is filled with tour groups of Indian men, each group in turn composed of groups of friends seated in different corners of Economy. Even those who haven't received a rallying cry realize that something is afoot, and keen not to miss whatever it is, percolate leftwards. I hunker down grimly in my seat in the middle block, hoping it might go some small way towards maintaining our centre of gravity. Disaster is averted by a matronly flight attendant who soon makes her harassed way down the left aisle despatching passengers to starboard while shouting 'Take a seat please! Take a seat please!'

This is only the latest (and not the last) of the flight attendant's troubles. While the plane is still on the tarmac at IGI airport, one of the tour-group Indians asks for cotton to stuff in his ears. The attendant considerately produces a mini-bale of cotton from the plane's first-aid supplies and asks the man to pinch some off. On seeing this others around him want cotton too, and the ensuing ripple effect requires the attendant to go down the entire length of Economy as passengers reach out for chunks of cotton, some of them all the way from the other aisle. She makes her way down the aisle with the diminishing roll of cotton in her hands and a look of bemusement and resignation combined, all the while chanting (since flight attendants are trained never to walk down an aisle without an incantatory phrase): 'It does not help. It does not help.' Then, just after take-off, with the plane still climbing, a passenger in front of me clicks open his safety-belt, stands up, stretches, and begins to trudge up to where his friend is seated, causing the aghast flight attendant to unfasten herself from her minder's chair and come hurtling downhill to put him in his place. Once the plane attains cruising altitude, she must deal with the overhead lights calling for her attention popping on faster than she can get them off: 'Water' is a universal cry, and from just the seats within earshot I hear one instance of 'I'm hungry' and one of 'AC not working'. Then, there's the propensity on the part of us tour-group Indians to constantly shuffle and sidle about the plane, either en route to huddled conclaves or as part of complex seat exchange arrangements. All this gets significantly in the way of the attendant's regular trolley-wheeling duties. She makes something like a dozen 'Take a seat please!' forays in the span of the three-hour flight, coming across as a hapless teacher-in-charge on a rowdy excursion bus.

It *is* a bit of a rowdy excursion. Right from the outset there's an air of impatience, of raring to go. One middle-aged man boards the plane and finds his friend already inside and buckled up. '*Kyon, badi jaldi hai jaane ki.* Why, you're in a hurry to leave,' he teases, and they slap palms together and laugh with a heartiness so intense that it sounds stagey. One man from my group negotiates a temporary mid-flight seat exchange to the seat in front of mine, next to the tour leader. '*Dekho,*' he tells the leader, preliminary to a logistical conversation, '*hum poora enjoy karne aaye hai.* Look, we've come to enjoy *completely.*' Which makes for as good a statement of our agenda as any. Almost to the man, we are a plane full of Indian men, and we are sex tourists bound for Uzbekistan.

Those who work in the travel industry seldom use words such as 'hotel' or 'resort'. 'How's the property?' they'll want to know, perhaps weary in the knowledge that the carapace is the only solid reality here, all else being design and decoration and branding and positioning and marketing. Likewise, using words such as 'tour' or 'trip' to describe a package tour immediately gives one away as an amateur. To the insider, those are *products*. Executives in charge of product development pore over maps and flight schedules and lists of properties to come up with combinations of itinerary and comfort and price-point (never just 'price') that are attractive to the package-touring public. 'No one else has a 12D/11N Europe product including both Spain and Germany with a price-point under 80k,' a travel executive may boast. Travel products are also differentiated by their target demographics. Tours designed for farmers may take in the sights of China or Israel while offering glimpses of how agriculture is conducted there. Other tours may have facilities and itineraries that keep in mind senior citizens. Women-only tours go with a woman guide. Group honeymoon tours allow newly-wed couples to enjoy a romantic (if somewhat crowded) European honeymoon without beginning their marriages in financial ruin. Some tour groups are united by language, often Gujarati or Marathi or Bengali. Or food, as with tours that serve Jain vegetarian food, no matter where in the world the group is travelling. And then, there are the somewhat lasciviously-undertoned men-only tours to various destinations around the world.

I'm at the Mumbai head-office of a popular travel company to enquire about their men-only tour of Thailand. Product name: Prince Charming. The ground floor is reserved for receiving customers and is reminiscent of the interior of a large branch of one of the foreign banks operating in India. A row of young women in red company T-shirts sits at desks to receive and guide customers. A level deeper, men in white shirts and ties sit behind computers, involved in endless counselling and option-checking for the prospective tourists in front of them. I explain my interest to one of the women in red, who calls someone upstairs. I'm directed to a lounge of sorts where customers wait to be seen by the men in ties. The room is rife with glossy brochures. A wall-mounted screen plays a looped video of ecstatic tour groups with foreign landscapes and European monuments in the background. Someone from Marketing and Promotion comes down to see me. I tell him I'm considering taking one of their tours for a travel book I'm working on. He's all for it and suggests they might give me a discount or even write off the tour's costs if I agree to mention the company's name. Which tour was I thinking of? Prince Charming, Thailand. He seems taken aback. 'It's not what people think,' he explains. 'Of course, people go for *that*, but it's not only that.' Would I be interested in any other tour? Not at the moment. He'll let me know in a few days, he says, and sends me off clutching tour itineraries and brochures.

I don't hear from him, and when I check by email a couple of times, I get such non-committal one-liners in response that it's clear they see no place for my charms on their tour. Of course, they aren't the only company that conducts tours of Thailand. Most travel agents would be able to book me on a similar tour, though perhaps not one as chivalrously branded. I mention to a friend that I'm looking for a men's tour of Thailand, and she says I should really go to—of all places—Uzbekistan. She tells me of how she was flying to Tashkent on work, and was taken aback to find the plane full of Indian men. Her male colleague, after being subject to much nudging and winking from his Indian neighbour on the flight, had asked what was going on, and learnt that he had been mistaken for a sex tourist because every other Indian man on the plane was one.

A travel agent in Bangalore books me onto one of these tours through a nameless entity in Delhi. I pay him and submit my passport and photographs for the visa. The sole requirement for a visa is a letter of application on a company letterhead. I offer to provide other bona fides since I'm not employed by anyone, but the agent is appalled. 'If we give them more documents they will start asking for them every time,' he says and implores me to somehow produce a letter on *any* company's letterhead. This I do, and my application is in Delhi when the Uzbek embassy decides to stop issuing group visas to Indian tourists for an indefinite period. Apparently there have been unsavoury incidents involving Indians, and the Uzbek government is worried. 'They don't want to get Thailand's reputation,' my agent explains. It only lasts a couple of months. Local businesses—hotels, restaurants, transport companies, guides—begin feeling the pinch and the Uzbek government is coaxed into resuming group visas for Indian tourists. The standard text of the visa application letter is identical to the previous one except for an appended undertaking: 'I assure you that during my stay in Uzbekistan, I will abide by the rules and regulations framed by the Government of Uzbekistan. I will respect the culture of the people of Uzbekistan and not indulge in any activity against the laws of the country.'

The group is to assemble at 8.15 on the morning of our departure in front of Gate 6, T3, IGI airport. This assembly is critical because our passports and visas are with the nameless Delhi entity that's organizing the tour. (Nameless to the extent that when I have to send my amended letter post-haste to Delhi, my Bangalore travel agent makes me address it to him, but at a Ghaziabad address.) Further, ours is a group visa that's valid only when accompanied by the tour leader. There are dozens of people milling about and after a small wait I notice a knot of people around a man. He nods when I say 'Uzbekistan?' but can't find my name on his list of fifty-odd people. I show him my printout with group and hotel details, and he tells me I must be with a different nameless operator. It's a revelation to me that there are actually multiple tour operators conducting men to Uzbekistan. (Later, on board the plane, it becomes clear that it's packed with tour groups—including one that is entirely Gujarati speaking—and a glance at the timetable in the in-flight magazine gives me an idea of the tourist volume: currently Uzbekistan Airways flies to Tashkent

five times a week from Delhi and three times from
Amritsar.)

I find my rightful contact person some distance away,
handing out passports from a kit-bag placed on a luggage
trolley. The group accumulates in twos and threes until
we reach our full strength of thirty-four. The nameless
entity's representative introduces us to our tour leader, a
young fellow with wavy hair and a sunny disposition.
The tour leader's role here is not that of tourist guide—
there will be a local guide in Tashkent—but that of
shepherd. The lone visa sticker is in his name and under
'Remarks' it says '+ 33 persons' with the attached sheets
detailing our names and passport numbers. The rest of
us only have photocopies of the group visa and must
stick closely to him if we are to pass Immigration at both
ends.

While waiting for the group to gather I've been diverted
by the presence just outside the airport's sliding doors of
what I take to be a sports coach waiting for his team. The
man, in his fifties, is wearing green trackpants, a green
cap, a tricolour-splashed white jacket with INDIA across
the chest, and has a green kit-bag hanging from one
shoulder. It turns out he's waiting not for his team but
for his passport—he's part of our group. In later
conversation he reveals himself to be an athlete who's
been a part of Indian Masters contingents at various
sports meets, and though he does not wear the tracksuit
again on the tour, the official cap remains a totemic
fixture, worn even indoors. Also part of our group is a
powerfully built man in his fifties, weighed down by a
massive potbelly. His arms, forearm on, are cluttered

with bracelets, a chunky watch, threads of religious significance, and heavy rings. There's further shiny metal around his neck, and a diamond encrusted trident glimmers in his collar's hairy vee. For his appearance, style, brashness, and an unsurpassed ability to spend money, he will come to be known among the group as Don. There are four sardars. And there's a group of three from Haryana who arrive at the airport identically dressed in white trousers and white full-sleeved shirts.

Geographically, the states/territories represented are Delhi, UP, MP, Uttarakhand, Haryana and Gujarat, with my presence adding the outlier Karnataka to the list. Age-wise (with precise tabulation made possible by the group visa), three of us are in our twenties, fourteen in our thirties, seven in our forties, eight in our fifties, one is in his sixties, and Kakaji as he will come to be known, often in the sentence 'Sab se zyaada toh Kakaji enjoy kar rahe hai. Kakaji is enjoying more than anyone else', is in his *seventies*. An impressionistic survey shows that pot-bellies are well-represented in the 30+ demographic, and the 40+ demographic shows evidence of recent application of unnaturally dark dye on facial hair and such hair on the head as remains unravaged by male pattern baldness.

In terms of occupation we are mostly businessmen—real estate dealers, government contractors for road and construction projects, a defence supplier, the owner of a transport company. A saree distributor from Gujarat named Paras one day tosses off an astute observation to the group at large: 'It's only people with *do number ka paisa*, unaccounted money, who go on a tour like this.' No one disputes him; two doctors in his immediate vicinity smile; and one impecunious writer seethes internally.

I haven't been able to purchase foreign exchange before coming to the airport because when I tried at my bank they wanted my passport and ticket, which were with the nameless Delhi entity, and so I must now buy dollars inside the airport at an extortionate mark-up. The very idea of going to a *bank* to buy foreign exchange would, I'm guessing, seem laughably naïve to my companions, all of whom have arrived pre-loaded with dollars. The tour leader announces that on arrival in Tashkent we will be asked to fill two copies of a form declaring the exact amounts of all currencies in our possession, and that this better be filled out diligently because 'checking *ho sakti hai*'—followed, in cases of discrepancy, by prolonged questioning. Someone asks, 'Do we need a forex receipt?' and a shiver of anxiety passes through the group with several members echoing the question in worried voices. But no, the tour leader assures us, no receipt required.

It takes a while inside the airport for everyone to fill out their Immigration forms. We are all bound to wait for each other owing to the group visa. During this time one of the younger guys (conspicuous for having his left arm in a cast) comes up to me and extends his right hand. Where am I from, what do I do. I tell him. Navin is a glass manufacturer from Delhi. How did he become a glass manufacturer I ask, and he takes over the conversation. 'Think you are in a job,' he starts. 'You may want to go home at 6, but your boss will come and say, "Brother, please do this work" and you will do it.

You may fall sick and then you may not be able to get leave.' 'Yes,' I say, thinking he has misunderstood my question, 'but how did you get into glass manufacturing?' He looks annoyed: 'That's what I'm telling you.' First, he makes a lengthy case for self-employment, then gives a blow-by-blow account of how he ended up in his line of work. I change the subject and ask him how he heard about this tour. He turns out to be a friend of the tour leader, with whom he will be sharing a room. At least that's the gist of an epic description detailing how his friend was going as tour leader, how the tour leader suggested to Navin that he join the group, the various considerations Navin had to make while deciding whether or not to go, and so on. One of the factors pushing Navin to go on the tour (as also previously into self-employment) appears to have been schadenfreude: 'My friend—he is working na? So he cannot enjoy. But I am free, I have no work. So I can enjoy.'

This is the first use of a word I will hear deployed many times a day on the tour, both in Hindi and in English sentences: the intransitive verb 'enjoy'. It will also be the key to what drives the group and perhaps all such tours: the idea of being able to enjoy absolutely and without object.

It takes a while to get through Customs at Tashkent International Airport. Every arriving passenger must fill two copies of a form with all the usual details plus exact amounts of all currencies in their possession. The Customs official pores over these details with uncommon attention to detail—ticking, circling, underlining, authoritatively scrawling, rubber-stamping—before turning over one copy to the passenger, who should preserve it for similar processing while leaving the country. The same official then scans passports and X-rays luggage before letting us loose on Uzbekistan.

We troop into a waiting bus and are soon face to face with our local guide Jabir, a lanky man in his early twenties who holds the mic of the in-bus PA system and begins: '*Namaste, Sat Sri Akaal, Salaam aleikum.*' Jabir, light-skinned with brownish hair and a native of Uzbekistan, goes on to welcome us in impressive Hindi. Later questioning reveals that he learnt the language in Tashkent in the service of subcontinental tourists, and later made a trip to India during which he honed his Hindi.

Even before the bus leaves the airport, Jabir addresses the question of local currency. The Uzbek currency is the soum and the official exchange rate at banks is currently 1950 soums per US dollar. Jabir will give us 2300 soums per USD. We will meet others who will offer to sell us soums, he tells us, but we might get into trouble with the law, so best to buy from him. Uzbekistan has severe problems with currency devaluation, and the highest denomination available—either because the government is trying to prevent currency-hoarding, or because the currency has slipped in value, or both—is a note of 1000 soums. Jabir has a backpack full of 1000 soum bundles and he goes through the bus stopping at each seat to exchange a few hundred dollar bills for towering stacks of soums. Over the next few days we discover that almost anyone who hangs around near a hotel or market or monument is a forex trader, and we develop a suspicion that we've been had by Jabir. Within a minute of my entering my hotel room a bellboy knocks and offers me 2400 soums per USD; later, a man at a market offers one of us 2800; one night the concierge at the hotel we're staying in is in need of a few USD 1 notes and he buys them from me for 3000 soums each. The official rate at this time is indeed 1950, and it doesn't take an economist to tell that this discrepancy in official and informal rates can't be good news for the soum, which, it ironically turns out, means 'pure' in Uzbek.

Tashkent is obviously doing much better than the currency. The roads are wide and lined with trees; the government offices look stately, the monuments impressive. The city exudes the clean, kempt, landscaped sparseness of a European city. During the twenty-minute bus-ride from the airport to our hotel in the centre of the city, Jabir (who addresses all of us as 'bhaijaan') gives us a quick introduction to Uzbekistan: independent in 1991 after the disintegration of the USSR; a country of 20 million people (though in fact closer to 30, if he looked it up on the Internet); languages spoken are Uzbek and Russian; Islam is the dominant religion. A glance outside the window is enough to learn that at least in matters of women's clothing this is not a conservative Islamic country. It's mid-afternoon, and the miniskirts and tight jeans on the footpaths elicit longing looks and neck-craning from our bus. Finally, someone asks Jabir to come to the point—what's the plan for the evening?

We're to first go to the hotel and settle in. Later we'll

go on a quick Tashkent City Glimpse tour before heading
to an Indian restaurant for a 'gala dinner'. A chorus of
voices wants to know the further plan for the evening:
'*Arre, kuch* setting *kara do yaar*. Fix something for us,
mate', '*Raat ka programme batao*. What's the plan for
the night?', and so on. Jabir tells us there will be 'night
managers' at the gala dinner. We are to manage our
night by dealing directly with them. Jabir won't involve
himself in procuring women, but for USD 60 per person,
subject to a minimum attendance of ten persons, he can
organize a private dance show.

It is perhaps because Jabir's Hindi has been learnt in
an environment of sex tourism that he is matter-of-fact
about vocalizing details that most Hindi speakers would
be slightly coy about. His description of the private
dance show is a marvel of specificity: '*Ladkiyaan poori
nangi hongi, aapke goad mein aake baithengi. Aap daba
sakte ho, kiss kar sakte ho, par zyada zor se nahin*. The
girls will be completely naked, they'll come and sit in
your lap. You can squeeze, you can kiss, but not too
hard.' He adds, 'No boom-boom.' Someone says '*Toh
kya faayda*. Then what's the use,' to which Jabir giggles
and says, '*Baad mein room jaake soap ke saath* . . . Later
in the room, with some soap . . .,' and moves his fist up
and down. I'm transfixed by the novelty of a 23-year-old
saying these things to a group in which everyone is older
than him, with a couple of men old enough to be his
grandfather. What's more, Jabir speaks Hindi with an
accent that knows no hard consonants, which makes
him sound like a particularly precocious and foul-mouthed
toddler, and renders him altogether irresistible.

Our hotel is one of the older five-star hotels in Tashkent. The rooms are palatial with plush carpeting, massive quantities of heavy wood, and brass fixtures. There's even a leather-upholstered writing desk the size of a ping-pong table (at which I sit down twice a day to ceremoniously make notes that are, as often as not on this trip, downright sleazy). The old-world stateliness is charming except for the fact that it extends to the hotel's technological preparedness as well. The television in my room is a gigantic boxy affair that has no doubt broadcast live the disintegration of the Soviet Union. This must also be one of the last five-star hotels in the world not to offer wireless Internet in its rooms, and Reception only shrugs when asked about a plug adapter for the power points in our rooms. The hotel lobby does have wireless Internet as well as scattered power strips that take various types of plugs, and the lobby is thus rendered an electronic refugee camp, full of people thumbing screens, charging phones and cameras, and tapping away at keyboards.

It is only later when I'm looking for some information about Samarkand and find Google blocked that I begin to wonder if this e-herding in the lobby is not just a sign of the hotel being out of date, but of something altogether more sinister. Uzbekistan is supposedly a democracy, but with an authoritarian president who was appointed just before the nation became independent, and who has since conducted four elections that he's won himself. 'We keep electing him because he is a very good man,' says Jabir with a straight face. There's no way of telling if this is a genuinely held belief or sophisticated sarcasm, but as an Internet search would show, there are human-rights activists and political opponents who disagree vehemently. And as I learn later from a guide in Samarkand, there are people in the shadows who keep an eye on what tourists and guides are up to.

Only three members of our group don't have a friend or relative accompanying them. One is Paras, who quickly teams up with a couple of other Gujaratis on the tour. The other two are Rajesh and I, who by default end up sitting next to each other on the bus and at the same table during meals. We chat for a while at the hotel while waiting for the City Glimpse tour to take off. Rajesh is a scrawny, sleepy-eyed man of twenty-seven. He comes across as somewhat jittery and constantly smokes cigarettes to calm himself. We get to talking about our families and what we do. Rajesh comes from a family of industrialists that is 'super-rich' according to him: 'House like a palace, lots of big cars.' But he is estranged from his family except for nominally being in charge of one of the family's factories and receiving a generous income for what he admits are very light duties. I ask him what he does with all that free time. 'I do a lot of meditation. I work on my consciousness.'

The group is so lackadaisical about sightseeing that Jabir has to call every room from Reception to get people into the bus for the tour. It's twilight by the time we set out to see the city. We begin with Independence Square, a vast fountain-studded garden at the centre of the city, surrounded by government buildings. We stop at a large sculpture of a woman cradling a baby in front of a globe set on a pedestal. This, Jabir tells us, is a monument marking the birth of Uzbekistan. At another corner is a flame kept burning constantly in memory of the Uzbek soldiers who died in World War II, this time with a grieving mother in the background. Nearby is a memorial along whose corridor the names of those fallen soldiers are engraved on brass plates that can be turned like the pages of a book. Around 330,000 Uzbek soldiers are estimated to have died in the war, a statistic made palpably real when one leafs through their names and sees (from the years book-ending their lives) that most of them died tragically young. The monuments scattered around Independence Square are impressive in scale, and I imagine it's all very powerful when seen during the day. Jabir is making a brave attempt to point at the barely distinguishable outlines in the dark and place them in the context of Uzbek history. But he's also having to quell internal rebellion in the group, which is (a) hungry, not having eaten anything since the not very appetizing airline meal; and (b) eager to get started with what is after all the tour's *raison d'être*. Even while Jabir spouts numbers and facts, I overhear Don complaining to one of his henchmen about how even now, after we're in Tashkent, there is a marked absence of any 'setting'. Don is also afflicted by peer pressure, notably by comparison with a friend back in India named Patlu who has previously toured Uzbekistan: '*Patlu ne toh pehle hi din kaam kar diya tha. Aaj kuch nahin hoga toh usko kya kahenge?* Patlu did the work on the first day itself. If nothing happens today, then what will we tell him?' Then, it turns out that someone in our group was offered a massage in his hotel room for USD 40 soon after arrival, which he immediately accepted. A few people gather round to find out what happened. '*Arre, woh* massage *massage tha*. It turned out to be a *massage* massage,' is the answer. A voice clarifies: '*Isne kapde utaare, lekin usne nahin*. He took off his clothes, but she didn't,' There's all-round chortling and someone says ruefully, '*Bangkok ki aadat pad gayi*. We've got used to Bangkok.' In between, while walking between the monuments around Independence Square, Jabir is being pressed about dinner and post-dinner plans, and he finally gives up and asks if we want to leave right now. The answer is a resounding yes and we wait for our bus beside what Jabir says is the Romanov Palace, where a Russian prince bided his exile in the nineteenth century. Of the glimpses listed on the tour programme—Independence Square, Broadway street with artists and souvenirs, Amir Temur Square, Victory Monument—I only have a recollection of walking around Independence Square.

Tour programmes are written with almost lawyerly precision to avoid disputes during and after the tour. The entry for our dinner reads: 'Gala Dinner at Indian restaurant with dance show, 2 veg + 2 non-veg snacks, soft drinks, local vodka and beer.' We troop into the restaurant looking adoringly at the waitresses greeting us with namastes, and sit at tables in ways that preserve the sub-groups among us. Most of the group can't be bothered with vodka or beer and have bought bottles of Chivas Regal and Johnnie Walker at Delhi duty-free. I sit at a table with Rajesh this first night, and we drink the local vodka (which, it must be said, is pretty good).

The first dance act is a gymnastics routine performed by a couple who wind themselves around each other in all sorts of impressive ways. They're followed by a group of girls who perform a folk-dance in hats and frilly skirts, and hoot in chorus at fixed points in the song. These are only the opening acts. Next is a group of girls in bodices and sheer pants who wriggle their hips and trace sinuous arcs with their sequined chests, and with the whisky beginning to make its presence felt, the evening begins in earnest.

Don gets up from his chair, a fan of notes in his upraised hand and dances his way to the clearing in the centre of the room. He's slow but surprisingly rhythmic, and looks like he does this every day. He picks a girl to dance with and hands her a few notes, the remaining cash still splayed in his hand. Jabir has told us there's no touching allowed, and Don shows himself to be an exponent of the art of close dancing while only occasionally and accidentally brushing against his partner. He periodically hands her notes or showers a few over her head with a flourish of the wrist. He dances with a consistently broad and rapturous grin on his face, and when he is not up close, his eyes ravish her body. When the song ends, he pats her on the extreme lower back and returns to his table to high-fives and hearty claps on the (upper) back.

It's soon a free-for-all with the girls dancing between the tables and the men either sitting down and leering while drinking and smoking, or getting up and joining them. Some of the men dance at a respectful distance; Kakaji, remarkably lithe for his age, holds both hands of a girl and jogs in place while the others cheer him on. Sharmaji, a fiftyish, balding, real-estate agent from

Haryana, holds his arms up in the air and skips from leg to leg, occasionally trying to grab at a girl. He's not the only one; there are plenty of clumsy attempts to break the no-touch rule, but the men are heavy with drink and bellies and lust and are no match for the girls, who shimmy and spin out of reach. The floor keeps getting littered with currency notes that are scooped up between songs by waiters. Don is easily the largest contributor here, having come with a large leather bag full of soums.

'*Aap enjoy nahin kar rahe ho?* You aren't enjoying?' asks the tour leader, concerned that I am not dancing. I shrug and after a while join him outside the restaurant, where he is waiting for the night managers to arrive. He's twenty-four, an MBA student in Delhi, and he does this part-time for the money. It's his second time as tour leader to Uzbekistan. He tells me that things have changed this time around. Previously the tour guide would manage the 'setting' but things are different now after the Uzbek government kicked up a fuss.

The night managers arrive in cars. There are four or five of them I'd guess, but it's hard to say exactly because they all seem to have emerged from a single mould: they're burly and bouncer-like in build with close cropped hair, wearing tracksuits or at least one half of a tracksuit; they're all freshly shaved with faces that are immobile except for darting eyes; they all have a cigarette going; the other hand is in a pocket and emerges every half-minute or so with a cell-phone that they hold to their ears impassively before ending the call with a single sentence, word or grunt. Some members of our group already seem to know where the action is. The sardars come across as particularly savvy, quietly taking off together in a taxi. (Contributing to their aura of savvy are the turbans they're wearing. This morning in Delhi they were all wearing regulation monochrome turbans, but here two of the younger sardars have donned multicoloured patterned things that sit nattily beret-like on their heads.) The unsavvy among us run back and forth between the night managers and the group. Navin adds himself to the mix, rushing between the night managers and the members of our group. The deal in the air is this: there's a farmhouse somewhere that interested parties can repair to, where there's a USD 50 charge to inspect the girls and then a further USD 150 for spending three hours with one of them. Some decide to return to the hotel and head to a nightclub from there. There's much confusion and Jabir tries to herd those returning to the hotel into the bus. Sharmaji is drunk and frustrated with the night managers and becomes livid when asked to get into the bus. '*Behenchod*,' he screams at Jabir on the street, furious at the prospect of a boom-boom-less night. '*Hum enjoy karne aaye hai. Park dekhne, daaru peene nahin.* We've come to enjoy. Not to see parks or to drink.' Jabir is immediately placatory and begs for forgiveness, saying he's only a child in front of Sharmaji. Some others in the group intervene, and peace is restored. Sharmaji goes off to relieve himself in the street while Jabir enters the bus and says into the mic: 'This is not India. We don't piss wherever we want.'

I'm walking into the hotel with Rajesh when the security guard at the hotel stops us to ask if we're looking for girls. Rajesh is, and he's told to go to the sixth floor of the hotel to make a selection. (Talking later with the security guard, I find that he thinks of himself as an artist. He's broken-hearted after being dumped by his girlfriend of four years, and has written a song about it. He also plans to write an English novel and has got as far as the title: *The Billionaire Living Inside of Me*. From him I learn that in addition to Indians, it's Pakistanis and Koreans who make up the bulk of sex tourists to Uzbekistan.)

I emerge from the hotel the next morning to see Rajesh in a red leather jacket and sunglasses, smoking a pensive cigarette on one of the benches outside. I join him and ask how last night went. 'So-so,' he says. He'd picked a blonde Russian girl and was told she'd come to his room, but a dark-haired Uzbek girl had showed up instead. He didn't want to kick up a fuss so he'd made do with her and paid up.

Today we're to go by bus to the Chimgan Mountains and the nearby Charvak Lake. The tour programme says we start at 9; Jabir has deferred it to 10; we finally set off at 11. There are many empty seats in the bus—Don and his henchmen are absent, as are the two beret-turbaned sardars and a few others. They're either recovering from the exertions of last night or resting in anticipation of tonight's. The bus is triumphant with stories of boom-boom from the previous night. Someone asks about Kakaji, and Paras says, a few rows behind Kakaji and out of his earshot, 'He was saying that he can't get it up any longer.' Someone shouts out, '*Arre Kakaji, Viagra le lo.*' Another recommends a magic 'chutney' that Don (who else?) has, that is guaranteed to work wonders.

The darker story from last night that's making the rounds of the bus is that three men from the group went to a farmhouse with one of the night managers and soon found themselves in the middle of a police raid. They were the only customers there, so it would seem that the whole thing was an inside job. The police had threatened the men with imprisonment and extracted from them all the money they had, even driving them to the hotel so they could fetch cash from the room. Total damage: USD 1900. Later in the day Jabir announces on the PA system that they needn't have paid anything at all because it's only the sex-workers and pimps who are vulnerable to prosecution, and if any of us finds ourselves in a similar quandary we have only to call Jabir and he'll arrive at any time of the night and—this communicated in his sweet, lisping Hindi—thrust a pole up the cops' rear ends.

'On the way enjoy view of mountains and life of local people,' suggests the tour programme. The two-hour bus ride to Chimgan Mountains does take us through a good cross-section of Uzbekistan. The roads in Tashkent, pleasantly wide and uncongested, are disproportionately full of Chevrolet cars (manufactured at General Motors' Uzbekistan plant that accounted for 94 per cent of all cars sold in the country in 2011). Outside the city there's little traffic, most conspicuous being the donkey-carts piled high with hay making their way along the side of the road. The landscape is flat with occasional patches of sparse green that give way easily to a rocky dusty brown. The only green here is scrub and shrub and frizzy trees with branches that rise upwards as if in surrender. Large expanses of land are given over to cultivating cotton, the export of which is one of Uzbekistan's main sources of income. Jabir tells us about how government employees and school and college students are marshalled for picking cotton by hand. (These are considered forced labour camps by human rights organizations. In general, cotton cultivation in Uzbekistan isn't a shining example of the liberties its citizens enjoy: in addition to these camps that ensure low-cost harvesting, farmers must meet quotas and sell only to a government agency which in turn exports cotton at huge profits that cynics claim line the pockets of the influential.) Besides cotton, there are large apple orchards; apricot trees seem to spring up anywhere there's space.

Uzbekistan happens to be blessed in the matter of fruits and nuts. This morning, on seeing the laden fruit table at the hotel's breakfast buffet, I'm reminded of what I've read about Babur, who founded the Mughal dynasty in India, but was to the end disdainful of the quality of fruit there. Babur, recorded as being obsessively passionate about fruit, spent his youth in what is now Uzbekistan. In his memoir *Baburnama* he credits the township of Akhsi in Fergana with producing a variety of melon that he suspects has no equal in the world. He should know, being a near-maniac about melons: he'd pit varieties of melons against each other at dinner parties, and once, when in fruit-deficient India a melon was brought to him from Kabul, he wept while eating it. At the hotel buffet I fill my plate with large grapes, slices of apple, and cubes of watermelon and musk melon. I manage to hold back the tears, but there's no doubt

Babur was on to something—there's a just-right combination of sweetness, juice and crunch to the fruits that's remarkably satisfying.

A little before we reach Chimgan we stop by the side of the road to buy slabs of roasted almonds, sun-dried with honey into a delicate lattice. They're being sold by a half-dozen scarf-wearing Kazakhi women whom Navin takes on single-handedly. He rushes around organizing us into impromptu buyers' collectives, and heaps packets of honey-almond in front of each of the women as he gauges demand from us in Hindi and forces the price down with peremptory motions of his unbroken right arm. When the bus is about to leave he initiates a parting high-stakes game that involves adding packets of the higher-priced variety of honey-almond to already full plastic bags and fishing them out when his price isn't agreed to. I notice that he's slipped in an extra packet in the frenzy and point it out thinking he's made a mistake, but he only grins. In the end, the Kazakhi women have sold plenty of honey-almond and our group has got a good price, but the most satisfied person here is Navin, who thrives on deal-making. Even without having too many words to serve him here, he's managed a transactional prolixity that's left everyone else exhausted.

Uzbekistan is a landlocked country bound on all sides by -stans: Afghanistan, Turkmenistan, Kyrgyzstan, Tajikistan and, in front of us, beyond the Chimgan Mountains, Kazhakhstan. The mountains are an upswelling of dust and craggy rock—the Central Asia of all that war footage from Afghanistan, of those expanses from Kairostami films. The 'Chimgan Mountains' of the tour programme are really the Western Tian-Shan range, with Chimgan being the name of a ski-resort as well as the tallest peak in the area. Our group hops onto chair-lifts in pairs to reach an elevation that now, without snow, simply serves as a viewing point. We take pictures of each other; Sharmaji and a couple of others look for a suitable place to pour midday pegs of whisky.

On the descent I share the chair-lift with Rajesh, who seems more fidgety than usual. I ask him if he's okay. He tells me, quite casually, that in a previous life he'd been killed by someone who chased him and hit him on the head. It comes back to him occasionally in the form of knocks at the back of his head, accompanied by the feeling that he's falling forwards. He's receiving those reminders now. 'Thak. Thak. Thak,' he says, holding the back of his head. We're suspended high above the mountainside—a terrible time to be talking of falling. I say something about how we don't have to completely believe everything our mind throws up. 'I don't believe. I know,' he says. The knocking soon grows fainter and we end up talking metaphysics all the way down. He talks about the Self with great conviction, almost entirely in unconnected aphorisms attributed to Osho. He considers himself a follower of Osho and has spent time in the Pune ashram. Returning to earth, he tells me: 'It's very easy to have sex there. In two months I had twelve girlfriends.'

A short drive away is the Charvak Lake, a water reservoir formed by damming the Chirchiq river. Its shores are lined by resorts, and it is at one of these that we have lunch. The resort is empty and the group hangs around aimlessly after lunch. I'm chatting with a couple of men who are government contractors and we're all surprised by the fact that Uzbekistan appears more developed than India. Tashkent has wide, clean tree-lined avenues with parks and squares, large buildings and monuments. One of the contractors certifies that the roads are even of good quality. Jabir joins us. He's had a couple of beers with his lunch and is in a frank and expansive mood. He tells us that people are hard-working in Uzbekistan and that's not the case in India: 'You won't throw rubbish in the bin because you have to walk a few metres.' And that is why, according to Jabir, India is dirty and poor. He's noticed something else about Indians for which he'd like an explanation, but none of us has an answer. *'Tum Indians na,'* he says, *'paani bahut peete ho aur susu bahut karte ho. Kyon?* You Indians drink a lot of water and you pee a lot. Why?'

The question is of significance to Jabir because: (a) he is pestered for frequent toilet stops by Indian tour groups; and (b) he is bound by the legalese of the tour programme to distribute 0.5 litre of water 'per pax' per day, which requirement he more than meets, but still finds himself besieged by parched pax who haven't received their water. As our tour progresses, discussions among the group will indicate that there are some who are sneaking multiple bottles of water into their bags for later use. More than one person's whispered testimony will implicate the athlete among us (who bears an uncanny resemblance to the actor Dilip Kumar, down to the jet-black dyed hair that becomes visible when his official cap comes off in moments of weakness). It is possible that Dilip Kumar, being an athlete, needs to maintain higher levels of hydration than your average sex tourist, but he and his companion also boast—whenever anyone in the group complains that the one thing they miss here is chai—about making cups of tea and coffee in their hotel room with an electric kettle for which the water must come from somewhere. The two also insist at the gala dinners that they occupy a separate table all by themselves. On occasions when those of us who aren't in a tightly-bound group try to join them, they conspicuously slink away to a new table to sit by themselves so that—it is speculated by the large and teddy-bear-like Gujarati government contractor—they can polish off an entire table's worth of snacks and fruit. Any doubts I have about DK's guilt in the water scam—Watergate?—vanish when I see, during one of the gala dinners, that DK has taken a two-litre bottle of Sprite from the bar counter and hidden it under his table. It's possible there are mitigating circumstances, and maybe this is some sort of each-man-for-himself attitude picked up in the past from touring in the company of hungry, thirsty sportsmen, but the duo's overall attitude earns it few friends in the group.

Something else that Dilip Kumar may have acquired during sports tours is the compulsion to be the life and soul of the party. After sitting quietly for a day and a half, he strides up to the front of the tour bus at a time when Jabir isn't speaking and takes the mike. 'From now on,' he announces, 'I'll always have the mike when Jabir isn't using it.' He bursts into *Kabhi alvida na kehna* even if it's a little premature (as he himself admits) for a goodbye song, and then launches into an elaborate joke presented here in precis:

Kakaji (for DK employs the jocular device of picking his characters from the group) *had a pair of shoes with singularly reflective uppers made at great expense before leaving for Uzbekistan. On the flight to Tashkent, when the young, pretty, short-skirted, female flight attendant served him a peg of whisky, Kakaji slyly inserted his foot into the aisle and accurately told her the colour of her underwear. The attendant, taken aback by Kakaji's guess, changed her underwear to test him and brought another peg, only to be humbled again. After this happened a few times the flustered attendant decided to outwit Kakaji by serving him a whisky while wearing no underwear. Kakaji burst into tears. Now concerned, the flight attendant asked if all was well, upon which Kakaji pointed to the foot of his outstretched leg and lamented between sobs the fact that his new shoe was already torn.*

There are several puzzled faces in the bus post the joke and this prompts Dilip Kumar to explain it in such excruciating detail that I suspect my mind switches off to cope. DK's subsequent jokes are only hazy memories when I later sit at the grand writing-table in my hotel room to make notes. I do remember however that DK introduces each new joke with the phrase '*Aur ek chutkula*' and that one of DK's chutkulas is a long-winded and atrocious meta-joke about how the very word chutkula derives from a Hindi vulgarism for a certain part of a woman's body.

The second evening's gala dinner, at another Indian restaurant, features dancers who would be considered outrageously beautiful in any part of the world. They're also accomplished belly dancers and the evening is a low-lit blur of skin and diaphanous fabric. The dancers are on a small stage in the middle of the dining area and there's a sign that says the stage is only for performers. This does not stop Don from clambering up with an ecstatic expression and a bundle of soums. Sharmaji is next. Soon, the girls are down among the group, dancing between tables to 'Sheela ki jawaani', 'Kajra re' and 'Munni baadnaam hui', and the floor is carpeted with soums. There are many attempts to chat up the dancers, who smile coyly and accept money, but will not disclose even their names. Paras, the sari distributor from Surat, is in his thirties but often boyish in behaviour. He tries to woo a waitress by looking longingly at her and saying 'Helllooo' but it only causes her to break out in giggles.

It's a drunk and slavering group that heads out of the restaurant. The sardars immediately get into a taxi outside the restaurant in the company of a mini-skirted woman. The rest have plans in or around the hotel, and head back to the bus. Four of us—Paras, Rajesh, a businessman from Gujarat in his mid-thirties, and I—are planning to sample a nightclub near our hotel. Kakaji, who has danced with abandon and is slightly drunk at the end of the evening takes us aside to give us some advice after we alight at the hotel. 'This body is all bones and flesh,' he tells us, extending his arms and looking at himself. 'It's nothing at all—here today, gone tomorrow. Enjoy everything; enjoy all you want. But just keep one thing in mind—never enjoy yourself at anyone else's cost; never hurt anyone else.'

Before we set off with the elder's blessings, we want to leave behind in our rooms our passports and money in excess of what we need for the night. In the hotel lobby we are stopped by the security guard who tells us there are girls waiting on the sixth floor. We stop by on the way down from our rooms. The sixth floor corridor is dense as a railway platform with members from our tour group. They're sprawled on the floor or sitting in small groups smoking and drinking whisky. They're the ones who are sharing rooms with one or two others, and they're waiting in the corridor while their friends are busy in the room. At one end of the corridor is a service entry passage where a half-dozen young women are waiting—leaning on the walls, sitting on the floor; one is seated on a toilet, the door to the stall open. A hotel security guard stands by smoking and checking his phone. The air is thick with perfume. The women array themselves invitingly as we arrive. Rajesh grins at the one resting on the toilet and asks if she's finished. They all laugh obligatorily and resume radiating allure at us. They're of different builds and hair colours, all in short skirts, high-heels and fresh make-up. From close up, there's something strangely unreal here—a mechanical coquettishness that brings to mind characters from video games, where if you stop playing and just look at one of the characters for a while, you'll see the rendered presence heave microscopically and twitch and blink in ways that are meant to aid verisimilitude but actually do the opposite once you pay any attention.

Rajesh is overcome with lust for one of the women. The transformation is startling—one moment he's casting a cool, appraising eye over the women and the next he's entranced by a blonde who's standing with her back arched against the wall. 'You're very pretty,' he says and kisses her tenderly on the cheek. He looks her over transfixed; he bites his lower lip and strokes the tattoo that's partially visible over the waist of her skirt. She can be his for an hour for USD 100. 'How much for full night?' he asks the security guard, who's also the pimp. USD 300. He turns to us like a man who cannot believe his luck. '*Yaar, yeh mast hai yaar*,' he says, and transfers his gaze back to her. Paras tells him to take her if he wants, the rest of us will go on to the club. Rajesh thinks for a minute and snaps out of it. It's only 11 p.m. He'll try his luck at the club and come back here if required.

A car with four women pulls up beside us as we walk to the club. A window rolls down and one of them asks: 'Boom-boom?' There's a short conversation. USD 100 for two hours; USD 150 for the whole night. 'Massage, boom-boom, everything,' the woman says. 'Exchange girls afterwards.' But the night is still young and we move on. One of the hotel's receptionists has given us directions to the club. When we get there, there's a club, but not the one we are looking for. Girls go in and out; burly men fitting the archetype of night managers stand outside in tracksuits or hoodies. One of them tells us the club now has a different owner, a new name and a fairly steep cover charge plus 'table deposit'. There's going to be a strip tease and there will be plenty of girls to be picked up. The other three are serious about following through, so I leave them there and walk back to the hotel. A couple of taxis slow down beside me: 'Boom-boom?' In the hotel elevator, a bell-boy asks, 'Sir, you want massage in your room?' It's an achievement to return to the room with the night unconsummated.

In the morning over breakfast I learn that Rajesh and the others picked up girls at the nightclub, took a taxi to one of their apartments at 4 a.m., and have only just returned. They paid the girls USD 80 and are subject to eager questioning by others in the group who feel this is more boom-boom for the buck than what they've been getting. Paras is adept at bargaining (no doubt from his experience in the saree business), and like all good strategists he knows when retreat is the best policy. He regales the group with an incident from last night when he invited four girls to sit at their table and asked if they'd like a drink. They wanted Red Bulls, which Paras, casting a quick eye on the menu, saw were USD 15 each. So he sprang up from his chair as if taken by the song that was playing, and lost himself in dancing until the girls were gone.

We are a depleted group again this morning as we head to the Lal Bahadur Shastri Memorial. Tashkent was the site for USSR-moderated peace negotiations in 1966 between the Indian Prime Minister Lal Bahadur Shastri and his Pakistani counterpart Muhammad Ayub Khan. Shastri died in Tashkent a day after the agreement was signed, and today a small landscaped plot with his bust serves as a memorial. Jabir has thoughtfully brought a couple of roses with him and members of the group have their photographs taken side-on, ostentatiously placing a rose at the base of the pedestal while twisting their necks to face the camera. We mill about and I hear some of the older members of the group talking about Shastri's integrity. The matter of his having resigned as Railway Minister after taking moral responsibility for a rail accident comes up. 'No one could point a finger at him,' one man says in admiration. Inevitably, a contrast is drawn between him and today's scam-ridden politicians, and there's much clucking and head-shaking about corruption (which I can't help thinking is a bit rich coming from a group composed in large measure of adulterers and tax-evaders).

We drive over to the *Shahidlar Xotirasi*—Memorial to the Victims of Repression—a museum and park that remembers the Uzbeks who resisted the regimes of the Tsars and the Soviets and were killed or incarcerated. We don't enter the museum, but we walk in the park laid around a soaring rotunda. This is also one of the few times we get to meet locals. Schoolboys ask for Indian cigarettes; schoolgirls want to pose with us for pictures to be taken on their phone-cameras. There is no common language for communication except Hindi cinema. Subtitled Hindi films were popular in the USSR and continue to be so now in Uzbekistan. So once it has been established that we are from India, an older man or woman might beam and say, 'Raj Kapoor!' to which the correct response could be a cheery 'Dilip Kumar!'; then a 'Rishi Kapoor!' possibly countered with an 'Amitabh Bachchan!' The schoolkids are more contemporary, bringing up Kareena Kapoor, Hrithik Roshan, Shah Rukh Khan and Salman Khan. As usual the most loquacious of our group turns out to be Navin, who in addition to never tiring of exchanging names of actors, has actually

Roadside vendors near Chorsu bazaar, Tashkent

made the effort to acquire a rudimentary Russian vocabulary. As a group of schoolgirls leaves after a long photo session in which Navin poses with them in various combinations, he calls out 'Dasvidaniya' and 'Ya tebya lublu', which elicits an uncomfortable blush from a couple of them.

If a lot of Tashkent looks new and shiny, it's because it is. An earthquake levelled Tashkent in April 1966 and today's Tashkent is mostly Soviet or Uzbek construction. We visit a monument marking the earthquake (one of the few Soviet era monuments to survive Uzbek independence): a larger-than-life couple with a child brace themselves against the earth splitting open at their feet. In the afternoon we go to Chorsu bazaar, a packed market in which pretty much anything one could want is on sale either in the shops or from the women in scarves seated on the pavements. Our interest is in the blue-green dome at the centre that houses the spices and dried fruits section. Dried fruits are what Indian tourists take back with them, and here are almonds, walnuts, raisins, apricots and dates available in varied sizes, shapes, combinations, and stages of processing. Competition among the sellers is so intense that they physically force potential customers to try samples and I walk out of the market with bags and stomach full of dried fruits. I see that several of the others have bought pomegranates at the fresh produce market nearby and am pleasantly surprised to find amidst us this Babur-like connoisseurship of fresh fruit until I overhear someone in the bus mention that it gives 'strength'.

In the evening I take a walk with Rajesh during which he tells me that he's looking for a larger purpose in life. He earns around ten lakh a month from his family business without much effort, but he doesn't want to go on like this, working half-heartedly at something he's not interested in. 'I want to do something,' he says. To that end he's planning some high-risk projects that should earn him a few crore in the span of a year or two. After that he'll be free of his family business and can work on something related to the arts.

The evening's gala dinner features the same performers as yesterday, so it's a joyful continuation from where everyone left off. Kakaji has body ache and is subdued—

the flesh and bones are making their presence felt after last night's drinking and dancing. I get up to use the toilet, find it occupied by someone who's taking inordinately long, and return to my table. Later I find out that one of the men from our group entered the toilet and found he had walked in on a woman who worked in the restaurant's kitchen. By force of habit he'd held out two thousand soum notes in apology. She'd looked at the notes and signalled five, upon which he'd locked the door behind him.

The fourth day of the tour is 'free at leisure' according to the tour programme. Some of us in the group have asked Jabir to organize a day-trip to Samarkand. It seems a shame to come all this way and not visit one of the most ancient and historically rich cities in the world. We're to leave early tomorrow morning. Navin asks Rajesh as we enter the hotel if he's going to Samarkand. '*Yeh history-wistory kuch kaam ka cheez nahin hai.* This history-wistory is of no use,' says Rajesh. 'I believe in only two things—sex and money.'

Nine of us have booked the Samarkand day trip: Dilip Kumar and his friend, Paras and two other Gujaratis, three Muslims from Delhi (whose religion plays a role in what transpires at Samarkand), and I. For USD 100 each—the price of a boom-boom—we will be driven to the railway station to board the non-stop bullet-train to Samarkand, where we will be met by a van and a guide who will take us around the sights of Samarkand and drop us off at the station in the evening.

The railway station is a large and impressive structure. As Paras puts it, Tashkent's railway station looks like an airport and the airport looks like a railway station. Our bags are X-rayed, our passports checked, and we get on to the platform where a sleek pointy-nosed train of Spanish construction is waiting. Outside the door to each compartment is a 'train-hostess'—a young woman in beige skirt and white shirt who looks at our tickets and smiles in welcome. We take pictures with the train, and then with the train-hostesses before taking our seats for the 344-km ride to Samarkand.

In about two and a half hours we are met in Samarkand by our guide for the day—the aptly named Bobur. He tells us that there are seven or eight sites that we shouldn't miss in Samarkand, but we don't have much time, and he'll do his best to show us as much as he can. One of the Muslims pipes up with a constraint—today is Friday and they need to be in a mosque at 1 p.m. for namaz. Which explains why one of them has today donned for the first time on the tour a white skull-cap.

First Bobur takes us to the Imam Al-Bukhari memorial complex. The Imam was a ninth-century scholar whose compilation of hadith is considered by many to be the most authoritative Islamic text after the Quran. The complex contains his mausoleum and a large mosque. The Muslims go to the washing rooms to cleanse themselves before entering. The Hindus—the rest of us—don't want to enter because we're not interested enough to pay the entrance fee. We hang around the grounds as Bobur tells us about how the ancient city of Samarkand was in ruins after being sacked by Genghis Khan until

Timur revived it by making it his capital in the fourteenth century. For that, and for his prolific military conquests, Bobur tells us, Timur is a national hero in Uzbekistan. Paras mutters: '*Lutera tha, daaku tha saala.*' (He's referring to the fact that Timur reached as far as Delhi when he attacked the ruling Sultanate in 1398 and returned with elephants—as many as ninety according to a source from the time—loaded with gold and precious stones.) In the meanwhile we're restless in the knowledge that we have all Samarkand left to see, but the Muslims are taking forever to emerge from the complex. When they finally do it's around 11.30 and they propose staying on till it's time for namaz. But Bobur tells them he'll make sure they get to another mosque on time.

It's a little after noon when we reach Gur-e Amir—tomb of the kings. Timur is buried here as are his sons and grandsons. The fifteenth-century structure features a single densely ridged dome with intricate patterns in blue mosaic, with the prominent pillars and ornate gateway being a later addition. The Gur-e Amir is regarded as the architectural predecessor of the mausoleums built in India—such as the Taj Mahal—by Timur's descendants, the Mughals.

While the Hindus look at Timur's tomb, Bobur leads the Muslims to the mosque a short distance away. The Hindus finish with the tomb, but there's a discourse going on at the mosque and namaz hasn't even started. So the Hindus go to the small Ruhabad mausoleum next to the mosque, which is said to contain a hair of the Prophet Mohammed. There's not much else to do and the afternoon sun is fierce, so all the Hindus except me repair to the van to wait. I chat with Bobur for a while

Gur-e-Amir (Tomb of the Kings), where Timur is buried

under the shade of a tree. He's a devout Muslim and if he weren't working right now he'd be at a mosque too. I ask him how, despite most of Uzbekistan's population being Muslim, the country feels quite liberal in the matter of alcohol or nightclubs or women's clothing. According to Bobur this is the case only in the cities, and even that is so because Islamic leaders cannot have their way. The Uzbek government is apparently wary of extremism, and ensures that religion stays low-key. He tells me of the time he showed a group of Pakistani tourists the sights of Samarkand. After they left he was picked up by the 'secret police' and questioned about the tourists' motives and interests. They'd never do that with Indian or Western tourists, he says.

Breakfast has been early and light, and I'm ravenous. There are no shops or restaurants nearby, so I walk back to the van to check if anyone has something to eat. I find the rest of the party around the van, tucking into biscuits, khakhra and pickle, reliably brought by the Gujaratis. Everyone's a little annoyed that the limited time we have here is being squandered like this, and there's something of an anti-Muslim sentiment being worked up. There's talk about the sudden Friday piety on display after all the boom-boom of the last few days. Then Paras says, 'I've heard they actually worship a *shivling* at Mecca.' Dilip Kumar nods vigorously. 'It's true,' he says, and adds, bizarrely, 'They also worship pigs there.' The namaz begins in the mosque and seems to go on and on. As do the khakhras, of which there's a seemingly endless supply. What was a stopgap snack until lunch becomes lunch. A plan is hatched to make the most of the afternoon: we'll give the Muslims what's left of the biscuits and khakhra and avoid stopping for lunch. They finally arrive with sheepish smiles: 'We thought it would be over in twenty minutes like in India, but it took a while.' Paras explains the plan to them: we don't have much time, so could they make do with snacks instead of lunch. 'I have to eat soon,' says one of the Muslims. 'I am diabetic and I am already getting chakkar.' There's no arguing with that, so we ask Bobur to take us someplace where we can pick up some food quickly. He claims to know of no such place, and says he'll take us to the one restaurant that he does know. On the way, the Hindus for some reason start talking politics. The doctor says to the Gujarati contractor: 'Modi has done an incredible job in Gujarat.

In ten years he's completely transformed the state.' There's general agreement on that, and further discussion in the van (during which the Muslims stay mum) leads to the consensus that Modi is by far the front runner for PM in 2014. There's a round of bashing the Congress-led government's policies, with Dilip Kumar calling the National Rural Employment Guarantee Act 'bakwaas' because it indulges the lazy. (He elaborates on this the next morning at breakfast. 'Who are the people who don't want to work?' he asks from beneath his INDIA cap, and answers his own question by counting off the indolent classes on two fingers: '*Chamaar aur Musalmaan*.')

At the restaurant, the Hindus wait outside wearily while the Muslims have lunch. Bobur is fed separately by the staff, and judging by his familiarity with them he comes here often with tourists and is likely incentivized to do so. While waiting outside, Paras, to kill time, asks a taxi-driver about the prospects for boom-boom in Samarkand. The prospects are unbelievably great. The taxi-driver, in his broken English, says he can arrange for boom-boom all right. 'What you like? 16 years, 17 years, 18 years?' How much? '25 dollars, 30 dollars.' Paras is goggle-eyed and wishes he'd known about this earlier. He and another Gujarati start making hectic plans to skip post-lunch sightseeing and instead squeeze in some boom-boom between now and the train's departure. But these plans are forgotten when Paras falls in love.

She's a young woman in a pink dress sipping cocktails with her friend in the outdoor section of the restaurant. Paras can't stop looking at her, but he can't muster up the courage to go talk to her either. The rest of us pass time by egging him on. Finally he goes up to their table, sits there for a minute, and returns. They speak no English at all, so there's nothing to be said. After an hour spent eating, Bobur and the Muslims emerge content from the restaurant. We pile into the van, but Paras has asked Bobur to interpret for him, and they head off to the girls' table. The rest of us sit in the van and watch Paras's translated wooing from afar. The diabetic Muslim, now energized, says to his cohort, pointedly and loud enough for the whole van to hear: '*Kyon, ab der nahi ho rahi?* Well, now aren't we getting late?' Paras returns triumphant. She's willing to go on a date with him in the evening. He can call her through Bobur and decide where to meet. But this will also mean that Paras will have to book a room in Samarkand and return by himself the next day. His Gujarati friends refuse to stay with him; he asks me, but I too say no. I ask him what his problem is with staying alone—anyway, if all goes well he'll have the girl for company. '*Foreign country hain yaar, dar lagta hain.* It's a foreign country, so one feels scared.'

We have time to visit just one more site, and it's to be the Registan, the main public square of Samarkand during the reign of Timur and his successors. What remains today is the tile-patterned expanse of the square bounded off on three sides by madrasas. One of the madrasas was built in the fifteenth century by Timur's grandson Ulugh Beg; the other two came in the seventeenth century. Each of these madrasas evokes awe with its size, elegance of form and density of ornamentation, but to stand in the middle of the square surrounded by three all at once is outright swoon-inducing. Towering gateways, minarets, cupolas and arches are all covered in coloured ceramic, most of it in vivid shades of blue. The motifs and inscriptions are intricate enough to be admirable on a teacup, but at this scale they are near-miraculous. It seems no exaggeration to say there's nothing quite like it in the world. The Registan is a kind of Mecca of Islamic architecture. Timur's military conquests took him far and wide and slaughtered far too many, but he brought back with him the best craftsmen and builders from wherever he went, and the eventual results of that confluence are the glistening blue wonders of Timurid Samarkand.

We make a hasty stop at a market to buy dry fruits and silks, and head to the railway station. Paras, after much introspection and discussion, decides not to take the risk of staying on in Samarkand. But its women, both professional and amateur, have made a mark on him. 'Next time I'm coming straight here,' he says.

Samarkand's history is ridiculously rich and varied: people have lived here for at least three and a half millennia, with a city being established in 700 BC; it's been ruled by Persians, Greeks, Turkics, Chinese and Russians; several larger-than-life figures in world history have been here—Alexander, Genghis Khan, Timur; it's had Zoroastrians, Buddhists and Nestorian Christians before becoming largely Islamic; and it's been an important staging post on the Silk Road, the network of trade routes that connected China with Europe until the fifteenth century. Our day in the most glorious city of Transoxiana has largely been spent waiting for people while they eat, pray or love, and we've left most of its riches unexplored. If there's a next time I'm coming straight here too.

There are perhaps five people in our entire tour group who are not here for boom-boom. I'm one of them, and I have to admit this whenever someone in the group wants to compare notes about how we're enjoying. One of the cool sardars asks me, '*Aap gay ho kya?* Are you gay?' More poetically, someone else asks, '*Mandir tak aaye, par pooja nahin ki?* Came till the temple, but did not worship?' I joke that maybe my temples are elsewhere, to which he says, '*Woh toh sabke hain.* That everyone has.'

I begin to feel, as the tour comes to an end, that despite all the fuss about boom-boom, maybe the group doesn't really enjoy it very much. Take Rajesh: one night he isn't happy because he's been sent the wrong girl; on the next night he's in a sex worker's apartment 15 km from the hotel and unable to have a good time because he's worried about safety. On the last night when someone asks if he's getting a girl, he just says, 'No, I'm bored.' (Instead we go to a nightclub where, between lap-dances, he tells me he doesn't approve of this sort of place: 'Sex is good. Sexuality is bad.') Or take Paras, who has no equal in the group when it comes to describing his experiences in queasy detail. He tells me that the sex workers here wear female condoms *and* get the man to wear a condom. Unable to help myself I ask him what that's like, and he says, 'It's okay. A little noisy'—which does not sound like much fun at all. When he falls in love with the girl in pink in Samarkand he outright denounces paid sex and tells me that just taking a girl out to dinner on one's own merits is far better than boom-boom with a sex-worker. Right at the beginning of the tour, even as the bus pulled out of the airport, Jabir told us about the show he organizes—naked women, fondling allowed, no boom-boom. When he found no takers, he'd said, presumably from past experience, 'Never mind. You'll all get bored of boom-boom in a couple of days. Then you can go for this.' This turns out to be exactly what happens.

I also come to suspect that there's a thrill that comes from exercising power over another that may be as or more enjoyable than the boom-boom itself. The delight on the faces of men as a girl dances for them is no doubt owing to some erotic self-validation, but also at the fact that the taunting clutch of currency notes in their hand gives them the power to acquire that validation at will. (This power dynamic is well-understood in dance-bars in India, where a feudal component is serviced as well: all the men working in these bars—the doormen, the waiters—in return for tips will affect a cowering smarminess intended to make the most hapless patron feel like Timur himself.) The pinnacle of power I'd guess is at the moment of selecting a girl from a fawning line-up, which might render the subsequent boom-boom somewhat anti-climactic. Unless there's a chance to throw one's weight around there too. Returning to the department of queasy details, Paras boasts over breakfast one morning of how he asserted himself in the night. He'd paid a night manager for a 'two-shot' session with a woman who, after the first shot, regretted her inability to go through with the second because she'd run out of condoms. Paras suspected she was shirking work and so he adopted a severe tone and asked her to call the night manager right now, upon which she found some condoms and readied herself for round two. Is the human element to be considered here at all, or does the situation have the same contractual obligations of, say, a tour programme that promises two non-veg snacks during a gala dinner and delivers only one? How do you go on to have sex with a woman who's clearly indicated she's unwilling, unless you don't see her as a person at all, or unless the very fact that she doesn't have a say is part of what's driving you?

At a nightclub I go to with Paras and Rajesh, there are about a dozen minimally clad women in impossible heels who take turns with the pole in the middle and stalk the room giving lap dances. At one point in the evening there's a cry from a table near ours and I turn to see a woman fly briefly through the air and crash to the floor. For some reason, the man she was straddling has thrown her off him. His table is at the edge of a slightly elevated section of the floor, making her fall all the more dramatic. She clambers back up onto her heels, looking at the man in disbelief. Gone is her strut, her inviting smile. It's a tired, frightened girl who totters away weeping. There are bouncers around but they say nothing to the man (who, burly and impassive, may well be some sort of alpha night manager). If this can happen in public, how vulnerable must women be behind a locked door with a stranger.

Jabir is defensive when I ask him how Uzbekistan

became a destination for sex tourists. He largely holds the tourists responsible. He says he's interested in showing people around his country, but they only care for one thing. According to him there aren't even that many women involved in sex work. He says, 'There are maybe around a hundred girls in Tashkent. Everyone comes here, fucks the same girls and goes back.' That sounds like a considerable understatement. There must be that number of sex workers from the former USSR in Delhi or Mumbai alone. The textbook explanation holds that the dissolution of the USSR created economic uncertainty in which many young women found it hard to support themselves, and ended up in different parts of the world as sex workers.

Why come all the way to Uzbekistan when it's easily possible to find women from the region in India? There are reasons of pragmatism, of course—there's no one who might recognize you here, and the country's relatively cheap. Beyond that, these four or five days are an opportunity to let oneself go. Here there are no responsibilities of family or work. The proscriptions of home are absent, so you can drink and smoke as much as you want. Everyone's a young man once again, giggling at adolescent jokes. There's the sex of course, but here it goes beyond simply servicing the libido. There's a jubilant revelling in sex and an air of constant bawdiness that can only come from the working-out of things long pent-up. Here you can unburden yourself comprehensively. You can enjoy.

It's the last gala dinner of the tour. The girls have danced and left; the notes have been swept off the floor.

But the group continues to dance in a small clearing in the restaurant. For the first time on the tour, it's only men. Everyone's drunk and there's a lightness, a playfulness in the air. Someone grabs Kakaji and mock-slow-dances with him; Don rushes for his money-bag and showers notes on them. Sharmaji is skipping with his arms in the air. The sardars are a joy to watch, especially the oldest of them, a man with a long white beard who's making rhythmic quotation marks in the air with eyes shut in intense concentration. One of the cool sardars dances up to my table and motions to me to join them. 'No one will ask you tomorrow. Get up,' he says firmly. Soon I'm flailing about amidst expressions of delight at seeing me on my feet for the first time. Tomorrow we will leave Tashkent and return to our regular lives, but for now—we are enjoying.

6
SANTA CLAUS AA RAHE HAI

Photo courtesy Reality Tours and Travels

Roof of a recycling unit in Dharavi

In his book of travel essays *Yoga for People Who Can't Be Bothered to Do It*, Geoff Dyer writes: 'All visitors to the developing world, if they are honest, will confess that they are actually quite keen on seeing a bit of squalor: people living on garbage dumps, shanty towns, that kind of thing.' He goes on to describe meeting a Swede in Bombay who had visited 'one of the worst slum districts', where a beggar woman had 'shoved her dead baby in his face'. Dyer writes that the half-dozen foreigners listening to the story were 'all horrified and, I think, more than a little envious'. Of course, that baby probably

wasn't dead. It's a common enough experience in Mumbai
or in any Indian city: if you look like you have a rupee or
two to spare, you can have a baby shoved in your face at
any traffic signal. Sometimes these babies have been
acquired on hire; sometimes they are sedated. It's likely
the Swede saw one of these babies asleep and believed
what he wanted to believe, or was tempted to embellish
the story to elicit exactly the sort of envious horror that
Dyer describes. After all, competition among travellers is
intense, and a story like this is a lifelong trump card at
dinner tables in hostels and guest houses across the
world.

Near the beginning of the 2008 film *Slumdog
Millionaire* is that much-talked-about flashback from
the protagonist Jamal's childhood in which he is locked
into a slum's hanging latrine by his brother just as his
idol Amitabh Bachchan's helicopter descends in the
vicinity. Jamal desperately wants Amitabh's autograph
and there's no way out of the latrine except for jumping
down into the pit. He emerges dripping with shit
(simulated in shooting with peanut butter and chocolate)
and makes his way through a gagging crowd to get the
autograph. The events that lead up to Jamal being locked
into the latrine feel so contrived that the whole point
seems to have been to somehow get a boy covered in shit
into the film.

The Swede's dead baby and *Slumdog*'s shit-covered
boy are both instances of a gaze that transforms squalor
into spectacle. The worse things are for the objects of
this gaze, the better it gets for the spectator. Here, the
dominant response to poverty and human suffering is

not pity or sorrow or compassion, but a kind of self-enchantment with witnessing or depicting it. So, it might seem bad enough that babies are used as begging accessories, but to raise it to a delightfully horrific pitch there's nothing like stumbling upon dead babies in the street and being in the presence of poverty so abject that a mother in her grief will shrewdly hold up her dead child's body to score a few rupees. And it's a matter of concern that open defecation and manual scavenging are well and alive in India, but how much more fun it is to personify this state of excretory affairs in a boy who glistens with shit from head to toe.

The travel writer Paul Theroux writes in his 2008 book *Ghost Train to the Eastern Star*, 'In Mumbai: a tourist would have been in a temple or a museum. I had been in a slum.' The boast is one that an increasing number of tourists can make today. If visitors from the developed world are 'quite keen on seeing a bit of squalor', the developing world indulges them readily through slum tourism—pay money to go and look at the living conditions of those less fortunate than yourself. There are organized tours of the favelas in Brazil, of townships in Johannesburg, of garbage dumps in Mexico, of slums in Mumbai, Jakarta, China, and plenty of other places across Asia, Africa and South America.

But slum tourism began in what is today the first world when affluent nineteenth-century Londoners began venturing forth into the seedier parts of town for a Dickensian fix. It wasn't long before the activity spread to the other side of the Atlantic. Here's the *New York Times* of 14 September 1884: '*Slumming, the latest fashionable idiosyncrasy in London—i.e., the visiting of the slums of the great city by parties of ladies and gentlemen for sightseeing—is mildly practiced here by a tour of the Bowery, winding up with a visit to an opium den or Harry Hill's.'* The post-slumming chit-chat feels remarkably contemporary: *'A quite well-known young English noble, returning from a tour of the east side the other night with some club friends, observed over his brandy and soda: "Ah, this is a great city, but you have no slums like we have. I have been in rickety condemned buildings that it was absolutely dangerous to go through! Found six families living in one miserably ventilated cellar—24 persons, 16 of them adults, living in the one room. No such slums here!"'* The article goes on to defend New York's honour by claiming that there are indeed such slums, places of *'misery, multitude and vice'*, and *'of the same squalor and suffering as anything ever seen in the English metropolis'*, but the inexperienced guides simply hadn't explored those routes. There's mention of how slum tourism led to charity work in London. Only one specific work is mentioned, and that seems utterly cosmetic and almost apologetic: *'The flower charities have done much good work among the poor in the tenements by distributing among them floral gifts. What a pleasure it must be to a sufferer imprisoned in one of these tenements to receive a flower, with its color and its green leaves and stems!'*

One may want to go see a slum because it is edifying to see how people poorer than oneself live, or because it presents a more complete social picture of the place one is visiting, or because, like Gandhi, one may at times want to recall the face of the poorest and the weakest person whom one has seen and ask oneself if the next step one is contemplating is going to be of any use to that person. A survey conducted in Mumbai's Dharavi by a researcher from the University of Pennsylvania found that most tourists who came to do a slum tour were motivated by simple curiosity, but though they were curious, they weren't interested in interacting with residents. In other words: they came to gawk. As the report states, 'The slum tourism experience was one of leisure rather than self-discovery.' The tour organizer was Reality Tours and Travel (RTT), founded jointly by an Englishman and an Indian in 2005 (and the subject of much media attention since).

RTT runs two tours of Dharavi—one long and one short. The Dharavi sections of the tours are identical, but the long tour starts in south Bombay and makes its way to Dharavi via the red-light area of Kamathipura and the dhobi ghat at Mahalaxmi. The walking tour of Dharavi aims to emphasize the economic vibrancy of the community and dispel myths about poverty and slums. Criticism that it's only a vehicle for first-world voyeurs crops up from time to time, but RTT counters this by saying that they use 80 per cent of their profits for the benefit of slum residents. In 2009, RTT consolidated their social work by starting an NGO—Reality Gives. Between them they run a nursery school, and a community centre in Dharavi where locals can learn English and computer skills. They also support other education and sports related activities. (We've come a long way from the token absolution of handing out flowers.) Tourists may well arrive at Dharavi with a keenness for squalor, but RTT aims to show them a different side of the slum, and in a way that ultimately benefits the community.

I find myself standing one morning at 8.15 in front of Cafe Leopold on Colaba Causeway. An alarmingly lean man shrouded in grimy clothes eyes me for a while before coming up to me: 'Dope-shope? Marijuana? Hashish? I have right now.' No. I'm waiting here because this is the pick-up point for RTT's long tour of Dharavi. Leopold is of course a well-known hangout for foreign tourists in Mumbai, and RTT's clientele happens to be almost entirely foreign. I will be disorientingly reminded of this at every step of the tour as I'm shown a part of my own country as if I were from elsewhere.

The RTT jeep is parked in the lane beside Leopold. Our guide is Dinesh, a hassled-looking young man of twenty or so. He has missed me in front of Leopold, perhaps because he wasn't expecting an Indian, and when I find him he is on the phone to the office complaining about the member who hasn't yet shown up. I get into the back of the jeep. Introductions follow. My fellow slummers are three women: Ulrika, a German woman in her thirties who lives in Australia; Nina and Andrea, in their twenties and from the French Reunion Islands.

As we drive from Colaba, I'm finding that Dinesh's commentary has a somewhat surreal defamiliarizing effect, given that I once lived in Mumbai for eight years. At Churchgate station: 'As you can see, people are bursting

out. You can also see dabbawallas here later in the day.'
Malabar Hill and Marine Drive: 'Land here costs 2100
US dollars per square foot.' Chowpatty: 'Here you can
eat a famous snack called bhelpuri.' Wankhede Stadium:
'Cricket is like a religion in India.' Chor Bazaar: 'If
something of yours is stolen—come here.' Kamathipura:
'This is the famous red-light district of Mumbai.'

As we turn into Falkland Road, Dinesh paints a
wretched picture of commercial sex work in the area. He
talks of how traffickers bring women, and often young
girls, from various parts of India and neighbouring
countries. 'The women are beaten by the brothel owners,'
he tells us. Ulrika fishes her camera out of her bag and
takes position at the window. Huddled doorways come
into view, open to varying degrees. 'These are the women,'
Dinesh says.

The depiction of sex workers in Indian films has always
seemed lazy and trite to me—the perennial combing of
hair, the constant lounging about clad only in blouse and
petticoat. On Falkland Road I discover that those films
are accurate, at least as far as Kamathipura goes. There
are any number of women wearing only petticoats and
blouses—sitting, legs akimbo, on steps framed by narrow
doors, or visible through the bars of windows. At one
door there's even a woman combing her long black hair.
We drive past, taking only a couple of minutes. Ulrika
clicks away with a predatory eagerness that I find
annoying. She wants to know, 'How much do the women
charge?' Dinesh pretends not to have heard. Ulrika repeats
her question and Dinesh is clearly offended. He replies
curtly, 'I don't know. I have never gone.' After a while he

turns around and adds, 'Here we believe in having girlfriends.'

We move on to the dhobi ghat at Mahalaxmi. 'This is the biggest open-air laundry in the world,' Dinesh says, adding, 'Your hotel will charge you a lot for laundry, but it will be washed here.' Our view is from a bridge overlooking the vast basin of the ghat and its panorama of laundering. Men, bare-chested or in vests, slosh about in troughs of murky water, flogging clothes in concrete cubicles. Bed sheets, pillow-covers, hospital gowns, uniforms, all dangle in orderly rows. It's a lucrative business according to Dinesh, and as with everything else in Mumbai, there is much competition for being allotted one of the cubicles here.

We drive past Girgaum, Phoenix Mills, Dadar station. Dinesh points out markets for fish, flowers and vegetables. Then there's a lull in his script. After a short silence, the driver breaks in: '*Reality khatam ho jaayega yaar ek-do saal mein.* Reality will be finished in a year or two.' For a second I think he's launching into a metaphysical discussion, but they're only talking about their employer. They're so used to having only foreign tourists that they're entirely unselfconscious conversing in Hindi. I learn that several others have now started Dharavi tours. The driver speculates that all this competition will ultimately shut down the company and tells Dinesh they better start looking for something else. Dinesh points out that RTT has begun to diversify by offering other tours—Indian village tours, Mumbai by night, Mumbai by public transport. 'But the main thing is Dharavi, na?' says the driver. The conversation is cut short when the jeep pulls up by a pile of garbage. We've reached Dharavi.

Dharavi is an area of around 550 acres wedged between the suburbs of Mahim, Sion and Bandra, contained by the tracks of Mumbai's Central and Western local railway lines, and by the Mithi river to the north. It is roughly heart-shaped, which allows RTT to sell nifty 'I ♥ Dharavi' t-shirts with the outline of Dharavi serving as a jittery, wonky heart. Somewhere between half to one million people live here. (The floating population makes them hard to count.) The land on which Dharavi stands is prime real estate in Mumbai, but this is today. In the nineteenth century the region largely comprised disjointed islands and mangrove swamp, and was reclaimed by filling rubble in the watery parts. This being the farthest edge of Bombay then, the civic authorities were just fine if migrants or the just-rendered-homeless from freshly demolished illegal settlements in Bombay came to live here. The original inhabitants of Dharavi, the Koli fisherfolk, were soon joined by others— migrants from other parts of Maharashtra, potters from Gujarat, tanners from Tamil Nadu, craftsmen from Uttar Pradesh, and ultimately by anyone who hoped to make a fresh beginning. In this sense Dharavi is a concentrated image of Mumbai, and it is fitting that it now finds itself not at the periphery but at the heart of the city.

Perhaps it is the assiduous ones who migrate? Or could it be that the very act of moving to another place leaves one with a residual momentum? Almost everywhere, migrants have been known for their enterprising ways, and Dharavi is no different, being a hive of unregulated industry. Dinesh tells us even as we're getting out of the jeep and stretching that the annual turnover of Dharavi is USD 665 million, and we are all suitably impressed.

Dinesh briefs us on how to behave and what to expect. 'We have to respect the people of the slum,' he says. 'So we have a strictly no cameras policy.' Some places may not be clean, and there may be strong odours at times. He addresses the women: 'I must warn you that people stare. But they are harmless.'

We set off down a road that really looks like it could have been anywhere in Mumbai—chai stalls, small hotels, vendors, a jumble of vehicles. The guide and I may well have been part of the scene, but clearly not the three women. '*Aao, aao*. Come, come,' drawls a young man who's made himself comfortable on a parked motorcycle; the two friends chatting with him make cheeping noises. They laugh after we pass. All through the rest of our walk, there's sustained staring and taunting. The comments aren't overly aggressive, and many of them aren't noticed by the women, being made in Hindi and usually just after we've passed. In fact, they feel almost *obligatory*, as if it's a territorial reiteration of sorts for the young men and teenagers who, every day, watch foreigners walk so earnestly through their turf.

The first part of the walking tour looks at the recycling industry, one of the economic mainstays of Dharavi. The considerable waste that Mumbai generates is sorted by scavengers and brought here to be renewed or repurposed. In one low-lit warehouse, stacks of empty oil tins tower over the workers. Dinesh tell us these come from restaurants all over Mumbai. This unit readies them for reuse by dunking them in hot water and scrubbing them with soap. In other places we see piles of cardboard, sacks, plastic odds and ends, bottles. The units are closely packed and storage space is limited, so everything tends to overflow, gather in mounds on the corrugated roofs, or line the paths in a casually ordered jumble. The recycling units look like makeshift arrangements with hastily drawn electrical wiring and equipment strewn about, but everything has a black lint of cobwebs and grime clinging to it, suggesting that this is how things have been for a while. From above, the zone feels like an urban analogue to one of nature's awesome cycles: detritus from the city around will keep flowing in, and this landscape of variegated rubble will somehow keep regenerating itself into things new and useful.

We are being treated to a view from above because we have stepped over sacks and climbed stairs so rudimentary as to count as a ladder to reach the tin roof of a plant that produces recycled plastic pellets. This roof is different from the roofs around in that it's been used less enthusiastically as a storage space, probably because it's a viewing point on RTT's tour. The roof is also different because it's the only one whose edge is cordoned off, with a sign that reads STOP. (In case someone decides to step off either from claustrophobia or first-world guilt?) Dinesh orients us, pointing out the surrounding suburbs and the path we will take for the rest of the tour. From here it's clear that there's nothing homogeneous about Dharavi. The construction ranges from precarious hovels to high-rise apartments, the latter the result of redevelopment projects. These are still exceptions in the otherwise squat topography, but may become commonplace if a comprehensive redevelopment plan goes through. Such plans have abounded, but have usually been stymied by their inability to get Dharavi residents on board. Dinesh tells us that, in general, people are happy to be living and working in Dharavi as it is. There are even people who've been allotted apartments, but have chosen to rent them out and start afresh at ground-level elsewhere in Dharavi.

It's not long before one of us asks Dinesh what *is* a slum anyway? He has a concise answer: 'House owned by people, land owned by government.' But there are some who own their land here—the original Koli residents, and others who at various times have been granted ownership of land they've occupied for long periods.

We move on to other industries. 'Can you guess what this is?' asks Dinesh pointing to a tray with brown cakes. Ulrika, after some thought: 'Brownies?' Dinesh: 'No, it's soap for washing clothes.' At an embroidery shop, a programmable Chinese machine is riddling patterns concurrently into several pieces of cloth. We stop by a bakery engaged in producing massive quantities of khari biscuits that none of us want to try. We see piles of tanned hides in a noticeably odoriferous quarter. Metal-work goes on in a room filled with heavy machinery. We enter a block printing unit just as a family from the UK is leaving—a couple with a teenage boy wearing a '7, David Villa' jersey. 'Isn't this incredible?' says David's mother as they pass. It is. No one thing here may be incredible by itself, but the presence of so many activities in such proximity conveys a sense of glorious vitality. It's the real-life equivalent of a mural that compresses an epic human drama onto a single wall.

Some idea of Dharavi's religious composition may be had from its places of worship. There are 27 temples, 11 mosques and 6 churches here (as Kalpana Sharma writes in *Rediscovering Dharavi* [2000]). Hindus and Muslims live in separate quarters of Dharavi. They've always co-existed in peace, Dinesh tells us, except for the communal riots that broke out in 1992–93 after the Babri Masjid demolition. We stop at a place where they make carved wooden altars that are used to hold images and statues of Hindu gods. This is in the Muslim area and all the workers here are Muslim. Dinesh dwells on the irony for a bit, but I seem to be the only one who's appreciative. Two boys of about ten wearing skullcaps and carrying satchels point at us and shout, '*Angrez! Angrez!*' They stop beside us, make swishing sibilant sounds meant to imitate a foreigner's English, and run off laughing.

We walk through a maze of narrow lanes in a residential area, an activity akin to some sort of urban spelunking. The paths are barely wide enough for a person to walk through, and sometimes not even that, necessitating adroit twisting and sidling. (Part of the fault no doubt lies with our party—I am of

A lane in Dharavi

fairly strapping build, and Ulrika may even be considered hefty.) Steps of houses, parked two-wheelers, and ad hoc electrical and water fixtures add a further level of navigational complexity. One section in particular is almost entirely dark, being between the rear-walls of houses, and one corner has a mass of water-pipes at ground level and a tangle of low-hanging electrical cables that take some tai chi style movements to get through.

It's mid-morning and there are few men about. Women are cooking, or sitting on the steps of their houses talking to neighbours, or washing clothes and vessels at nearby taps. Through open doors I can see homes created in the space of a tiny room or two—patterned floor-tiles, TVs, steel utensils on wall-mounted shelves, beds, rolled up mattresses. There are children everywhere—on doorsteps, at the corners of lanes. They constantly crowd around us, proffering their hands with delight and great ceremony. Mothers and elder siblings sometimes push kids forward, saying to them, 'What should you say?' The kids say 'hi' or 'hello' and stick their hands out. The foreigners shake hands and reach for their bottles of hand-sanitizers.

Maybe it's the concentrated quality of life here, but surrounded by these homes I'm reminded of my own. I grew up in a larger house with more amenities, but it's a difference only of degree. These are middle-class homes, a world I know well: the steel vessels, the televisions, the clutter of odds and ends hoarded because they might come in use one day; the sounds of pressure cookers going off, pans being scraped with a piece of brick, clothes being rinsed by hand. These are part of my consciousness. In a sense that the foreigners on the tour cannot possibly share, I am among my own.

More precisely, I appear to be on some kind of safari among my own, an observer in the midst of spaces that feel private. Most of the women here are wearing the national dress of the middle-class homemaker: the baggy nightgown. When they squat to wash vessels or clothes, these gowns are rolled up to mid-thigh to avoid getting them wet. I feel as if I shouldn't be here, but the women are oblivious of us as we pass. Two women sitting on steps across a lane continue their conversation as we walk *between* them. In one Muslim household there's a group of women sitting on the floor, watching TV, who hardly glance at us as we crowd the doorway and peep in. This may be from the conditioning of living in a place as densely populated as Dharavi, but I suspect it has more to do with being inured to tour groups passing through, as well as the realization that these groups consist almost entirely of foreigners. Such frictionless passage can occur only between people who are sufficiently remote. If Indian tour groups started passing through these lanes with regularity, Indians with the cultural bases to judge and slot and appraise, I doubt the people here would be as unconcerned. I'm here only because my being with the group turns me into a foreigner.

We've seen no real squalor so far (if we ignore a wide drain of slow-flowing dark sludge that is a choice blend of human and industrial waste). There have been flies, smells, people working and living in cramped-to-the-point-of-bonsai conditions, but nothing remotely abject.

I'd noticed earlier that Ulrika furtively got out her camera and took pictures of the aforementioned drain, and she's seemed impatient when Dharavi's industrial achievements are recounted. So, when she asks Dinesh if there's a toilet she can use, I can't help wondering if she's really angling for some *Slumdog*-level squalor. If she is, she's disappointed. Dinesh conducts us to a solidly constructed public toilet connected to a municipal sewage system. Not far away is a clearing that seems to be used as a local garbage dump. A few children are using it as an open-air toilet. People here use either a public toilet, of which there aren't enough to go around, or defecate in the open.

Municipal water connections are available, as are 'private' ones—illegal operations that draw pipes from the main municipal water pipes. Both can be unreliable, and water is hoarded, usually in big blue plastic drums.

We stop for chai. I ask Ulrika how she's finding the tour. She's not impressed. 'This is like a residential area,' she says. 'There are *buildings* here.' And there are computers and televisions and air-conditioners too. There's even a BMW that belongs to one of the factory owners. Ulrika visited another slum, near Colaba, just yesterday. 'That was like a real slum,' she says. 'It was right next to where Shanty-ram lived.' (That conflation of Shanti, Shantaram, and shanty might serve as the perfect description for a certain type of tourist in India.) How did she learn about the place? From a taxi driver. Apparently some taxi drivers in South Bombay offer their foreign passengers an informal slum tour.

She signed up for Dharavi expecting more, but is now disappointed.

I ask Dinesh if there are others who conduct slum tours in Dharavi. 'After *Slumdog* others have started,' he tells me. Some of them used to be guides with RTT who saw the increased interest in Dharavi and decided to start their own tours. 'But they don't do charity work.'

We move on. Dinesh points to a woman flattening dough with a rolling pin and trimming it into neat circles. 'She is making poppadum,' he tells us, something many women in Dharavi do to supplement their household's income. Dinesh gives us a compressed sociological account of Indian womanhood: 'Women are not allowed to go out. Cook, marriage, children. Little bit allowed now, but Muslims are still same.'

As we pass through a lane my attention is drawn to a scattered group of obviously affluent teenagers. They're wearing sneakers and colourful T-shirts and shorts that stand out in these surroundings for being ruthlessly unfaded. At one door there are three of them talking to a harried-looking boy wearing a school uniform of navy blue trousers and indigo-smudged white shirt. '*Aapke paas bijli hai, paani hai?* Do you have electricity, water?' one is asking. Another: '*Textbooks ke liye koi problem hai?* Any problems getting textbooks?' I surmise they're on one of the school visits that RTT organizes. I ask one of the boys and learn that they're from Bangalore International School, here on a class project. They watched a documentary on Dharavi as part of one of their classes and felt they should go to Mumbai and see

the slum first-hand. He tells me, 'We just wanna find out
what their needs are, why they don't wanna move, and
why they're not into development.' Then, with a shrug,
'And maybe do something about it.'

By the time I've scrawled down some notes the others
have moved out of sight. I rush down the lane and catch
up with them. We will visit a preschool run by RTT,
make a quick stop at a potter's house, and end the tour
at RTT's community centre and office where we will
receive a cold Coke to help us recover.

The preschool is a single room, cheerful with charts
and streamers. Around twenty kids, aged three or four,
are being taught rhymes. A group of young women are
present—trainee teachers according to Dinesh. David
Villa and his parents are already inside. The room is
full and we cram in at the door. The teacher doing the
training tells us that they try to get the kids learning
English as soon as possible. One of the ways they do
this is to teach them English rhymes as well as the Hindi
translations of those rhymes. Right now they're learning
Jingle Bells. A woman is singing in a clear, loud, high
voice, one line at a time. The kids repeat indistinctly
after her:

Ghanti bajao, ghanti bajao
Saare raaste mein
Santa Claus aa rahe hai
Khulli gaadi mein

I'm sure the school is doing a fine job in general, but
I find the selection of rhyme so dismaying that I stagger

away from the cluster at the door and wait for the others some distance away. Who is Santa Claus and why is he coming? Why should I sound a bell (as the Hindi words exhort)? In the absence of a culture in which Santa Claus is a keenly awaited bearer of presents, asking kids to learn this rhyme makes about as much sense as riding a sleigh in Mumbai. Worse, when the first units of one's formal education turn out to be bewildering things with no relation to the world around, they send the message that education really isn't about very much, just a series of sounds or symbols to be memorized. If English must be taught here to toddlers, it might make more sense to translate Hindi rhymes into English, not the other way round.

But then, maybe an early familiarity with bewilderment is a good thing if the kids are going to routinely have strangers from distant lands peeking into their homes. And maybe it makes sense that this part of their education is being sponsored by those very tourists. If slum tourism must exist at all, this model—the Santa Claus model?— would seem the way to go. There's something for everyone: the tourists have their curiosity sated, their minds broadened; the slum residents benefit from the proceeds in various ways; and a few enterprising enablers make a living.

In the case of RTT, the guides (a couple of whom I've spoken to) and founders (one of whom I talk to after the tour) exude a genuine sense of affection for Dharavi. They could easily put together a tour of Dharavi that would satisfy Ulrika and those looking for something more gritty, but they choose instead to showcase its

industriousness. People may take the tour with vague
expectations of squalor, but what they get is something
else that's fascinating in its own right.

7
ACCORDING TO THEIR OWN GENIUS

Living root bridges, Nongriat, Cherrapunji

The tour of Assam and Meghalaya conducted by a travel outfit called Journeys with Meaning (JwM) turns out to be so free-form that it barely feels like a conducted tour. The other bus tours I'd been on had older people who seemed to have led scripted lives and were sure—sometimes infuriatingly sure—of their place in the world. Here the tourists are in their twenties and thirties, idealistic, and at crossroads of one kind or the other in their personal and professional lives.

In fact my fellow tourists here might well be the children

of the tourists I'd met on the Tamil Nadu or Europe tours. They are representatives of a younger generation that is trying to travel on its own terms even while opting for the convenience of a conducted tour. A few dozen travel companies have sprung up in the last decade to cater to this segment. Most are run by a handful of young people and reach out to potential customers through the Internet. As expected, wildlife and adventure sport are hugely popular. Some companies also offer more idiosyncratic tours, such as G-Sharp, which combines guitar lessons with travel to a scenic location so their clients can (according to their website) 'experience the greatness of music coupled with nature'. Girls On The Go organizes women-only trips to 'new, exotic destinations', noting on their website that 'with changing times more and more women want to break free from domestic monotony or corporate stress and explore the world around them, without necessarily being accompanied by men or having to drag along busy friends'. The Blueberry Trails calls itself an 'experiential travel company', and promises to take you 'beyond boardroom politics, the malls, the traffic snarls' as a 'fellow traveller and NOT as a tourist'. The Mumbai-based Grassroutes aims to put city dwellers in touch with rural India, and organizes village tours with featured activities such as drawing water from a well, chopping wood, ploughing fields and milking a goat. Wild Trotters has among its offerings group tours of haunted places in Rajasthan and Karnataka. Among other tours, Getoff Ur Ass conducts photography workshops in photogenic places such as Spiti, the ghats of Varanasi, Goa during the carnival, and Alleppey during the boat race. The names of these travel companies—Nirvana Nomads, Gypsy Feet, Roads Less Travelled—tell the story of who the travellers are and what their aspired-to self-image might be, but perhaps none better than an outfit that promises 'incredible off-beat travel' and calls itself White Collar Hippie.

The Mumbai-based JwM offers tours to Kashmir, Ladakh and the North-East that feature a varied mix of activities. Their North-East tour to Assam and Meghalaya includes wildlife and adventure, and meetings and visits that yield insights into the region's society, culture and ecology. Time is set aside for discussions and for watching documentaries, and guidance is available for those who might want to improve their photography skills. When I call to enquire about details, JwM's founder, Vinod Sreedhar, comes across as so pleasantly straightforward that I decide to look no further. In two weeks I'm on a train bound for Guwahati, where the tour begins.

I learn about JwM's inception over a tour's worth of conversations with Vinod, an earnest-looking bespectacled man in his mid-thirties. While in college, he realized that he wasn't cut out for the standard get-a-degree-then-a-job path, dropped out, and went on to become a musician. He played keyboards for a couple of rock bands and later became one half of a duo that composed ad jingles and background scores for television serials. He'd all along been interested in environmental issues, so he began conducting workshops on what he calls Whole Systems Thinking and Earth-friendly Living, with commercial music fading into the background. He says about the workshops he was giving: 'I found that the classroom experience wasn't enough. Turning it into a travelling workshop felt like a good idea, as it would help participants make deeper connections between what they were learning, the places they were visiting, and the people they were meeting.' And so, in 2007, JwM was born. Vinod also began conducting a workshop called Inside Out to help young people identify their aspirations and work towards them. His own priorities are working with the environment and helping people become self-aware, and it's evident during the Assam and Meghalaya tour that he feels these are connected: it's the same system of thinking—or unthinking—that creates ecological imbalances as well as causes people in cities to be stuck in unfulfilling jobs.

The idealism behind JwM is apparent in its working. For the first four years of its existence, JwM experimented with operating tours at cost, with the company supported by voluntary donations made by participants at the end of a trip. This changed when they felt the need for a more reliable stream of income. Now, participants pay the company a fixed price to reserve their place on a tour, and then share all expenses during travel. JwM tries to keep its carbon footprint low, and the considerable travel required for scouting new locations and making local arrangements is all done by rail and road. An email sent to the participants of the Assam and Meghalaya tour encourages us to take a train to Guwahati rather than fly.

At Guwahati, people trickle in through the day into the Assam Tourism hotel. There's Homi—a tall, lean frizzy-haired man in his early twenties who works for JwM. He's a journalist by training who attended one of Vinod's Inside Out workshops. There he was asked what he would do if he knew he had only five years left to live. He'd travel, and so he now works for JwM. The other just-joined member of JwM is Moresha, also a journalist. She recently lost her parents in quick succession, and in the ensuing period of introspection and adjustment has decided to throw in her lot with travel. There's Ankita, a 23-year-old from Mumbai who's a law student and a teacher of French, who tells me that for a while now she's been feeling 'cynical and jaded' and unable to enjoy anything. She's hoping this trip will help revive her spirits. She heard about JwM from her cousin Preeti, who's here too. Preeti, in her mid-twenties, took a break from her hectic corporate job and went on the JwM tour of Ladakh. She recalls being amazed at how much the locals smiled as they went about their day. That, combined with the open spaces and the discussions during the tour, had an effect on her. She returned to Mumbai and fell ill. 'It was probably psychosomatic,' she says, but it gave her a long break from work and time to reflect, and she eventually quit her job to spend more time on travel and her hobbies. Ramesh and Priya are a couple in their mid-thirties who work at corporate jobs in Delhi. They've been meaning to do one of these trips for a while, and they have a window of opportunity now that Ramesh is in between jobs and wondering whether to take up a corporate gig he has lined up or go do a Ph.D. Moon Moon and Saurabh are colleagues at an advertising firm in Delhi. Snigdha works for an NGO in Delhi and exudes such a calm, ever-smiling demeanour that I half-suspect she's part of the tour, brought along as a role model for harried white-collars.

It's early in the morning and still misty when we leave Guwahati in a Tempo Traveller. On either side of the highway is a rowdy lushness relieved at places by clumps of bamboo or the suddenly ordered green of areca nut or plantain groves. Small tin-roofed houses abut groves, their fences of interlaced bamboo staving off the engulfing vegetation. These signs of habitation grow infrequent as the morning progresses. When the view flattens itself out into a tree-fringed grassland, and when we see distant boulders that turn out to be rhinos, we know we've arrived at Kaziranga.

We head out on safari in the afternoon. It's exhilarating to stand in an open jeep and course through the expanse of tall rippling grass. Lone, bare trees and the odd observation tower only serve to accentuate the ranging flatness. In there somewhere are rhinos, tigers and elephants, but also thousands, millions, of smaller living things. There's the buzzing of insects, assorted bird-calls rising above the jungle's thrum, lakes and rivulets with secrets of their own. It's something we seldom get to feel in the city, this palpable sense of mutually sustaining, interconnected life. It's the ideal setting for communion with nature.

But safaris are funny things, and the mood permeating them is almost always one of grim vigilance arising from a just-below-the-surface competitiveness about spotting and identifying animals and birds. Our afternoon is filled with urgent stage-whispers and sharp taps on shoulders. We see hog deer, wild buffalo, a couple of snakes, elephants, plenty of rhinos; we just miss seeing a tiger by a rivulet, but see its pictures taken from another jeep. The trees are full of remarkably pretty birds, aggressively photographed so that disagreements about their identity can later be resolved with the Internet's help.

A rhino blocks our path

Where does it come from—this eagerness to identify, catalogue, and document; this urge to dominate one's environment rather than be a part of it? Is it a reflex acquired from the patterns of our education and work—finding, naming, sorting? Or is it more atavistic, a remnant from our hunter-gatherer past when to be the last to spot and identify an animal must have marked one out as a loser? In any case, both the hunter and the modern safari-goer may have much in common. The jeep's engine off, waiting in a state of high alert, our vocabulary on spotting an animal is similar to a hunter's: whispers of 'wait, wait, let him come closer'; muttered exhortations to the animals to 'turn around, turn around, turn around'; and then, 'Got him!' We capture the animals we see by taking their photographs, and we do so compulsively. Homi says, curtly, 'Rhino. Three o'clock,' and I swivel with my finger on the shutter release and click almost without volition though I know that this photo is just like any of the other fifty photos of rhinos I've already taken today.

But this state of high alert can last for only so long. When we stop at a viewing-point, Snigdha brings out a packet of theplas and we grow relaxed as we feast. The hunter's edge is dulled by food, and the rest of the safari is spent chatting and laughing, driving away any animals that might have come our way.

In the evening we meet Kamal, a researcher working on tiger conservation in Kaziranga. He gives us an overview of the national park and his work here, and asks if there's anything specific we'd like to know. The first question he gets is a lengthy one about 'human–animal conflict' which seems to take him by surprise. He says, gently, 'There are many good things also,' before going on to answer the question. He is asked about tiger poaching, but it turns out that tiger poaching isn't a problem in Assam, and the national animal is doing well at least in the Kaziranga and Orang reserves. Rhinos are in more danger though, given that dehorning a rhino is quicker than skinning a tiger, and two poachers were caught earlier in the day. 'Are militants involved in poaching? What about politicians? Forest rangers?' Kamal smiles and shakes his head: 'No, no, no.'

After dinner Homi, Ramesh and I discover that we are all fans of the Mithun Chakraborty cult-classic *Gunda*. It's the sort of film that's impossible to watch only once, and then, when it has been watched a few times, it is impossible to forget. The others are unaware of the film, so the three of us try to set things right by providing a re-enactment, beginning with the hero's introduction as a coolie in an airport (in what turns out to be one of the film's more realistic scenes). We'd begun the evening with a serious discussion about ecology, and when we end, late at night, it's with an absurd debate about whether or not *Gunda*'s director Kanti Shah can be considered a Gandhian film-maker.

Our first visit in Shillong is to an NGO called Impulse that works with child rights and human trafficking (among other things). The discussion here is largely about children employed in the nearby Garo and Jaintia hills to work what are called rat-hole mines—small, ad hoc coal mines that are often no more than a burrow. These mines are unregulated, and accidents and deaths are all too common. Impulse estimates that 70,000 children work in these mines, some from the North-East, the rest brought from Bengal, Orissa, Nepal and Bangladesh.

The Meghalaya government claims that it's only a handful of children who work in these mines. Impulse doesn't find this surprising given that many of the mine owners are part of the government. A project manager at Impulse speaks of the need for a mining policy and better enforcement, but also, she points out, the Sixth Schedule needs to be revisited.

As I learn on the trip, there is no discussion about the North-East in which the words 'Sixth Schedule' will not sooner or later be uttered. The Sixth Schedule of the Indian constitution aims to ease the integration of the north-eastern states with the rest of India by providing for some autonomy in local administration. To protect the interests of tribal peoples, land transfer to outsiders is regulated. It's also hard for the government to acquire land for mining and other 'public good' projects, and local landowners are entitled to any resources their land may hold. This state of affairs has also allowed the creation of tribal land-barons who buy up coal-rich land and operate an informal and more or less unregulated mining industry.

If we weren't staying in the relatively sedate area of Kench's Trace, we may have altogether missed the pretty Shillong of pine trees and flowers, of steep lanes and dreamy light. More central parts of the city are overrun by obtrusive new construction and traffic. One evening at Police Bazar, vehicles are so hopelessly gridlocked that it looks like an Escher drawing come to life. After dinner there, we take taxis to return to our guest house. The driver of the taxi I'm in turns on to the Guwahati–Shillong road (NH-44) and soon comes upon a line of stationary trucks. He lets out a feral scream and darts into a narrow high-risk lane of his own fashioning on the right edge of the road. After a brief, hair-raising stretch he realizes it's a false alarm when the line of trucks ends at a traffic signal. What feels like a colossal over-reaction on his part sounds perfectly reasonable when we later learn that traffic jams caused by coal trucks on this road have at times lasted the better part of a day. A report from *The Shillong Times* of 5 December 2011 headlined *Chronic Traffic Jam: Government at Wits' End* begins with a plaintively self-referential lead: 'In the last few months since the beginning of the peak coal business season in the state not a single issue of *The Shillong Times* was without any reference to the traffic jam on the National Highway 44.'

'Property is owned by individuals, not the government. So development is very difficult here,' says Bah J.E. Tariang, almost as a prologue to talking about Meghalaya. We're seated in the hall of his house, where I suspect many delegations and supplicants have been received. Bah Tariang is a Khasi elder, a long-time Congress Party leader in the North-East, and a former MP. Now ninety, he still looks dapper in his grey full-sleeved sweater, red tie, and beret. (From its children to its senior citizens, the people of Shillong would have to be the best-dressed in the country.) He has a carrying voice that's obviously had some practice. When Nehru visited Garo Hills in 1955, it fell to Bah Tariang to interpret his speech. He goes back in time as he repeats Nehru's words of reassurance that the region did not have to fear being overrun by the rest of India: 'I wish the hill people to grow according to their own genius.'

Not all this genius is for the best, according to Bah Tariang. The two most populous indigenous peoples of Meghalaya, Khasi and Garo, are both matrilineal. 'Property was traditionally owned by women,' says Bah Tariang, and he feels that this left men with no incentive to work. 'I built this house, but it belongs to my wife. It's difficult for families to grow. The men get spoiled; they don't take care of children; they leave it to the women. That's why Khasi Hills is not growing as fast as it should.'

He speaks about the difficulty of being accepted as Indian. When he went to Bombay as a young man, he was asked if he'd come from Nepal. 'I said, "No, Shillong". They said, "Oh, Ceylon". They knew another country but not their own!' A generation on, his daughter went to Delhi as a student: 'The Hindu girls called her "chink"! Chinese! We think we are Indian, but they say we are Chinese!' Bah Tariang feels there's a growing acceptance of Indian identity in the North-East today. 'I thank god,' he says, 'that the hill people now realize that they are part of India and that India is a great country.' And somehow, the very fact that he has to say it is telling. It's common here to hear the rest of India being referred to as India, as if this place were outside it.

Mayfereen Ryntathiang, who took us to meet Bah Tariang, runs an NGO called Grassroot. She's a bustling woman with an explosive laugh, and at her house she tells us about Grassroot's work. Forthcoming is a food festival of the north-eastern states, with the underlying aim of preserving local cuisines. 'People have started eating fast food, Indian food,' she says. As a result, she feels they're forgetting their own cuisines. Grassroot also works to educate women about their rights, and in this context May adds to what Bah Tariang told us about the sexes: 'Historically, we were a matrilineal, patriarchal society. Property moved from the mother to the youngest daughter. But she had to defer to her eldest maternal uncle.' Matrilineal property apart, she says that these days the parents' property is usually inherited by all the children. To the extent one can tell by simply looking around, women do enjoy a more emancipated position here relative to the rest of the country. And despite her pointing out flaws in the way the matrilineal system is practised in Meghalaya, May's work and comportment could themselves be seen as good advertisements for it. Also associated with Grassroot is an NGO that opposes uranium mining in Meghalaya, where deposits have been found. According to May, it is suspected that illegal 'yellow-cake' mining has already begun. The government too has taken samples that they say are to be sent to the United States for testing, but the suspicion around here is that 'it will go somewhere in India and be used for nuclear weapons'.

A half-hour's drive from Shillong is Smit, the seat of Hima Khyrim (loosely, the Khyrim kingdom). We are received by a man in his early thirties, a friend of Vinod from previous visits, who now, after marriage, holds the title of Duke of Smit. (The resigned tone in which he reels off this title suggests he has all too often to introduce himself to tourists. In reality, he explains later, he's the consort of the future high priestess and spiritual head of the kingdom, the Syiem Sad.) We've alighted from our

van at a sprawling, uneven field of grass with boxy three-
or four-storeyed buildings to one side, and clusters of
stately conifers on the other. In between are sixteen
lackadaisical archers—hunched or squatting or kneeling
awkwardly on the grass, some smoking as they take aim,
shooting with no discernible technique or interest at tiny
cylindrical targets. Duke soon explains that for all the
seeming listlessness, there is high intrigue going on just
beneath the surface. People have placed bets on these
archers, and scores are being kept discreetly through
colour-coded arrows. The apparent lack of technique
and the clumsy stances all sort themselves into two
schools of archery—shoot from the heart vs. shoot from
the eye. And the feigned insouciance, according to Duke,
is part of a mind game: 'They are silent outwardly, but
inside they are willing the other guys not to hit the target.
This is the most important part.' They're all expert archers
we're told, and looking beyond the apparent disarray, it
is true that arrows are thwacking into targets with
impressive regularity.

We walk to the Iing Sad, a large wooden structure with
a thatched roof. This is the official residence of the high
priestess and her consort, and also serves as the ceremonial
and administrative centre of the kingdom. It's constructed
without any metal, not even nails, and we have to divest
ourselves of all metal before entering. At one end of the
main hall is the stout tree trunk considered divine and
believed to be from the time kingdoms were first formed
here. According to legend the first Syiems or kings in the
area were the sons of the first high priestess, Ka Pah
Syntiew, who took her origin from a rock near Shillong

Peak (where the creator U Lei Shillong resides, and where, according to some agitating Khasi leaders, he is disturbed by the mobile phone towers that have sprung up at the conveniently elevated spot). The main hall of the Iing Sad, where we're sitting, is where the Syiem presides over his council and where ritual festivities and worship occur, notably those connected with the annual Nongkrem dance. The Khyrim kingdom is not just a ceremonial entity like the other princely states of India. Here, in Sixth Schedule territory, the royals have an administrative and judicial function in the villages of Hima Khyrim that runs parallel to modern government structures. For instance, though courts exist, many disputes here tend to be resolved by village elders, with the trickier cases brought to the council of ministers that meets in this room. The royals here tend to have parallel roles too—when they're not being functionaries of the kingdom, both Duke and his wife teach in colleges in Shillong.

We head back to Shillong, and for dinner go to a restaurant called City Hut Family Dhaba that's so packed that it would appear May's concerns about Indian food taking over the North-East are true. But we have a test for them in Snigdha and Preeti, whose diet is 'pure Jain'. The waiter is clueless about Jain interpretations of the menu, and when the concept is explained it proves mind-bendingly hard to understand. He goes to the kitchen a couple of times with enquiries about whether certain items on the menu can be made without certain ingredients, and returns more confused each time. It being a busy day, he's having to rush around serving other tables too, and he finally blurts out in frustration,

'Ma'am, this is a non-veg restaurant.' The Jains then write a note to the cook with lists of allowed and proscribed ingredients, the latter much longer than the former—onion, garlic, potato, ginger, carrot, brinjal, radish. When their 'curry' arrives it's clear that an annoyed cook within has made a statement by sending plain boiled vegetables. The Jains are not amused at all.

When we met Bah Tariang, he'd said, 'We were fortunate, I'm sorry to say, that the missionaries came. They brought us education. No one cared for the tribal people before the missionaries came. That's why we love the missionaries.' It was a Welsh missionary in the mid-nineteenth century who gave the Khasi language its script—Latin—and it was missionaries who established the first schools, colleges and hospitals in the area.

A more recent addition is the elaborate seven-storey Museum of Indigenous Cultures put together by the Salesians of Don Bosco. It begins with information about languages of the North-East, and moves on to a clinically anthropological photo-gallery of tribes from the region. The exhibits on the first few levels of the museum have much to say about the clothes, weapons, crafts and music of various peoples of the North-East. The upper levels begin to show the strain of trying to be both objective and devout. The pre-history gallery states that there are two ways of approaching the origins of life—creation and evolution—and there need be no conflict between the two because even evolution needs a moving force. Then the museum changes tack and celebrates the history of Christianity and Don Bosco. A comparison of the world's religions lists pros and cons of each, except for the clear winner Christianity, represented by a large painting of Christ. The section on Cultures of the World contains a mural in three parts: in the first, a missionary arrives at an island inhabited by savages who are attacking him with spears and arrows; in the next panel, the savages accept him; in the third, the savages are kneeling as Christ looms over the mountains in the background. Such representation is itself a part of the history of indigenous people here and elsewhere. In this sense, the most illuminating exhibit here may be the museum itself. Near its entrance is a placard with a glowing and somewhat cagey testimonial from Sonia Gandhi, who inaugurated the museum in 2010. It begins: 'I have travelled many parts of the world and I have seen many museums, but I must frankly admit that this is the best museum, and I say so even though I have seen just two floors.' A skywalk on the terrace provides a panoramic view of Shillong. 'Is this some new religion?' asks a dazed Preeti, pointing to a spiked metal ball that crests the building, but it's only a lightning conductor.

We leave Shillong and go to one of the many sacred forests that dot the Khasi Hills. This particular forest at Mawphlang occupies an area of 75 hectares, and the contrast with the rest of the surroundings is stark. The thick forest, marked off by megaliths that represent ancestors, erupts from a grassland so flat there are football goalposts on it. Presumably all of it was forest once, and what has survived is only the part considered sacred, which the locals will not indiscriminately raid. (They can cut dead trees and ritually collect certain vegetables and herbs, but no more.) The deterrent is fear, instilled by all the mysterious power of legend. A woman wearing a pink jainsem who's from the nearby village tells me that 'something very bad' will happen to anyone who misbehaves within the sacred forest. 'Like what?' She twists her neck as far as it will go and says, 'Like the head will turn around.' She says a group of Indian Air Force personnel once disregarded the warnings of villagers and chopped two truckloads of wood. As they drove back to their base they were gripped by a strange and overwhelming fear, so they returned in a panic and dumped all the wood back where it belonged.

From Mawphlang we take the David Scott trail to Lad Mawphlang, near Cherrapunji. This is a 14-km-long, single-day section of Scott's nineteenth-century mule trail that goes all the way to Bangladesh. Duke, who's originally from Cherrapunji, joins us for the trek. We descend into a wooded valley, cross a cold rivulet at its vee, drink from it, and rest on the rocks. It's uphill from there on, and our party begins to get winded. Since we're trying to reach Lad Mawphlang before it's dark, our pace can't be slowed beyond a point. Homi and I take on others' bags. I'm trudging along determinedly when Preeti, whose backpack is one of the three I'm carrying (in addition to a bulky DSLR whose owner has decided that breathing is more important right now than taking photographs), calls out to me from a distance to wait— she needs something from her bag. She skips up, unzips her bag, withdraws a large bag of popcorn, and offers me some.

We settle into our rooms in Cherrapunji, and while we wait for dinner, there's mutual leg-pulling and general silliness and laughter. It happens often on the tour—the specifics are too inane to recount or even remember, but the mood is unmistakable: it's the lightness that comes from being among people who *get* you.

In the morning we set out for Tyrna, from where a steep butterfly-surrounded descent of 3000 steps takes us to Nongriat and the gnarled miracles that are the living root bridges. Bridges built of bamboo or wood tend to rot here because of the prodigious rainfall. The War-Khasi people have learnt to guide the secondary roots of the fig tree across rivers and streams using hollow areca nut trunks. Roots from either side intertwine to form a bridge that can then be paved with earth or stone slabs. Some of the bridges here are hundreds of years old and utterly beautiful. We lounge about in the water for a little, eat our packed lunches and begin the agonizing climb back. (Last year, Duke took the Shodh Yatra group down these 3000 steps, then up 5000 to Nohkalikai Falls, and the effort, he says with some pride, almost killed them. When I tell him I'm going on the next yatra, he asks me to convey his respects to Prof. Gupta, the yatra's leader, and adds, 'I'm sure he will remember me.')

We're supposed to go caving, but the guide never shows up, and the morning is a pleasant washout. We laze about the hotel we're staying in, talking about music. Vinod turns DJ and plays pieces to illustrate whatever we're talking about: the life and work of A.R. Rahman; Bach's mastery of counterpoint. In the afternoon we walk around the market in upper Cherrapunji, then head for the Mawsmai cave complex to duck and crawl amidst mineral fingers and craggy rock for some token caving.

Next to the cave complex is another sacred forest. For some reason, Homi gets two of the girls to preen here as if they were on a catwalk. Our driver, Vijay, prances about monkey-like and swings from vines. All this must not count as being disrespectful of the forest, because no one's head turns around. In fact, at least as far as Vijay is concerned, it puts him in a buoyant mood since he can show off his skills. He may work as a driver, but his true calling is that of action film star. He's even been an extra in a film as part of a crowd in which a bomb goes off. He was asked to fall wounded to the ground, and he does so passionately in all his several re-enactments of the scene. If one of the participants on the tour felt they had to be an actor they'd be agonized about having to do something else for a living. Perhaps it's Vijay's economic background that makes him pragmatic. He's completely clear about what he's going to do in the future. He's twenty-four now, and he wants to make enough money to buy his own Tempo Traveller. Then, if he earns a little more money, he can think of getting married.

It's a subject we return to constantly on the tour: how we live and how we make our living. Some of us have abandoned what seems to be the default path—a well-paying corporate job—for somewhat more adventurous, if unremunerative, activities. Four of us work for corporates, but are dissatisfied to various degrees. Among these are Ramesh and Priya, who want out. They don't particularly enjoy the work they're doing, and they have other interests, notably music, that they don't find time for, but they're trapped by having to pay the monthly instalments on their house. After we've returned from

Mawsmai and had dinner, Priya becomes emotional about this—she tells me and Vinod that she's sick of her job, but has no alternative. Vinod says, sage-like, 'You always have a choice.' For instance, he suggests, if she's so distressed by the situation, why not sell the house and go to live in a place smaller than Delhi? A quick calculation reveals that there's a tidy profit in it for Ramesh and Priya, but then, it's too radical a solution.

One of those nights in Cherrapunji four of us—Vinod, Homi, Sourav and I—are sharing a large room. After the lights have been out for a while, Sourav sits up in bed and cries out, 'Yaar, I want to freelance.' He's not happy in his job, and so we have a discussion about the logistics of freelancing. Moon Moon has been in the same job for almost four years, but she's begun to feel insignificant at work. In Cherrapunji she gets an email at midnight from her Japanese boss saying he knows she's on vacation, but could she make some changes to a document. Moon Moon is annoyed because she sent it to him for comments two weeks in advance precisely because she was going on leave, and now she's going to have to look at it. The rest of us encourage her to rebel. Homi is volubly outraged on her behalf. Vinod says, 'What's the worst that could happen if you don't do it? Earthquake in Japan? Floods?'

The last four days of the tour have constituted an untaught class about man's relationship with the environment. We walked carefully down a slope into a vast wooded valley; we crossed a narrow, swaying rope-bridge high above a gorge, moving slowly with meditative or petrified attention; we climbed stair after endless stair, reduced after a few hundred to panting thoughtlessness. In each case the surroundings rushed in to fill the blank aftermath. The natural world here is so dense and teeming, its scale—from towering canopy to birds and butterflies and columns of ants—so vast, it's intricacy so overwhelming, its interconnectedness so evident and unfathomable, that it seems only proper that all forests be thought sacred.

But they're not. Deforestation is a problem here, caused by logging, mining and cultivation for an ever-increasing population. The result is that Cherrapunji, despite signboards proclaiming it the wettest place on earth, today faces water shortage. The rain is still considerable, but the water can't be held without enough vegetation, and it rushes down the hill-slopes. The last place we visit on the tour is Mawlynnong, that proclaims itself the cleanest village in India. From atop a towering, creaking, bamboo platform, we look over the trees down to the plains of Bangladesh. Standing here, it's hard not to sense, at least vaguely, that it's all somehow connected—the traffic in Shillong, those kids in the mines, the water shortage in Cherrapunji, the floods in Bangladesh. And if we're to look for hope, we might think of the living root bridges nearby. To grow one of those bridges takes decades, and it's likely that a bridge will be used only by the generations that follow the ones who built it. In a way these are bridges across time as well, reminders that we are custodians of the land we live on.

Had our tour-group sat down to draw up a manifesto, it might have gone something like this: We—the young

Crossing a rope bridge

urban middle-class—tend to lead a rushed life working for corporates that care more for their bottom-lines than for their employees or the environment. As stressed, unfulfilled, moneyed individuals we then seek satiety in consumption, a treadmill which, besides drawing us further into the same trap, is environmentally unsustainable and has far-reaching consequences. If we'd only be willing to lead a slower, simpler life, we might not have all the shiny stuff, but our work might be better aligned with our talents and dispositions, and we'd have the opportunity and time to introspect, explore and lead more fulfilling lives. Everyone would then be growing according to their own genius.

A year later, I reached out to several of my fellow travellers to ask what effect the tour had had on them. They all reminisced about the fun they had on the tour, and how they gained new friends. This latter aspect is actually quite unusual: all conducted tours seem to end on a note of friendship, with promises to stay in touch that are seldom acted upon. This is perhaps the only tour group I've been with where people are still in touch a year later and meet when they visit each other's cities.

Ramesh, who was deciding between a corporate job and a Ph.D. at the time, decided to go with the corporate job. This was determined largely by the constraints of his home loan: 'Reality continues to ruin my life,' he wrote, quoting Calvin and Hobbes. But he and Priya have a plan in place to begin easing out of their white collars in about another year. Ankita, who'd been laid low by ennui, found that being around people who were passionate about music or the environment or animals stirred her and she returned from the tour 'a lot more sorted'. Moon Moon was feeling 'a little rootless' when she came on the tour. She feels it was because she was in limbo in Delhi, away from her friends and family, and in a job where she was stagnating. She's changed jobs now and moved to Mumbai, where she feels at home. Sourav too has changed jobs and moved to Bangalore. Preeti, whose stressful job had got her down, now feels 'the stress was mostly self-inflicted'. She has spent the last year travelling, introspecting and doing volunteer work. She says she's gradually returning to more remunerative work, while asking herself: 'Can I be the same carefree and intuitive person that I am when I am not shouldering any responsibilities?' Homi continues to travel and work for JwM and is convinced that it's the best thing that could have happened to him. He says he was confused and directionless when he went to Vinod's Inside Out workshop, but now, four years later, he's happy with his life, and believes this is in large measure due to his travel experiences. He says, 'From a position of having absolutely no faith in myself, I know and love who I am more than ever before.' Moresha, who had just begun working for JwM at the time of the North-East tour also went on to do the same workshop, during which she realized that she wanted her work to be centred around writing and that at this stage of her life she needed a more steady income. So she left JwM. (Vinod, who'd like to see more people quit their jobs and attempt something they're passionate about, jokes that one of the few people he's succeeded with was his own employee.) The North-East experience was important to Moresha because it came at what was a hard time for her personally, following the loss of her parents. She speaks of the tour as being a way of getting out into the world again: 'I wanted to see—can I be by myself?' And she's been busy since, travelling and doing freelance projects, and is about to begin working for a weekly magazine. Vinod still runs workshops and tours. In the last year he and a friend have bought a plot of land in Kerala, where they're building a cob house and experimenting with growing grains, fruits and vegetables. He tells me these things are likely to make their way into JwM workshops or tours in the future.

As for me—I was already doing what I wanted to do. But after I returned from the North-East, I insisted on using public transport in Bangalore. I found myself waiting so long for buses that I soon abandoned the project. In any case, what it would have trimmed off my carbon footprint was negligible given that my work entails a few international flights every year. I normally take trains within India, but while returning from the JwM tour, I flew from Guwahati to Delhi. The plane took off in the evening as the sun was beginning to set outside my window. For the next couple of hours, the sun set in slow motion as we flew west, and there were still faint wisps of coral in the sky as we landed. I know I'd have found the scene as beautiful before the JwM tour, but I can't be sure about that hint of the transcendental I sensed.

8
THE SAME WATER EVERYWHERE

Prahlad Tippaniya and group perform on a cold night in Momasar

The soundtrack to one of the few epiphanies of my life was the blues. Or at least a blues scale that I was practising on my guitar. I'd been reading about the origins of blues music the previous day—about its welling up in the cotton and indigo plantations of the southern United States from chants and ditties and work-songs, about how the first blues performers were only adding their twists and flourishes to a form their audiences already knew and owned. Sitting there in my hostel room in Mumbai, going up and down the notes of that scale, what I was doing suddenly seemed inauthentic. This music was transplanted from elsewhere, and most people around me wouldn't be able to respond to it. This wasn't *my* music, and to pursue it determinedly felt like both theft and an affectation.

By then I'd played with a couple of college bands, doing clumsy covers of rock staples. There were other bands that would produce note-perfect imitations of songs by Led Zeppelin or Pink Floyd and drive audiences wild. If a band could play something exactly as it was on tape, the consensus was that they must be good. But after a period of proving themselves this way, most bands became a little more ambitious, and a day would come when they'd go up on stage during a college festival and introduce a song with the dreaded words, 'This is an original composition.' Almost always, these originals were listless pastiches of the covers the band played, the lyrics apparently not about anything at all. These were skilled musicians, but their chosen form seemed to preclude any real engagement with their own lives or the lives of their audience. This was most evident in the Death Metal bands, where you might have a good Hindu boy growling menacingly about his affinity for Satan. This was a cargo-cult, a mimicking of someone else's rebellion.

I had been noticing such incongruities for a while, but once it all sank in with awful clarity I found I couldn't bring myself to play the guitar with any degree of earnestness. I tried to fill this musical void by learning Hindustani classical singing, but that didn't last for long. Other things came up to claim my attention, and my life of music, such as it was, faded out.

More than a decade later I signed up for the Rajasthan Kabir Yatra. Folk musicians from different parts of India would perform in villages near Bikaner, and the yatra was a chance to travel with them in the company of others who were passionate about music. Somewhere within me I suppose was the vague hope that this week-long immersion in music that was clearly rooted in this land would wake the musician inside me and give him some direction.

The air in Bikaner is fragrant with frying when I step out of the railway station on a pleasant February afternoon. Every other shop here sells sweets and snacks, and outside each of them are mounds of pakoras, mathri, kachoris, and most conspicuously, about ten different types of bhujiya, from filamental to ropy. These piles outside the shop seem to be there not so much for display as for simply being impossible to fit inside. Can a single town really snack its way through all that? If the link between fried foods and heart disease is indeed established, then why aren't people keeling over all around me? I walk about for a while and taste some of the snacks before taking an auto to Lokayan, an NGO that is the local host for the yatra. The auto judders through narrow lanes past densely nestled homes and havelis, the yellows and oranges outside sweet shops blurring into the creams and sandstones of the walls until it feels like all Bikaner is built from fried besan.

Lokayan is offering logistical support to the Kabir Project, Bangalore, which conducts the yatra. With a day

to go before we start, their office resembles a war
headquarters. Volunteers rush in and out; participants
and musicians arrive; someone has to be picked up at an
odd hour; equipment is on its way; concert venues have
to be readied; arrangements must be made for food and
accommodation at each of the villages the yatra will
visit. Coordinating all this is a diminutive man named
Gopal who is seldom without a cell phone at one ear. (As
the yatra progresses, he keeps a charger dangling from
the phone so it can be charged wherever he can find a
plug point.)

The yatra is a two-bus caravan of singers, accompanying
musicians and participants like me who are along for the
ride. But it's all somewhat freewheeling: some participants
will join late; some will drop in for a couple of days and
leave; some will follow the bus in a car for a leg or two.
Halfway through the yatra, I'm talking to a new arrival,
on a break from his job as a BBC cameraman. Suddenly,
he glances at his phone, says, 'Oh, I have to go to
Afghanistan,' and rushes off. Most of the yatris are
youngish people from cities across India, many of them
working in creative disciplines such as art, design,
advertising and photography (which is particularly well
represented). We also have a half-dozen foreigners—a
journalist, a few who are engaged in South Asian studies
at universities in the United States or Europe, a couple of
residents of Auroville, near Pondicherry—and some of
them will turn out to be the most enthusiastic of the
yatris.

Only a few participants trickle in on the day I arrive,
and they're mostly volunteers. But the one who makes

the most striking first impression on me is Oum-Hani, a retired opera singer of French-Moroccan origin. She often travels to Sufi festivals, and here she's an ethereal presence floating about in white robes. She comes upon Rahul, a photographer from Ahmedabad who's wearing a Guns N' Roses T-shirt that reads Appetite for Destruction and has the image of a skull-encrusted cross. Oum-Hani looks sadly at Rahul's T-shirt and says, 'You will invite asuras.' She goes on to inform us that it's the *kaliyuga* and she can sense bad energies swirling about us. Rahul looks hurt. I try to lighten the situation by saying that he obviously doesn't mean whatever the T-shirt seems to be saying. This offends Rahul further, who says he means exactly what the T-shirt says, and we all leave it at that. Later, at dinner, Oum-Hani isn't eating because the food has spices in it, and when someone comments about it, she says, beatifically, 'I'm fine. I'm eating prana.' One of the organizers runs to get her a couple of chapattis with sugar so she can supplement the prana. And my breath catches when she lets drop with a faraway gaze, 'Water is my sister. The ocean is my mother.' Kabir was the only mystic I was expecting to encounter on the yatra, but Oum-Hani outdoes him comfortably.

That night, about a dozen of us sleep on mattresses laid out on the floor of one of the rooms in the office. A participant arrives in the middle of the night and settles in next to me in the dark. Later I wake up to loud machine-gun noises. It's the guy next to me. He gets up on his knees, says in Hindi, 'No one woke up? Good,' and raises his arms, as if he's in a trench with someone pointing a gun down at him. 'Finish me off, *chutiye*!' he screams. 'I cannot stand up.' After that, it's a restless night for me in the trenches. First, Oum-Hani's strangeness, and now this person beside me fighting imaginary battles. It's as if I'm in one of Kabir's *ulatbansis*, 'upside-down' poems that challenge conventional reality. (It turns out there's a slightly less upside-down explanation for the events of the night. After receiving many strange and fearful looks the next day, the warrior reveals that he's just recovered from a back injury after being laid up in bed for six months, that the journey here has aggravated the problem, and that this can result in seizures during which he doesn't know what he's doing. But such is his enthusiasm for the yatra that he alternates between resting in Bikaner and travelling on the bus, which he sometimes does standing up to protect his back from bumpy roads.)

We set off in the late afternoon. Over the next week, we will travel to the villages of Momasar, Napasar, Pugal and Diyatra, returning to Bikaner twice for concerts in between and at the end.

At Momasar, the concert is at the school ground and goes on late into the chilly night. The village audience isn't the most enthusiastic, but they stick around anyway, wrapped in shawls. The performers here include Prahlad Tippaniya, who is perhaps the best-known Kabir singer in India today. He began singing Kabir when he found himself drawn to music in his twenties and now, more than three decades later, he's a star who can draw audiences in tens of thousands in his home region of Malwa. Other singers include the flamboyantly moustached Muralala Marwada from Kutch, the founder of the Kabir Project Shabnam Virmani, the Meghwal singer from Jaisalmer Mahesha Ram, and a popular folk singer from Sikar in Rajasthan, Bhanwari Devi, whose namesake has been in the news lately. When she begins singing, a few people from the village stop to ask me in puzzlement if Bhanwari Devi hasn't just been murdered.

As if to prove otherwise, Bhanwari Devi's is the feistiest performance. Part of her act has a man in gaudy traditional attire strutting about for comic effect and enacting the words as they're sung. This loosens people up. A couple of villagers go up to the front and hand him money in appreciation. Some of the accompanying musicians, who after their performances are clearly in high spirits of one sort or the other, break out into their own jigs. Some of the participants join them, and the night develops a festive air.

The yatra organizers hold a meeting in Momasar after the performances. Their concern is that all the dancing that's been happening may be detracting from the spiritual element, with the words getting lost in all the ebullience. Does the yatra really want to put entertainment before (?) of the spiritual? Perhaps Bhanwari Devi should be asked to drop the prancing jester from her act; maybe some of the more enthusiastic participants should be asked to tone it down a little. There's a call to reflect upon what the yatra is really about.

At least to the village audiences I see over the following week, the music seems largely to be about entertainment. There exists a culture of all-night satsangs and jagrans here, and some of the performers on the yatra make their living in this way, but from what I can tell, the knowledge that profound things underlie the music may give it a halo of virtue, but it doesn't necessarily make people delve deeper. The musicians seem to know it too, and the songs are sung to hold attention—fast-paced or dramatic with dense percussion and busy harmonium fills. The lyrics are seldom decipherable, and it is only Prahlad Tippaniya (who happens to have been a schoolteacher) who pauses to explain what he's singing about.

Those of us who have travelled here may claim a somewhat more deliberate seeking out of Kabir and his music. The milieu in which this re-engagement has come about is alluded to in *Had Anhad*, one of the four luminous Shabnam Virmani-directed documentaries to emerge from the Kabir Project. The film's title juxtaposes Kabir's metaphysical sense of boundary with a (perhaps equally intangible) geographical one—the India–Pakistan border. Near the beginning of the film Virmani states that turning to Kabir may have been a 'turning away from . . . that militant Ram used to stoke Hindu-Muslim hatred in India'.

The Kabir Project was started in 2003. This was in the fraught aftermath of Godhra and the horrific communal violence that ensued in Gujarat in 2002. For many young urban Indians, this was when it became apparent that religion was being hijacked for political ends. Those who had appointed themselves as the public face of religion were so obviously distant from anything that could be called sacred or spiritual that some people grew disenchanted with religion itself. These were perfect times to look to the fifteenth century mystic-poet Kabir, who has never been far from the Indian consciousness, but whose vigorous mockery of orthodox religion and its hypocrisies now felt particularly apt. His words leaped over the narrowness of any single faith while laying out spiritual goals that were hard to disagree with. With Kabir, you could feel that you were rooted in your own culture, and that you had a connection to the spiritual. And if you liked, you could keep wearing your G N' R T-shirt.

Of course, Kabir has been co-opted by others at various times. The *Adi Granth* of the Sikhs draws heavily upon Kabir. The Kabir Panthis have turned him into a god immaculately sprung from a lotus. Legend has it that after Kabir died, his Hindu and Muslim followers (not having absorbed a shred of what he taught) argued over whose he was and whether the body was to be cremated or buried, and while they argued, the body turned into a pile of flowers that could be divided. Even all of Kabir's poetry isn't necessarily written by the man: not a single song or poem can be definitively attributed to the historical Kabir; most of his work exists in multiple versions; there exist references in his poetry to distinctly post-fifteenth-century inventions like the railway train. Kabir is a winking, shimmering presence, an idea, a way of thinking that can manifest itself variously.

The Kabir Project began by looking for Kabir's presence in the subcontinent and found him thriving in the interiors. Kabir is sung widely in Madhya Pradesh, Rajasthan, Gujarat, Uttar Pradesh and Pakistan. The Project's idea of Kabir has since grown beyond the man—any folk musician who sings of the attribute-less divine is in a sense singing Kabir, and so the Sufi singer or the Baul also come within his ambit. The Project has ensured a wider platform for several folk musicians who previously had a restricted audience. Performances have been organized in Indian cities and abroad; CDs and concert DVDs are available through the Project. Musicians and audiences from different parts of India have been brought together by the Kabir yatras. At present the Project is engaged in assembling a comprehensive archive of Kabir in performance.

Many of the people I speak to during the yatra have done a vipassana course or are planning to. It is the most advanced spiritual recourse today for the young secular English-speaking Indian urbanite: it cannot be suspected of being a money-making racket since one can only make a voluntary donation; the aesthetics are clean and modern, with the technique involving no idols, no prayer, no surrender, and no chanting, only quiet meditation. Though the technique is meant to be practised regularly after the course, few seem to persist (at least among my peers). But doing the course itself is a badge of identity and it's spoken about in the same terms as a travel experience—one 'does' a vipassana course just as one might do Ladakh or the North-East. One of the reasons Kabir is so attractive to this demographic—which includes me—is that he asks nothing of us. He pokes savage fun at rituals, at discrimination based on religion and caste, and since this happens to be exactly how we feel, Kabir provides an authoritative reaffirmation of our beliefs. In return, there is nothing in our lifestyles that we are asked to give up, no practice or observance that we are required to take up. And this suits us just fine—a form of spirituality that demands nothing more than the passive glow of thinking of oneself as being spiritual.

Yet, Kabir's is a voice that relentlessly hammers in the spiritual basics: you are going to die; everything you think of as important really isn't; transcendence is within your reach. But these big, hard assertions are sublimated in music or even in the bright cadences of a *doha*, just as grief or longing is sublimated in a ghazal. It is tempting to appreciate the teachings in the manner of a *rasika*, with a hint of self-congratulation. Today Kabir's words are cast in diverse forms: Indian classical music; folk music; he's the go-to person for lyrics when it comes to high-minded Indian rock. There's the Zen Buddhist idea about teachings only being the finger pointing at the moon, and there's no denying that Kabir has a distractingly pretty finger. But there's always the chance that those words will occasionally slip through, and that in place of a pleasantly distant Kabir talking about weavers or potters or the inevitability of other people dying, we find him pointing straight at us.

He'd first have to break through the shell of our preoccupations. We, here on the yatra, are a busy lot. Some of us are helping out with arrangements, putting up banners or running the merchandise stall. Many of us are involved in projects related to the yatra and we proceed with the conviction that the unrecorded moment is not worth living. The yatra has to be the most intensively documented event I have ever seen. For starters, about half the participants seem to be semi-professional photographers or better. A couple are on assignment, and the rest are not blind to the portfolio-plumping opportunities afforded by a folk music event in rural Rajasthan. There is seldom a moment, even as a mere

Gawra Devi sings, is documented

participant, when someone or the other isn't looking keenly at you through a DSLR. Those who aren't yet serious photographers are no less enthusiastic with their point-and-shoots and phone cameras. Audio recorders are rampant, and a singer only has to open his mouth to find a couple of microphones and a dozen digital recorders and mobile phones thrust at him. An Australian radio journalist doing a segment about the yatra moves briskly about cornering musicians and participants for interviews. Two camerawomen are filming the yatra on behalf of the Kabir Project, and they're seen day and night with bulky cameras, walking with the videographer's steady, curtailed gait. The two writers on the yatra, both grave, bearded men, trail the others when it comes to technology, but no one can say we don't whip out our notepads with flair.

Since there's no shortage of self-created distractions, an aspect of the yatra I particularly come to appreciate is the chance to listen to the singers every day. It's the first time I'm hearing most of them, and this repetition lets the songs grow on me. Prahlad Tippaniya and his group of seven accompanists fill the breadth of the stage and are reliably energetic and full-throated. Gawra Devi, a singer from around here, who's now in her sixties, sings with an abandon, a heightened sense of drama, that blind singers so often seem to possess. She's accompanied by a *manjira* player who sits glumly, a wad of tobacco in one bulging cheek, and clatters his tiny cymbals furiously until they vanish along with his hands. We may have PA systems now, but most of the singers here come from a tradition in which a singer's voice had to carry to the audience without assistance. Bhanwari Devi is particularly strong at throwing out her voice. But the most notable exponent of both volume and pitch on the yatra is Muralala Marwada from Kutch, who quickly becomes one of my favourites. His songs have undulating drawn-out melodies that he renders with great joy (while singing higher and louder than anyone else).

One morning the Australian radio journalist wants me to act as interpreter for an interview with Muralala, so we repair to a relatively quiet room of the dharamshala in which we're staying. Muralala's been singing since he was a child, and he says his family has been singing Kabir for perhaps ten generations now. Shabnam Virmani visited him in Kutch after hearing about him, and invited him to Bangalore to sing in a Kabir festival. Muralala says he arrived in Bangalore with a harmonium because he thought it was expected of him, but he was told by Virmani that his group should perform in the traditional style of Kutch—no harmonium, just the *manjira*, *dholak* and *santara*, and wearing turbans typical of the region. I continue talking to Muralala after the interview is over. He's been on all three Kabir yatras, and has had his music released by the Kabir Project. Here he's been singing Kabir, Mirabai, and the Sufi Bhitai Shah, but back home he also sings a variety of other bhajans. I ask if he misses performing those other songs in his repertoire. 'You have to give people what they want,' he says, with his sweet gap-toothed smile.

What we want on the yatra is usually more music, and there's no better way to get this than living and travelling with musicians. In Napasar I wake up to the singing of women—a wedding sangeet is on in a room nearby. But what has really woken me is Muralala standing outside by himself, looking delighted, clapping and adding the high-pitched blast of his voice to the women's chorus. The fact that the musicians on the yatra are performing every night doesn't prevent them from frequently breaking out into song during the day. Singing on a bus journey to pass time takes on an entirely new dimension when the bus is packed with folk singers. We also have a couple of sessions when just the yatris gather round to listen to songs and explanations of the words being sung. One of the people on the yatra is Abdulla-kaka, a quiet, unassuming elder from Kutch who is not performing, but is a repository of knowledge when it comes to Sufi songs. He talks of the content of some of those songs, which on the surface are fables with princes and horses and lovers, but are really rife with symbolism. These informal sessions usually end on a high note with the music building up to a crescendo and everyone breaking out into dance.

Muralala Marwada in song on one of the tour buses

Not all these interactions take place in a group setting. Having the musicians around means that we're free to walk up to them and express appreciation or ask what a song means. And really, there's no telling what each one is experiencing. One of the American students comes up to me and asks if I'll translate for him while he speaks to Abdulla-kaka. We find him just as he is getting on to the tour bus. 'Ask him: If I go to Kutch and stay with him, will he teach me how to be compassionate?' I ask. Abdulla-kaka turns his palms upwards and looks at the sky, then writes down his address.

I'm surprised to find, as the yatra progresses, that I'm beginning to develop quite a rapport with Oum-Hani. Over a few days of desultory chats, I've actually come to see her way of thinking—all this talk of strange energies and asuras—as more than just Indophile kookiness. As metaphors for going about life, they work well enough for her to flash blissful smiles and find long stretches of tranquillity. Why should anyone complain (as long as their T-shirts are not being maligned)? She's not one of the performers on the yatra, but she occasionally gets out her small travelling tanpura and sings—unclassifiably, and beautifully. There are no words in her singing. She tells me she gave up her career as an opera singer in Europe to work with 'pure vibrations'.

While I'd expected to be awash in pure vibrations and poetry by coming on the yatra, I had not imagined that it would lead to my debut in retail. As it happens, the yatra puts up a merchandise stall with CDs, DVDs and T-shirts at every performance venue, and the in-charge, Deepa, is on the lookout for a cashier. 'We need someone responsible,' she tells me, which is just the sort of flattery I fall for.

The first evening at Momasar, a sea of young men surge around the stall even as it is being set up. I ready myself for an avalanche of cash that does not come. It quickly becomes clear that the crowd isn't here to buy but to gawk. The two women at the stall are a revelation to the young men of Momasar—Deepa has ultra-short hair, and Nimisha is wearing a little hat. From where we're sitting, behind an arc of tables displaying our wares, all we can see are torsos in jackets or shawls, and faces wrapped in mufflers. Occasionally someone asks what a T-shirt or CD costs just for the thrill of it; now and then someone draws out a mobile phone to take a photograph. A man with a fixed delirious grin rushes up to Deepa every half-hour or so, says 'I love you' and rushes off again. A policeman appears periodically and shoos people away, but they accumulate again after a while.

It is decided that the women will not front the stall at Napasar. So my role expands to cashier-cum-T-shirt-salesman. On the third day, at Bikaner, we're short of manpower to set up the stall, so I have to lug around large boxes of CDs, which weigh about the same as similarly sized blocks of metal. At Jamsar, I find myself crawling about inside the boot of a bus with a weak cell-phone flashlight, looking for vanished inventory. They say jobs inevitably go downhill, but by any standard the descent from what I thought was a cushy desk-job has been precipitous.

The film *Had Anhad* is screened thrice on the yatra, and at about the same time that our stall begins to open for business. The Pakistani qawwal Farid Ayyaz makes a swashbuckling appearance in the film. He stirringly recites the Kabir doha about there being different wells and vessels, but '*paani sab mein ek*', it's the same water everywhere. All humanity, all existence, is one in its essence. He goes on to sing:

> *It's a good thing my pot burst:*
> *I needn't fill water any more.*
> *It's a good thing my rosary broke:*
> *I needn't chant the lord's name any more.*

More than once, even as Ayyaz implores '*paani sab mein ek*', we at the merchandise stall are trying to differentiate the vessels. We must classify our potential customers as villagers or city-dwellers. This is because we have two rates for our wares—urban and rural. The same CD or T-shirt is sold at a lower price to villagers to make it affordable for them, and to city folk at three or four times the village price. It is usually not too difficult to make the distinction: any woman who comes up to the stall is from the city; the shawl-swaddled men are villagers; those who wear smart jackets or sport kurta-waistcoat combos while connecting with their roots are city-dwellers. But not always. A particularly dandy villager might get quoted the city rate. Sometimes, a person in a crumpled kurta pays Rs 50 for a CD, while his friend in a coat is asked Rs 200, causing some awkwardness when the discrepancy has to be explained.

I've been hearing from Kabir that the body counts for nothing, but my lower back will not listen and eventually begins to issue a sharp twinge when I try to lift anything. Rahul, with whom I'm doing most of this lifting (and who is one of the mildest people ever to wear an Appetite for Destruction T-shirt), also declares that his back hurts. So we're given a rest, and stall manager Deepa runs off to get a few others. 'What about them?' grunts one of the new recruits, seeing us sitting around while he's hefting an improbably heavy box of CDs. We've earned the rest. '*Un donon ka back hai*,' says Deepa.

The last day at Bikaner, there's a good-sized crowd and everything is tagged at city rates. For the first time on the yatra I come into my own as cashier—organizing notes by denomination in a box, curtly asking people to give change, sending people out to break a note. I've often grumbled at the peremptory manner of those who sit at cash tills, but really, it's unavoidable.

Our living arrangements are simple. At different places we sleep in marriage-halls, a dharamshala, a temple-cum-samadhi, a school. Usually we reach the place of our night-halt in the evening, before the performances begin. Mattresses and blankets are piled in a corner or spread out on the floor and we 'reserve' places to sleep using our luggage. These reservations aren't always respected, so sometimes there's nothing to do at night except fling oneself into a row of sleeping people.

We have little interaction with the villagers, except at Pugal, close to the Pakistan border. This may be because Pugal is the village of the singer Mukhtiyar Ali, who has been associated with the Kabir Project. (He was to be one of the headliners of this year's yatra, being from the region, but he backed out.) It's the most rousing welcome we've received so far. The buses are stopped outside the village, and the sarpanch—a woman—enters the bus to greet us. We alight and walk a couple of kilometres through the village in a procession led by a drummer striking up a noisy drum roll. Pugal is a sandy village that looks like it's struggled out of the desert. Its inhabitants line up along the streets or at compound walls to look at us; tied camels give us bored sidelong glances. At the school, the venue for the concert, little girls tie threads on our wrists, apply tilaks. A policeman at the venue looks as unconvinced as the camels. 'It's a village of thieves,' he says to me, looking at all the equipment we're bringing in. 'You'll be lucky if you return with half the things you came with.'

One of the villagers at Pugal gets talking with me. 'What's your caste?' he asks, in a matter-of-fact way. It's a question I'm used to answering in villages. But now, I turn indignant. 'You can't ask me this on the Kabir Yatra,' I tell him. 'I won't tell you.' His face falls, and I realize it's me who's being rude here, not him. He's just being friendly as best as he knows, and in the name of Kabir, *mujhse bura na koi*, I'm the one who's at fault.

Despite the policeman's warning, we leave Pugal with all our equipment. There *are* things going missing on the yatra though. The *paani sab mein ek* line appears to have sunk powerfully and literally into the consciousness of the participants—there are too few water-bottles on the yatra, and you can't leave one unguarded for a moment without it disappearing. Other boundaries are dissolving too—slippers that are lying around are freely borrowed, setting off a chain reaction that has many of the yatris wearing other people's slippers while looking for their own. At Pugal, some of the guys are looking for marijuana, but haven't been able to find any. One of the girls on the yatra comes to their aid. She has in her possession a small stash, and she hands it over after making plans to smoke with them later. But the brotherhood of smokers is unable to wait, and they partake freely, forgetting all about the original source. A steady stream of cheerful red-eyed young men makes the girl suspicious. She investigates and finds that the last vestiges of her stash are being smoked behind one of the yatra's buses. She screams at them for this treachery: do they have no consideration that it's harder for a girl to buy the stuff? What kind of men are they if they can't score a little marijuana in a place where it's being smoked in every other temple?

The food on the yatra has, with a few exceptions, been puri and an oily potato curry. The more urbane among the yatris haven't much taken to this diet, and can be seen holding pieces of puri with the tips of their fingers, poking daintily at the gravy. (This is a genuine culture clash. Once, even as I was trying to ladle out a piece of potato without getting too much of the oil onto it, the cook beamed in admiration at his own work and said to me, 'Whatever I prepare, I prepare well. Tell me, is there any hotel where they'd add this much oil?')

On the way from Pugal to Diyatra, we're to have lunch at a temple in the village Jageri, but there's been some miscommunication, and there's no food waiting for us there. Arrangements have to be made from scratch. The much-awaited Parvathy Baul has just arrived, and she starts an impromptu satsang in a room in the temple, talking about sacrifice and dedication and singing of those themes. It's nearing four in the afternoon, and we're desperately hungry. Outside, someone gets out a large packet of bhujiya from his bag, and soon there are more people surrounding him than are listening to Parvathy Baul. And when the puri-sabzi is finally served, at least this once no one seems to be picking at their food.

Parvathy Baul is to perform on the last two evenings of

the yatra. There's something almost regal about the simplicity of her appearance as she takes the stage at Diyatra—the saffron robes, the knee-length matted hair, the musical self-sufficiency of an *ektara* in one hand and a *duggi* at the waist. While other musicians sit still on stage, here's one who's going to prance and whirl as she sings. After all that expectation, it turns out her cordless microphone doesn't work. So about half an hour is spent in positioning all available mics in a circle, creating an arena within which she will sing. She's barely begun when her foot gets caught in a cable or something and she stumbles. 'It's better I don't sing today,' she says, folds her hands to the audience, and walks off the stage. I wonder why she didn't simply come down among the audience and sing—if anything that would be closer to the tradition of the wandering Bauls. The villagers are restless with the long lull in the music; the sound-man is in tears. The breathless anticipation when she takes the stage on the last day at Bikaner is all about whether the sound set-up will cooperate. It does.

Two singers from the south—Vedanth and Bindhumalini—join the yatra midway. They sing Kabir to the accompaniment of Vedanth's guitar. I've never seen anyone playing a guitar sing with as much nuance as Vedanth, and Bindhumalini has a powerful rounded voice that she deploys to stunning effect. It helps I suppose that they are both accomplished musicians, having trained in both Hindustani and Carnatic classical singing. Vedanth composed for a film and went through a phase of playing with rock bands before he found himself recalling the songs he'd sing in his school assembly. He began to sing these songs again to the accompaniment of his guitar, and this eventually led to his first album, a compilation of songs by Bhakti poet-saints. He then began a collaboration with Bindhu, and the result was a Kabir album called *Suno Bhai*. They make extensive use of harmony in their singing, something relatively rare on the yatra. This music is the most exciting I've heard in a long time.

I abandon my duties at the merchandise stall when Vedanth and Bindhu sing. One evening I happen to go sit behind Muralala and Abdulla-kaka, and it's moving to see their childlike rapture when they hear voices harmonize. Muralala breaks out in his gap-toothed smile, twists his arm with a jerk and looks at Abdulla-kaka in wonderment; Abdulla-kaka looks back, biting the tip of his tongue, furrowing his brows, continually nodding in disbelief. They've spent their lives with music, but its riches are not yet exhausted.

In fact, I'm learning that you never know where good music will turn up. At Pugal, a man from the village had been pestering Vedanth to accompany him on the guitar. Vedanth relented just before we boarded the bus, and this small man squatting on the ground outside the school ended up singing in his high, clear voice a Kabir song that was one of the best things I heard on the yatra.

After that late lunch at Jageri, a few of us sit beside a lake outside the temple, where there's a mild breeze going. Vedanth and Bindhu begin to sing. After a few songs that are familiar from the evening performances,

Vedanth begins a song he hasn't played yet on the yatra. The languid walkdown intro on the guitar is all too familiar to me—it's my old nemesis, the blues. The words are Kabir's: '*Bhajo re bhaiyya, Rama Govinda Hari*'. The form and guitar-playing are typical blues, the vocal flourishes Indian classical. But they flow naturally into each other, and putting aside classification for a moment, it's just a beautiful, unforced song, which in the end is all that counts.

Music works in strange ways. When I was sixteen, I borrowed the collected works of Kafka from a library, a big book with a black cover that hadn't been issued in years and which smelt not just musty but downright loamy. For a week I stayed in bed reading it while listening on my Walkman to an Iron Maiden album I'd just managed to lay my hands on. I have only fleeting memories of both the book and the music. But every once in a while, I hear a snatch of song from that album emanating from a passing car or a house I'm walking past, and I find myself overwhelmed by the recollection of that book's smell.

A book—Kafka is said to have written to a friend—must be the axe for the frozen sea within us. The same can be said of music, of art in general, and perhaps also of activities considered to be in the realm of the spiritual. They all hack away at things rigid inside us, and rearrange the pieces in ways not apparent from the outside. (And maybe, when their work is completely done, they leave behind the same water?) It is impossible to say who took back what from that week of music and Kabir—even the most preoccupied, the most hardened of us might, years later, recollect a stray line, or chance upon a tune, and realize that it has been at work all along. When I decided to come on the yatra I imagined I might return with a song or two (and I did pester Muralala to teach me the words of a song I particularly liked). But when I returned, I found myself picking up my guitar that had lain fallow for so long, and playing not what I'd just heard, but anything at all that took my fancy. I wasn't playing particularly well, but I was doing so with lightness, without shame. Whether this is a step forward musically, spiritually, both, or neither, I cannot say.

9
REAL INDIA

Professor leads the yatra into a village

It's an unconsciously hot May in Madhya Pradesh, the landscape all dust and glare. In the sun it takes only a few minutes to be sapped into dissociated stupor, after which one can walk on in a daze, unconcerned with self-preservation. In the breezeless shade, sweat refuses to dry, coating arms and faces with a thick oily sheen. For the first time I realize my palms are capable of producing sweat, and I can bring the tips of my fingers together to watch a drop form. My clothes, limp and moist, bunch up along my body in maximally annoying configurations. I frequently wish I could rip them off and plunge into water, but there isn't any water around. Once, someone mentions a lake, and when I ask where it is, I'm told that it's the expanse of cracked soil we're walking on.

We are on the Shodh Yatra, a week-long walking tour of villages in search of traditional knowledge and local innovations. It's conducted twice a year, once in summer and once in winter, and each time in a different part of India, by an organization called SRISTI (Society for Research and Initiatives for Sustainable Technologies and Institutions). The hottest places are visited in summer and the coldest in winter, the method behind this madness being that adversity brings out the best in people when it comes to innovation. The present yatra is to villages in Sehore district, Madhya Pradesh.

From Bhopal's Lalghati a bus takes me to Sehore, and from there a combination of two ramshackle buses takes me to the farm in Jamonia Talab where the group is convening. Introductions are already underway beneath a shamiana when I reach. There are around forty people here of whom about half are affiliated with the organizers: a biologist, an intellectual property rights lawyer, research assistants, people in charge of logistics, a few established rural innovators from other places. Anyone who's interested can join the yatra for a small fee, and the rest are a varied lot from all over the country, mostly from cities: two young men from Chandigarh who have just graduated and are travelling for a couple of months because they feel they haven't seen enough of India; a few people associated with NGOs that work in rural areas; some students—a couple of them from IITs, a couple with civil service aspirations; a handful of young professionals. We have two students of innovation—one a German doing her Ph.D. field-work in India, another an Indian man studying in a French university. We are gathered at Rishabh Vatika, a farm where we will spend the night.

In the morning, we are herded together by Chetan Patel, a wiry hyper-energetic man in his early twenties who's been in the area for six weeks, laying out the groundwork for the yatra. He implores, shouts, furiously blows the whistle around his neck, and eventually manages to get us to load our luggage onto the truck and set out walking towards Sehore. In front is a banner that announces the procession as the 29th Shodh Yatra. It outlines the main stops we will make over the week: Rishabh Vatika—Jamonia—Dhaboti—Mogra—Pipalthon—Sankota—Bhadakui—Sotia—Neelkanth. At three corners of the banner are the logos of SRISTI and the closely allied Honey Bee Network and the National Innovation Foundation (NIF). These organizations and the Shodh Yatra owe their existence in large part to the efforts of one man, Prof. Anil Kumar Gupta, who in addition to holding various positions in those organizations, is a faculty member at IIM Ahmedabad. He is to lead the yatra, but Professor—which is how yatra veterans and the organizing team refer to him—is arriving straight from China and has been slightly delayed.

We've been walking for fifteen minutes or so when a car pulls up and out hops Professor to lead the walk. He's hitched a ride with an Associated Press team that's covering the yatra. Professor is a lean, bespectacled man in kurta-pyjama, with a grey beard and swept-back hair that give him a gurudev-type mien. He walks quickly with long strides, is impatient of any dawdling, and is clearly a man on a mission. In fact, there are times on the yatra when, in heat-induced delirium, I feel as if I'm one of the followers in those black-and-white newsreels who's trying to catch up as Gandhi darts from village to village at a high frame rate.

As we reach the town of Sehore, Professor stops frequently to talk to people in shops and in the streets. He asks if they've done anything novel, if they know anyone who has, if they face any problems in their work. Some of those accosted simply shake their heads, unsure how to respond. One man, who works as a *mistri*, a construction supervisor, revels in his well-adjustedness: 'I have done nothing new. These days the companies make everything convenient. There's nothing else I need.' The group huddles around as Professor tries to make the mistri and his friend see that there surely must be some scope for improvement in the way he works. But they're adamant that things are fine as they are. A passer-by asks me, '*Aapko paise milte hai yeh karne ke liye*? Are you paid to do this?'

In the market at Sehore, Professor finds the yatra's first innovation. At Mohammed Iqbal's metal-work shop he encounters a seed-drill that can drop seed and fertilizer at one go. It's a simple modification—an additional outlet for the fertilizer at a height appropriate for sowing wheat in the soil around here—but it can save a farmer an entire pass over the field. Iqbal's details are recorded; pictures are taken; the AP photographer and videographer squat and stoop and loom to capture the farm equipment in the tiny shop. The yatris move in quick leaps and arcs to avoid getting in the way.

Six kilometres from Sehore is the village of Jahangirpura, where there's a village meeting. These meetings are the heart of the yatra. They're usually held in a public place such as the school or the temple to ensure that village politics does not discourage anyone from attending. Here the meeting is in the shade of a tree near the school. Around thirty villagers are seated on the ground in a circle along with the rest of us. Chetan, perky despite the heat, introduces the purpose of the yatra: we're all walking in the sun so we can understand the villagers' lives. In times past, people practised agriculture without chemical pesticides, raised animals without veterinary doctors, managed with what water was available, kept healthy with herbs found around the village, and knew which local plants could be used for food in times of scarcity. But people have begun to forget these things. We're here to document such practices of traditional knowledge so they can be preserved, developed, and shared.

For some reason, many men have chosen to stay away from the meeting in Jahangirpura, but the women participate with enthusiasm. Plants named *pamal* and *silbili* that grow around here can be used for food. *Channa* leaves are dried for later use. A young girl says that water in which *sitaphal* leaves have been steeped makes for a good pesticide. An *anganwadi* worker reveals that *kaner* leaves of the red-flowering variety can be boiled in oil to yield a cure for baldness, and swears that if her daughter has hair today it's only because of this.

The yatra also looks to encourage local innovation. So Mohammed Iqbal, who makes the fertilizer-dropping seed drill is felicitated. Travelling with us as sources of inspiration are some rural innovators from other parts of

Amrutbhai (left) demonstrates his pulley-with-brake

India, along with their innovations. Amritbhai from
Gujarat once saw an old woman struggling to draw
water from a well and decided there must be a better
way. He went on to design a pulley with a simple
mechanical brake that allows a person to rest mid-draw
without letting the bucket or pot crash down into the
well. Khimjibhai has made a frame that distributes the
weight of a pot carried on the head to the shoulders and
reduces neck-strain. We demonstrate the devices and
present one of the pulleys to the village.

Professor introduces the assembly to Dharamvir, a
farmer from Damla village, Haryana, who's made a
multipurpose processing machine for which he received
an award from the President of India. If the yatra is a
travelling show, its star is Dharamvir. He's had an
extraordinary life, and has the storytelling ability to do
justice to it. He's a man of around fifty with a versatile
black-and-white checked towel that he uses as a turban,
or to wipe the sweat from his ruddy face, or to fan
himself, or to sit on, or as a fashion accessory, hanging
over one shoulder or dangling around his neck. With his
appearance, his Haryanvi-tinged Hindi, his high voice,
and the fact that he affects an expression of mock
wretchedness while speaking, he gets the villagers' rapt
attention.

As a young man, Dharamvir found he couldn't meet
the needs of his family through farming, so he left his
village to ply a cycle-ricksha in Delhi. An accident left
him seriously injured, and he was brought back to his
village, where it took a year for him to recover. In Delhi
he'd seen large sums of money being shelled out for

herbs, so he decided to use his half-acre of land to experiment with the organic cultivation of lucrative crops: herbs, strawberry, mushrooms; later, aloe vera and *amla*. Soon, Dharamvir realized that his produce was going into expensive products and that the real money was in processing, not selling the raw material. The machinery to process aloe vera and amla was expensive, so he designed his own machine with the help of a local mechanic. Soon he was making shampoos and creams with the aloe vera extract he produced. He was selling the juice from his amlas at a good price and—he affects incredulity—even the remaining fibre was being snapped up for making candy. Processing proved so lucrative that Dharamvir modified his machine to be versatile enough to produce a supermarket's worth of goods. He stopped selling herbs and went into herbal oils. 'Thanda thanda cool cool,' he says, tousling his hair, to amazed laughter from the villagers. Then he began buying produce from surrounding farms and turning them into products. Strawberry juice. Pomegranate jam. A brand of tomato ketchup named after his son. Turmeric and ginger paste. The list is endless. His appeal to his '*kisan bhaiyon*, brother farmers' is simple: stop selling raw material, start processing it yourself. He is his own testimonial: '*Ab meri badi badi makaanein hain. Bachchon ka MBA karvaya.* Now I own big-big houses. I got my kids to do their MBAs.' Dharamvir sits down to riotous applause. And of course, Dharamvir has made a smaller version of his 'multipurpose processing machine' that the villagers can buy from him. A sample—a shiny steel affair dense with tubes, chambers and gauges—is being lugged around in one of the yatra trucks for the villagers to inspect.

After lunch we walk to Nayapura, a village that's decrepit in comparison to the others we've seen so far. The meeting here is again attended mostly by children and women, and Professor begins with a question to the kids: he holds up a matchstick and asks how the wood could be better utilized. A girl, perhaps seven or eight years old, says softly that it could be tipped at both ends. Professor lights up with joy. '*Shabash bachche, shabash!*' he cries out and leads a round of clapping for the girl. Later he tells us that it takes a while for him to elicit this answer from even his IIM students. The pulley-with-brake is demonstrated, and an old woman squatting opposite me who has no doubt pulled up water from deep wells far too many times breaks into a toothless smile of wonderment. Professor emphasizes the innovative aspect of the pulley, saying that the simple modification that saves so much effort has 'come after 2000 years.' But it might be just a little late. A woman speaks up, saying that the water in wells is so deep these days that they mostly use electric pumps. As we're leaving, an old woman from the village corners me and asks, with some bitterness, what sense there is in telling them about these things when most of the village owns no land and works elsewhere for a daily wage. I have no answers, so I make sympathetic noises and escape. Perhaps that's why there are so few men around at this time of the day. Perhaps that's why the houses in this village are ramshackle.

Our night-halt is at Dhaboti, a village of 2000-odd people. The village meeting is at the school, where we'll also spend the night. The night meetings (here and in other villages) are in a sense lit by innovation—the locals in charge snag metal hooks onto the power lines outside and run wires into the school. (Given the number of such wires we see running into homes all through the yatra, this is a wildly popular arrangement in these parts.) After the meeting, there's a touch of drama. Dinner is being cooked in a makeshift kitchen, where one of the gas-stoves erupts in flames. The cooks rush out of the room in time, and there's nothing left to do but watch from a distance as the gas cylinder expends itself with roof-high flames. Then, everyone's attention is drawn towards the school's entrance—from somewhere just beyond, a woman is screaming as if she's being beaten. It's dark, and some of the yatris start moving towards the entrance to investigate. But they're called back by the organizers— we're not here to interfere with the village. Hoarse, pathetic wails rend the night and subside after a few minutes, as do the flames on the other side.

About half the yatris here are affiliated with the organizations on the yatra's banner, and are mostly preoccupied with work. Some of them have been in the area for a month and a half, doing the groundwork for the yatra, and they're weary—sometimes to the point of surliness. Talking to the others, I learn that most of them are from cities, and like me have been led here by a curiosity about villages. Two or three are semi-regulars on the yatra, and don't shy away from calling these surroundings the 'real India'. The younger lot, mostly in college or just out, have a shiny-eyed enthusiasm for rurality that's well-served by the yatra's policy of planning routes to avoid roads and highways. For a week we hardly see any buses or cars, and for all we know India lives in her villages and is connected by hot, dusty paths.

Village life—at least the version of it we're living—has a rhythm that induces a simple sense of well-being. Tired from the day's exertions, our attentions unclaimed by television and the Internet, we sleep early and rise with the first rays of the sun. Then we head out into the open spaces, a bottle of water in hand. Since the terrain is mostly flat, and since there's not much greenery for cover, it often takes a significant walk to find an appropriate bush or tree or boulder, and even then, there's a good chance that there's already someone ensconced behind it. Some bushes have tinny mobile-phone renditions of film-songs emanating from behind them to announce occupancy, surely a recent innovation. There are government-painted signs in some villages that read *Gaon ko khule mein shauch se mukti dilana hai / Ghar mein shauchalay banwana hai* (The village needs freedom from alfresco defecation / Start in your homes a toilet's construction), but judging by the open-air turnout, not enough villagers have taken it to heart. The morning excursion is easily combined with dental care by chewing on a neem twig, a method that's particularly attractive here since it requires little to no water to rinse.

As is to be expected, the natural world figures in a big way. Even the traditional mud houses here look like the landscape has gathered itself into functional order. The scrub turns into a fence of uneven pickets and bramble, and the rough earth becomes a smooth and swept courtyard from which rises a house. These structures need regular maintenance, but are much cooler than the boxy concrete affairs that are schools, panchayat offices and other government-sponsored pukka buildings. In one village I come across someone who declares that the best shade is obtained under either neem or bargad trees. I've never thought about quality of shade, but if there's one place where such discernment is required, it's here, where a tree's shade is the only remotely comfortable place during the day. In another village, I overhear a man saying to another in a worried voice, '*Usko chakkar aane lagi hai*. He's started feeling dizzy.' He goes on to discuss the patient's restlessness and lack of appetite, and it's a while before I realize he's talking about a bullock.

Water is hard to come by. We sleep in the open, usually in or around village schools. Even when there are taps in the schools, there's no water in them. In one village there's a deep well from which we draw small buckets to bathe. (Drawing water with soapy hands and feeling the rope beginning to slip, I long for a brake on the pulley.) In a couple of places we find borewells not far from where we're camped, and take turns working the handle. In one village, some of us bathe from a drinking-trough for cattle, after which we're flecked with hay. In Dhaboti, a tanker has to be summoned for the yatris to bathe, but women from the village start filling their pots and buckets, and the local organizers chase them away after a high-pitched confrontation. It obviously takes some effort for the people living in these parts to get water in summer, but still, people think nothing of offering us water when we stop at a house, shop or field. Of course, it's a tradition across India to offer water to someone who's come in from outside, but here I begin to see poetry in it: when one has walked a few kilometres in the summer sun, there's no gesture of kindness or acknowledgement of shared humanity greater than a vessel of cool water.

The government is evidently helpless when it comes to supplying water, and in desperation has emblazoned the villages here with slogan after slogan emphasizing the importance of water (which one would think these people already know): *Bhoojal hai anmol / Samjho iska mol* (It's time you got a clue / Groundwater's beyond value); *Jo jal ko bachayega / Wahi sukh samriddhi payega* (Only he who's frugal with water / Will be able to prosper); *Jal hi jeevan hai* (Water is life); *Jal hai iswar ka vardaan / Jo hai is dharti ki jaan* (Water is a gift from god / The life of the earth clod); Rahim is co-opted for the cause—*Rahiman paani raakhiye / Bin paani sab soon* (Practise water conservation / Without it only desolation); and somewhat apocalyptically, *Jal hai to kal hai* (No water, no tomorrow).

Even if water isn't flowing like water, paint is. There are so many public awareness slogans on the walls that they serve as literal signs of the times, a digest of what's happening here these days. The National Rural Employment Guarantee Act announces: *Sau din ki nischit majdoori rojgaar gaaranti* (Hundred days of assured labour is a job guarantee). Malaria is going strong, according to the dire *Koi bhi bukhaar malaria ho sakta hai* (Any fever can be malaria). School education needs pushing to judge by the ubiquitous benediction of *Sab padhe sab badhe* (May everyone study, may everyone

grow) below an image of a boy and a girl straddling a
pencil; also a reminder that *Shiksha ka adhikaar mila
hai / Poora labh uthana hai* (Education is your rightful
due / Take from it its full value) if not for anything else,
then because *Jo naata titli ka phool se / Wahi rishta bachche
ka school se* (What a butterfly is to a bloom / A child is to
a school). A sign left over from the Socio-economic and
Caste Census of 2011 cheerfully reminds people that it's
their right to be included in the census, and by doing so
hints that some people in these parts may not count at
all: *Meri ganana mera adhikaar / Sahi ganana sahi vikaas.*
And perhaps for those who want out of it all, a phone
number below the clearly non-governmental sign:
FOREIGN INSTITUTE—Ab English bole bina ruke
(Now speak English without hesitation).

There's much here that's pretty to city eyes: turbaned
men at the reins of bullock-carts that raise dust as they
trundle down rough roads; hut-sized mounds of packed
cow-dung cakes; heaps of firewood; neat mud houses
painted with folk motifs. One afternoon the AP
photographer chases and circles at close range a woman
who's walking alone in a field with a bundle of dry brush
on her head. She's the personification of rustic charm,
but doesn't know it and grows increasingly flustered.
Beyond the picturesque, there's something inscrutable
about the terrain we're walking through, and there are
occasional hints of a complex world that lies just beyond
our field of vision: like the house in Bicholi I enter to
admire a painted grain-store, and where I learn by chance
that the children who live in it are not served the midday
meal at school because of their caste; like the sarpanch

Decorated grain store inside a mud house, Bicholi

we felicitated at Kalapipal who turned out to be the husband of the real sarpanch who was sitting quietly at a distance with the other women; like that woman screaming in the dark.

For much of the yatra I find myself walking next to Brigadier Ganesham—a retired army-man who now works with rural and grass-roots innovators in Andhra Pradesh. The Brigadier is a spirited conversationalist and we have long discussions about tradition and modernity, about the quality of life in rural and urban surroundings. These matters seem to be on the minds of a few other young urban yatris as well, who walk with us, listening to our arguments and occasionally contributing their views. The Brigadier is a staunch ruralist based on his experience growing up in a village in Andhra Pradesh in the 1950s and 1960s. In his village, he says people were healthy and happy, and usually died of old age. Hardly any women died during midwife-supervised childbirth, and infant mortality was negligible. There was no crime or abuse of any sort in the village. Such health and prosperity, the Brigadier feels, was largely a result of eating food cultivated without pesticides and other chemicals, traditional medicine, and a close-knit and supportive community. He believes that a return to such a natural, rural life will solve many problems of health and poverty that the country faces today. His position is so entrenched that I'm forced to become an apologist for modernity and urban life. I suggest that his village might be an exception, that statistics do show that life expectancy has more than doubled since the early 1940s, and this is no doubt in large part due to access to modern medicine, including vaccinations, antibiotics, and better care for infants and mothers. But the Brigadier is sceptical of government statistics, saying he knows exactly how they're generated. In support of the city, I make the point that one of its main advantages may precisely be that it offers freedom from a defined community, that it allows people to remake themselves as individuals if they want to. I narrate the story of the Satyajit Ray film *Mahanagar*, in which the stresses of city life force a housewife to go against her family's wishes and get a job, and how this ultimately results in her coming into her own. The rural idyll may be fine for many people, but there may be those who wish to escape for various reasons. What future is there today, I ask, for a gay person in a close-knit village community? It is the anonymity and bustle of the city that allows diverse cultures to co-exist and affords people who are different to be fulfilled as individuals. The Brigadier sees some merit in this, but also feels that it is precisely the single-minded focus on individual fulfilment that's destroying the institutions of marriage and community and leaving people unhappy. Maybe some institutions deserve to be shaken up I counter, and so on, and so on.

As we're passing through a village called Phagiya, the Brigadier and I stop to talk to Moti Singh, an elderly man sitting on a charpoy under the awning of his house. The Brigadier might as well have planted him here to illustrate his views. Moti Singh has moved here relatively recently, two years ago, after his land near another village was acquired as part of a dam project. (He got Rs 1.2 lakhs as compensation for his ten bighas, and here he has six bighas, purchased for Rs 1.35 lakhs.) I ask him what his general perception is—are things better now than they were. He has no doubt at all that things are worse: 'No one was *dukhi* back then. Now they are.' In earlier days, they relied on the rains and had a single annual harvest. But now, using chemical pesticides and fertilizers, and water from borewells, they try to squeeze in as many harvests as they can in a year. (The Brigadier mutters to me: 'They are raping the land.') But this means more work and expense. When he was younger, Moti Singh says, they bought some local manure, perhaps a little urea, and kerosene for the house; foodgrains and milk seldom had to be purchased. But now, expenses related to living and farming have increased, and though they're cultivating more than ever, Moti Singh says they don't get very much for their produce. He recalls his elders saying, '*Doodh aur poot*, milk and son—these two things are not to be sold.' But now they do sell milk, and their sons often try to find jobs elsewhere. (Oldies in a couple of other villages make a stronger *doodh-poot* connection, claiming that children these days are being given watered-down chai in place of the for-sale milk, and the result is the weak, feckless youth of today.)

The pattern of agriculture in these parts (as described by one of the residents of Pipalthon), is something like this: in June, with the first monsoon rains, they plant soybean, which can grow with just rainwater and is ready to harvest by September. Later they grow wheat or channa on the same land. The richer farmers cultivate sugarcane, a thirsty crop that demands splurging on borewells and pumps. The water tables are low, and at some places they have to drill up to 450 feet at considerable expense, without any guarantee that water will be struck.

Farmers are constantly experimenting with hybrids and isolating useful strains of crops. A popular variety of soybean is the 70-day 'Patel Pichchassi', named (I'm told) for its isolation in 1985 by a man called Patel. Others include varieties called Sonia and Atal. When I ask a farmer how these got their names, he tells me: '*Sonia ki speed achchi hai. Atal late se aati hai.* Sonia's speed is good. Atal comes late.' In addition to Iqbal and his two-in-one seed drill, we come across Abdul Rahim, who's made a simpler version of a machine to extract seeds from cotton. He's now working on a gentler cutter for soybean that won't scatter the seeds, and Professor promises money and technical help for seeing the idea through. Farmers here in recent years have taken to filling their tractor tyres with water when they plough on dry soil. This ensures better traction and longer-lasting tyres without farmers having to buy the weights sold for the purpose by tractor companies. This technology is apparently unheard of in Haryana, and Dharamvir is thrilled to learn of it. 'Chalo,' he says, 'I learnt at least one thing by coming here.'

At every village, the yatra felicitates the oldest members of the village and asks them about the secret of their longevity. At Dhabamata a 105-year-old man recommends, in addition to eating and drinking well, that pointless talk is to be avoided: *'Faltu batein mat karo. Tension ho jata hai.'* Hemraj Singh of Lasudiya Kangar is so spry at 110 that Professor points to him as a specimen and says, 'Good teeth, erect posture, no spectacles. You should all be able to eat food grown free of chemicals.' (But sometimes, when villagers declare with pride the ages of their elders, I get the feeling that the figures are slightly inflated from affection, respect and an eagerness not to disappoint us.)

It's the village medicine-men who are the key to potentially useful local herbs. But this knowledge is often hopelessly mixed up with magic and mysticism. At Kudi, Bhanwar Singh tells us about a herb that's effective in stopping bleeding, but he also talks about keeping the village safe by having its residents run to the village boundary holding burning pieces of wood that are then hurled across. Since these torches are made from a specific kind of wood, Professor thinks at first that the smoke may have a disinfectant property. It soon becomes clear that Bhanwar Singh is speaking of an altogether different sort of safety. Then Dharamvir softly asks one of the villagers something that causes Professor to pounce on him and change the subject. I later ask Dharamvir, who is as rational as they come, what he said. 'I asked,' he says, '*Yahan bhoot-woot toh nahin hai*? Maybe you have ghosts and spirits around here?' He explains: 'What else will it be if they're screaming and running around with burning sticks? It shows the mentality of the people.' Dharamvir's entire village in Haryana is an Arya Samaj village. 'We don't even believe in idols,' he tells me proudly.

Elsewhere, a sarpanch tells us when we ask about traditional medicine: '*Yahan hum jhaad phoonkte hain.* We exorcize spirits here.' At Phagiya we learn from one of the villagers about a plant whose extract cures sunstroke in five minutes when applied to the forehead, eye problems instantly with a drop, and stomach ailments when taken orally. It turns out to be aloe vera. At Guradi, Komal Bai suggests that a flatulent buffalo can be treated by feeding it oil in which bhujiya has been fried. In Samapura a young man wearing an 'NY Sports' cap back-to-front says he gives women medicine that will make them conceive a male child. An older man recommends egg-yolk mixed with hair shed by women while bathing as a balm for broken cattle horns. In Nayapura the medicine-man is willing to share a mantra that ensures the survival of premature calves and babies. He also knows a panacea—a mixture of three herbs in milk—that will, he jokes, 'make even a dead man come alive.' And if a scorpion bites you, you only have to cut your fingernails off and smoke them in a beedi. He's also a palmist, and he can accurately predict rainfall—in the short term by counting the twitches on the blackened neck of a chameleon, and in the long term by observing the fraction of cloud cover on the four days after *Holika dahan*, each of which is indicative of one of the four monsoon months. Felicitating him as is the usual practice, Professor drapes a shawl around him and says to the youngsters of the village, ' Preserve this knowledge, respect him,' upon which one of the boys shouts out, 'We go to the doctor when we're ill,' to laughter from the others. At Lodhri we're told, 'We never go to doctors. It's only *dev-babas*, godmen, who can cure us.' Professor argues gently, but is told of a shrine nearby that is so powerful that when the then chief minister of Madhya Pradesh, Digvijay Singh, visited after a flood, his helicopter would not start until he announced funds for repairing the shrine.

It's painstaking work to sift the useful from the useless—even an extravagant claim may have a kernel of truth to it, as in the case of the medicine-man singing the praises of aloe vera. (And who's to say fingernail smoke has no active ingredients against scorpion venom?) The yatra has a botanist who will identify and take samples of potentially useful herbs and plants; researchers at the NIF will test them and, in some cases, develop products. There's also an IP lawyer on the yatra, and when something does prove useful, patents will be filed to ensure that the sources are acknowledged and rewarded.

Some products that were developed this way are being given away at village meetings—among others, a mosquito repellent and a dietary supplement for cows to improve milk-yield. Professor also draws from his experience on yatras in other parts of the country to provide advice on natural cultivation and livestock care, but the villagers are sometimes sceptical. In Kalapipal, a farmer complains about *pala* afflicting his wheat, and Professor tells him it's a common problem in Haryana, UP, and Punjab, and that it can be addressed by watering the crop at night and burning cow-dung cakes along the perimeter of the field. The farmer is visibly disappointed, and says, '*Kuch practical bataiyen!* Tell us something practical!' And sometimes there are deeper misgivings, as in Guradi, when a bearded man with a prominent tilak summons a couple of the yatris and grills them under the impression that we're a group of Christian missionaries.

The yatra conducts a recipe contest at every village it visits. We come across much interesting food as a result: laddus and malpua made of the mahua flower, kheer from wheat and coconut, a biscuit made from flour, dates and cream, rotis made of channa, curries made of local greens. Professor asks the women at one village if they'd visit Ahmedabad to participate in a food festival, and one says, 'Definitely—if you'll pay us crores as in Masterchef.' But no TV show judge can match the yatris' enthusiasm for this fare. With our sensitivity to food heightened by a diet that's primarily dal and rice, we scuffle for scraps of recipe contest entries.

While the yatra may not be Christian, it does come across as puritan in some respects. At Samapura, Dharamvir turns to one of the villagers at the meeting and asks him if they eat meat. It turns out they do—fish, chicken, jungle birds. On Durgashtami they slaughter a goat and the village feasts on it. 'Excellent,' Dharamvir says. 'After all, animals are created to be eaten by us.' I later ask Chetan, who knows all the villages along the yatra route, and is the one who goads women into entering the recipe contest, about why we're seeing only vegetarian dishes. He tells me the yatra simply doesn't do non-veg, and he's been instructing women to bring only vegetarian preparations. This does seem a shame from the perspective of documenting traditional knowledge, given the complexities of cooking and curing meat. On one occasion, I go out into a village with Chetan while he drums up entries for the recipe contest. 'Can you make something that's not commonly prepared anymore? Can you make something that's different?' he asks a group of women with whom he's interacted during his visits to the village. 'Chicken,' says a coy teenage girl, causing the women to break out into giggles around an exasperated-looking Chetan. At Nayapura, the villagers announce that no one drinks there. Professor asks everyone to clap and announces that they'll work with Nayapura on a processing project: 'There's no alcohol here, so it's a good village. It's a good place to start good work from.' Most of the organizers are from Gujarat, but one of them is from Assam. He's expressed disdain previously at the yatra's squeamishness about meat, but as we leave Nayapura he's livid at what he sees as a needless vilification of alcohol. He feels it's an insult to his culture, where he says it's customary for babies to be given a drop of rice wine before even mother's milk. He has a tart sense of humour though, and gets his revenge soon enough when he's offered channa and jaggery by one of the other organizers. 'Am I a horse to eat channa?' he asks. 'Then have some jaggery.' 'Am I a Gujju to eat jaggery?'

As we're leaving Nayapura, I ask one of the villagers if it's true that no one drinks there. It's been true for a few generations now, he says. 'But the Mamas eat-drink everything.' Who are the 'Mamas'? It turns out that the panchayat is called Kuri-Nayapura, and is made of two abutting villages. Nayapura is Yadav Gawli in composition; Kuri is Bhil (or 'Mama'). We've seen several Yadav villages, but none that are Bhil. The Bhils are an ancient people from this region, and some of their hunting-gathering traditions still survive. It does seem like a missed opportunity if we're interested in traditional knowledge.

As we walk from Nayapura, I get talking to a fellow yatri named Garima, an electronics engineer who's just started working for a multinational in Bangalore. She asks me how I'm finding the yatra. Among other things I mention that I'm finding the yatra's outlook on eating-drinking a little too wholesome, and immediately get a counterview. She feels it's good to stay away from anything to do with drinking because—she says it with uncomplicated clarity—alcohol ruins lives. She has friends who 'sometimes drink beer', but they're different because they are educated and have self-control, which is lacking in many villagers. So, when it comes to villagers, it's best to steer clear of alcohol. I tell her a little heatedly that she's being patronizing—who are we to tell anyone how they should lead their lives? But that's not an easy view to defend when grim stories of families ruined by alcohol are brought out. (For instance Professor, in talking about how happy he was to come across a village that doesn't drink, mentioned a schoolgirl he spoke to in Chhattisgarh. He'd asked her if there was anything she needed, and she'd said that all she wanted was a room of her own. Her father drank and beat her mother every night, so it was hard for her to study in their one-room house.) Garima finds her current job all right, but she wants to do something more meaningful in the future, maybe social work of some kind, and I can easily imagine her ridding entire villages of alcohol.

Dharamvir's stature grows day by day in my eyes. His talk exhorting farmers to process their produce acquires more colour and detail with every village he delivers it in. By the time the yatra ends, he's so persuasive that I'm half inclined to begin farming just so I can process. He thunders about the injustice of it all: 'It takes a year to grow sugarcane, but sugar gets made overnight.' He talks about the craze for 'farm-fresh' products, and declares to loud applause that it's only the kisan who can make anything farm-fresh. In addition to rhetoric, Dharamvir is one of the keenest minds on the yatra. He sees that my camera has an articulating screen that can be flipped to face the same direction as the lens, and asks if he can borrow it to shave. He's a no-nonsense rationalist, certainly more so than many of the urban yatris. At Sanukota, some of us are bathing at a borewell, when someone teases the two yatris there who are wearing sacred threads by asking if they loop it over the ear when they head for the fields in the morning. There's a scientific reason behind it, says one of the thread-wearers, the IP lawyer (of all people). The thread presses upon a nerve behind the ear and helps protect against hydrocele. Dharamvir, threadless, butts in: 'Arre, what about those who don't wear a thread? Will everyone get hydrocele?' And the matter ends there.

On the last afternoon of the yatra, I fall in with a few organizers and a couple of regulars who constitute the tail of the walking group. Trailing the others allows us to indulge in vices such as chai and soft drinks along the way, and file in unobtrusively when the village meetings are well underway. We're so far behind at one stage that the luggage truck comes to pick us up, and to cause maximum embarrassment it drops us right in front of Professor. The red-facedness of my fellow slackers suggests our transgression is of the same order as being caught scarfing British chocolates on the Dandi March by Gandhi himself. The one among us who's most bothered by this is Arun, a yatra regular from Mumbai. Perhaps to salvage his reputation, he decides to deliver the introductory talk at Sotia, the penultimate stop of the yatra. Arun is a formidable and somewhat glib talker, but in English. (He's the only one among the yatris who seems to have read the Constitution of India, and he wins debates about development and policy from losing positions by luring his opponents into asking, 'Who says so?' in response to a tangential statement. Arun's answer is, 'The Constitution of India. Read it first; we'll talk later.') Here he'll have to speak in Hindi and so he takes quick tips from the NIF's PR person. It's almost dark by the time he begins, and he begins in populist fashion by asking everyone to put their hands together for the good people of Sotia. Then he mangles the Hindi for National Innovation Foundation (hardly his fault considering it's *Rashtriya Navpravartan Pratishthan*) to a few titters from the back. Arun's Hindi is of the Bambaiyya variety, and here in a village in Madhya Pradesh it sounds hilariously off-key. He introduces our mission: '*Hum buddhe logon se seekhne aaye hain.* We've come to learn from old fogies.' The yatris are by now shaking with quiet laughter. Then he comments on the absence of women. He tells us later that he had wanted to say that he understood it was an inconvenient time for the women since they'd be busy with housework. But what he comes up with is this: '*Maataein aur behenen hoti to achha hota. Lekin mujhe pata hai ki unke dhande ka time hai.* It would have been nice if the mothers and sisters were here too. But I know it's time for them to begin plying their trade.' Half the yatris are stunned into incredulity and the other half collapse in laughter. Some of us laugh all the way to the last stop of the yatra—Neelkanth, on the banks of the Narmada.

We spend the night in a temple in Neelkanth. In the morning, we take a dip in the Narmada, after which Professor addresses the group. He begins with three sonorous incantations of Om followed by the Gayatri Mantra, and goes on to talk about the yatra. He says it's an 'attempt to inculcate a sense of responsibility towards the coming generations' as also to empty oneself in order to be receptive. He likens the yatra's relationship to the villagers as that of Jambavan to Hanuman. Jambavan made Hanuman aware of the prodigious powers he already possessed and this enabled him to leap across the sea. 'Knowledge,' Professor says, 'has eyes, ears, brains, but no legs.' And so, we have walked for a week.

The participants all speak about their experience on the yatra. Many of us mention the generosity of the villagers with water even when it's clear there's not much to go around. For many of us the walking in the sun has been physically taxing—a few had to be driven back to Jamonia to rest for a couple of days; Professor was himself laid low for a day—and there are accounts of personal physical limits being extended. Arun makes a point about how women villagers should be pushed to participate more, even at the risk of offending cultural sensibilities. Last to speak, and only when she's forced, is a nineteen-year-old student of mass communication who's been documenting the yatra through photographs and video. Yesterday, she was asked to ride in the luggage van for her safety because the walk to Neelkanth was after sunset. She'd insisted on walking, but one of the organizers—the same one who earlier in the day had dropped us stragglers in front of Professor—ordered her to get in. 'For the first time in my life I wished I was a boy,' she says, weeping.

Among those present is the schoolmaster from Sotia—he wasn't in the village last evening, and so has come to Neelkanth to pay his respects to Professor and the yatris. He requests the opportunity to say 'do panktiyaan, two lines' (which I've learnt, in a week of listening to sarpanches and masterjis, is code for an epic oration studded with quotations from the Gita, Ramayana, Mahabharata, Kabir's poetry, and snatches of song). He begins by rebutting Arun's point about getting more women in villages to participate, saying that it's not due to any innate reluctance. If we visit a village as a group of fifty men and four women—and it's true that there are only four or five women among the yatris—it hardly inspires women to come out. He shows his regard for women with an aphorism about three things that both warm you in winter and cool you in summer: a well, a banyan tree and a woman. He then quotes a poem that casts people, weather, food, marriage, and pretty much everything in villages in a favourable light compared to cities. When he's finally done, Chetan shouts out, '*Savdhaan-vishraam-savdhaan*,' to which we shuffle our feet, and then we all—city dwellers, villagers—together sing the national anthem and go our respective ways.

10
THE TASTE OF SUGAR

On the road to Pandharpur

I must have been seven or eight when my mother first told me the story of Sakhubai, devotee of Panduranga. Sakhu was a young woman much put upon by her mother-in-law, who made her slave away at household chores and beat her when she fell short. The mother-in-law also interposed herself freely between Sakhu and the object of her devotion Panduranga, directing Sakhu away from worship and towards housework. On one occasion the mother-in-law perversely assigned Sakhu to grind a sack of jowar overnight. Sakhu was overcome by the effort and fell asleep having barely made a dent in the sack. Panduranga, ever solicitous about his devotees, realizing she was going to be in for it in the morning, manifested himself beside Sakhu and set his nose to the grindstone. When Sakhu awoke in the morning, the entire contents of the sack had turned to flour.

A god who looked out for his devotees so assiduously seemed someone useful to have on one's side (not even to mention the tantalizing implications of that Sakhubai story when it came to school homework). I was stirred enough to begin a post-bath routine involving joining my palms in front of a ledge of assorted gods while holding my mind in a state of blank thrall, but this lasted only a week or so. At around the same time I had what was a less calculated impulse to prayer. My kid brother was knocked over by a car in front of our house and rushed off to hospital. I found myself at home alone and scared, and I bypassed that godly ledge and ran up the stairs to the terrace where I tearfully pleaded to some formless thing in the sky for my brother to be all right. He was— barring scratches and a concussion. Still, I suppose my aptitude for faith in both a personal god and a more nebulous interventionary beyond was limited, because it ran out soon after. Today, if you swore that the Sakhubai jowar-grinding story really happened and asked me to explain it, I'd guess that she did all the grinding herself, perhaps in a trance-like state in which Panduranga figured.

But even the more or less faithless can feel an attraction for the cultural concomitants of faith. Over the years I have frequently travelled by road in Maharashtra, and during these journeys I'd often see small groups of people walking by the side of the road, the men dressed in white, the women carrying tulsi plants on their heads. I learnt that these were Warkaris, devotees of Panduranga who walk on pilgrimage from their towns and villages to the temple at Pandharpur. Some Warkaris walk to Pandharpur several times a year and spend more time on the road than they do at home, but the most important pilgrimage for Warkaris comes in early monsoon. The 220-km march begins from Alandi and Dehu, places associated with the prominent poet-saints of the tradition, Gnyaneshwar and Tukaram. Warkaris join in along the way and numbers swell over the eighteen-day walk until lakhs arrive at the Pandharpur temple on *ekadashi*, the eleventh, of the Hindu calendar's *Aashaadha* month, a date that falls sometime in late June or July.

As I learnt more about the Wari, I began to be intrigued by the idea of a pilgrimage in which the journey was as or more important than the shrine at the end of it. To do the Wari was to walk to Pandharpur. Those who couldn't walk the whole way would join in for one leg or two and return having felt that they had participated in the Wari. It was a joyous procession, filled with singing and chanting, and it embodied the 700-year-old bhakti tradition of the Warkaris in Maharashtra. I told myself this was something I had to experience at first hand. But then there's always a good reason to postpone a really long walk. This time it was a trip to Uzbekistan, scheduled right in the middle of the Wari. Then, on the day the Wari began, I heard from my travel agent: the Uzbek embassy had stopped issuing visas to Indian tour-groups, so the trip was off until further notice. Even as I got off the phone, the Warkaris were walking from Dehu and Alandi to meet at Pune, where they'd halt for a couple of days. If I rushed I might be able to join them there.

It is possible to simply join the throng of Warkaris, sleep wherever one finds space, eat whatever comes one's way through the kindness of strangers, and be borne to Pandharpur. But the hardships of the Wari are eased somewhat by group travel. Those who can afford it—and the charges are very reasonable—set out in organized groups called *dindis*. Each dindi is accompanied by a truck laden with supplies, and staff who ensure that the dindi's members get their meals on the road and have a place to sleep at night, usually a tent in a hard-won clearing. In an environment where people regularly undertake the Wari, people are roped into dindis without even having to try, but I was in distant Bangalore. Frantic emails and phone calls to people I knew in Pune yielded the phone number of someone who knew of a dindi. 'They are educated people,' was the only detail he would disclose over the phone, but if I managed to reach Pune before the Wari moved on, he would put me in touch.

The Indian Railways e-booking website is at the best of times a Rube Goldberg machine that throws one back to the login page if any number of technical variables and cosmic forces are not in alignment. It came through on the first attempt. My wait-listed ticket for the next day was soon confirmed. And after I'd thrown into a backpack all the white and off-white clothes I possessed, I was ready to leave. For the first time in years my mother looked at her refractory son with approval, even a touch of reluctant admiration. 'Some people plan for years to go to Pandharpur and still don't manage,' she said, 'and you've planned the trip in two days.' I'd barely begun to bask in the glow of such rare approbation, when she, on further reflection, decided that even if credit were due, it could not be to this edition of me. 'You must have accumulated some *punya*,' she said. This sort of diminishment of individual agency would be all around me for the next couple of weeks.

I reached Pune—or Pune was reached by me—and was soon riding pillion on my dindi-liaison's scooter through the lanes of Shaniwar Peth looking for the house in which the dindi was camped. The dindi *pramukh*, G. Mauli, turned out to be a stocky, leonine man with a curt, authoritative air. They had just finished a session of chanting the lord's name in front of an altar, and about the room were a dozen men wearing white clothes and Gandhi caps, tottering in the manner of those who have been sitting cross-legged for too long. I watched G. Mauli order people around regarding arrangements for the next day, all the while apprehensive about putting forth my case. I'd shown up there ponytailed, clad in jeans, severely handicapped in the bhakti department, and hoping they'd allow me to accompany them on a pilgrimage. But none of this mattered since my case had already been made at a higher level. 'If you've come all the way, it means mauli wants you,' said G. Mauli. 'It's now our duty to take you with us.' I was told to return within an hour with my luggage so it could be loaded onto the dindi's truck. We'd leave at four the next morning.

The single most frequently heard word on the Wari is 'mauli'. It means 'mother', with connotations of reverence and affection, and refers to Sant Gnyaneshwar, the thirteenth-century poet-saint who can be said to have started the Warkari tradition. Mauli also refers to the lord Vitthala (aka Vithoba/Panduranga/Pandharinath), considered the *swarupa* or original form of Vishnu (as opposed to an avatar). And mauli also refers to *everyone* who's on the Wari, because it is believed that the spirit of Gnyanoba can descend on anyone who's walking. So everyone on the Wari—man, woman, child—addresses one another as mauli, whether it's while making a request or enquiry, or simply while heaping abuse on the person who's crushed your foot in one of the small melees that are a near-constant occurrence on the Wari. With the regulation uniform and the common appellation, it becomes hard to tell one mauli apart from the other, and it's a while before I can confidently distinguish even the members of my own dindi.

We're around twenty people in our dindi, including five staff members who have left with the truck at 3 a.m. The rest of us leave at 4.30 a.m. dressed in white clothes and Gandhi caps (mine presented by G. Mauli, who correctly surmised that it was unlikely I owned one). The pre-dawn streets of Pune are packed with groups in white who appear to be walking purposefully in random directions. As we reach a junction, one group charges across us to the right, while we carry on straight. This is explained to some extent by the fact that different people take different routes to the point of assembly, but more pertinently, there are actually two groups leaving Pune today. The nucleus around which dindis on the Wari assemble themselves is a *palkhi* or palanquin that bears a poet-saint's *padukas*—the minimalist wooden slippers customarily worn by ascetics. The two largest groups accompany the palkhis of Gnyaneshwar and Tukaram, which depart respectively from Alandi and Dehu, converge at Pune, and then take independent routes till they meet again close to Pandharpur. Palkhis of other saints join in along the way with their own followers.

Our dindi walks with the Gnyaneshwar palkhi. The dindi was started by a doctor from Pune who's thought of by the group as almost being a saint himself, but who is now too old and infirm to join the Wari. (He still keeps a close eye on arrangements though, having even issued a menu for each meal of the Wari.) In his absence, the leadership of the group will be divided among other experienced members, with G. Mauli going first. The group itself has come together over the years through word of mouth. At its core are several PWD employees serving in different parts of Maharashtra, and they're joined every year by a floating population of people in their circle of friends, relatives and colleagues.

For my first day on the Wari I've been asked to stick close to R. Mauli to keep from getting lost. R. Mauli is an engineer in his mid-twenties who works in Mumbai, and since he can't afford to miss work he'll only walk with the Wari for a few days before taking a bus back. It's faint daylight by the time we reach the throng that leads to the Gnyaneshwar palkhi. The procession moves in fits and starts, the crowd thickening and rarefying every time the palkhi stops or resumes, and R. Mauli and I jostle through the crowd for a half hour to reach the palkhi. The palanquin is in a festooned, ornate silver chariot that runs on rubber tyres. There are about a dozen people sitting around the palanquin—fanning the padukas, throwing flowers or prasad to the masses, or just looking important—and the combined weight of the chariot and its occupants is pulled by a pair of hulking bullocks. (As hulking as they are, this is obviously very hard work: a bullock collapsed and died while the palkhi was entering Pune, due to—as the *Sakaal Times* puts it—'sunstroke and extra burden'; and later today, when the palkhi needs to ascend a hill, I'll count six pairs of strapping bullocks aided by a column of tugging Warkaris.) People are constantly lunging at the padukas over, under and beside each other, ensuring that there's always a tight scrum around the centre of the chariot. When the chariot needs to move on, the harassed-looking policemen who surround it tear people away and the bullocks charge ahead.

R. Mauli and I hurry on until we can walk without being subject to the tidal effects of the human ocean surging around the palkhi. Near Hadapsar we wait by the side of the road to take our place in the official procession. It so happens that our dindi is independent in the matter of food and accommodation, but when it comes to marching in the procession to Pandharpur we're part of a larger dindi. The procession is composed as follows: at the head, a bullock cart followed by two horses, one apparently riderless but believed to carry the mauli's spirit; then, twenty-seven dindis marching in columns four- or five-wide; the mauli's palkhi; and then 200-odd more dindis. Each dindi is made up of anywhere from a couple dozen to a few hundred men and women.

The Mauli's padukas are in a palanquin borne in a chariot

At the head of each dindi are the *patakadharis*, men carrying staffs with long saffron pennants that twist and writhe in the breeze unless it's raining and they're rolled up and enclosed in a water-proof sheath. One of them carries a small board with the position of the dindi relative to the palkhi. (For instance, R. Mauli and I are waiting for the board that reads in Marathi: '8—in front of the palkhi'.) The men of the dindi are arrayed behind the leaders, many carrying bell-metal hand cymbals, and at least one a pakhawaj. These are used in the singing of *abhangs*, devotional songs composed by the tradition's poet-saints down the ages. At least one person in each dindi also carries what is known here as a veen, really a small tanpura symbolic of the singing poet-saints, but not of much practical use amidst the pakhawaj and the clanging three-quarter kilogram hand-cymbals. The women of a dindi follow in a colourful cluster behind the men, wearing bright nine-yard sarees in the Maharashtrian style, some bearing on their heads a pot of water or a tulsi plant in a small metal pot.

If the procession sounds somewhat like a troop in its configuration, that's because it is so. The present look-and-feel of the Wari follows largely from rules for its organization laid out in 1831 by a devotee named Haibat Baba who also happened to be a chieftain under the Shinde rulers of Gwalior. There's a schedule of abhangs to be sung by a dindi through the day; the padukas will be washed at specific places and times; tradition dictates which noble families hold various positions of honour in the Wari hierarchy; which families supply oxen or horses for the Wari; and so on unto the most minor details. The coexistence on the Wari of unbridled god-addled joy and stark militaristic discipline is perhaps best illustrated at the evening arati, just before the palkhi rests for the night. The dindis amass in an open space, singing and swaying and clanging their cymbals, and when an official called the *chopdar* (who even dresses like a nineteenth century Maratha commander) raises his silver staff and shouts 'Ho!', the tens of thousands assembled there go deathly quiet. All this might have been deemed excessive even up until a few decades ago, when the people participating in the Wari could be counted in the thousands, but now, with eight lakh people officially registered this year, it seems visionary of Haibat Baba to have gone about the Wari as if he were undertaking a massive troop deployment.

Before Haibat Baba the Wari festivities had been shaped by Tukaram's son, Narayan Maharaj, who in 1685 began the practice of carrying Tukaram's padukas to Alandi, from where a procession would commence to Pandharpur along with Gnyaneshwar's padukas. Before him it is thought to be Gnyaneshwar's chief disciple, Namdev, who began the 700-year-old tradition of walking to Pandharpur in the company of other poet-saints. With the guru's padukas worn around the necks of prominent disciples, the Wari turned into a collective march of saints from the past and present.

As dictated by tradition, R. Mauli and I touch the dust of the road to our foreheads and slip into our marching dindi. All along the way, residents of Pune have been holding out food for the walkers. It's ekadashi today, observed by the Warkaris by consuming no grains. So families stand by the road handing out bananas or *rajgira* laddus or tea or bottles of water. Larger groups and businesses have kiosks where the Warkaris line up to receive *sabudana khichdi*. The most gaudy and raucous of these food kiosks are the ones run by political parties hungry for mileage. All the prominent parties have a presence, marked by the larger-than-life hoarding of an esteemed leader around whom ostentatiously tilak-ed minions are in orbit. Recorded abhangs blare from loudspeakers, drowning out the singing in the dindis and causing them to walk listlessly until they're out of range. Mercifully, all this is restricted to a three- or four-kilometre stretch around the place the palkhi halts for breakfast.

It's considered exceptionally meritorious to feed

someone who is on a Wari, so families and institutions approach dindis and book them in advance to consume a meal. Our entire marching dindi assembles in a school ground where a family serves us an elaborate ekadashi breakfast. After I've eaten, a woman from the family falls at my feet. I leap back in horror, but she thinks I'm playing hard to get, says imploringly, 'Don't do that, Kaka,' and lunges again for my feet. This will turn out to be a regular occurrence—it so happens that to be a mauli is considered the same as being the mauli, who in turn is no less than the mauli himself. I quickly learn from others in the dindi that the appropriate response to someone touching one's feet is to touch theirs in turn (though this is easier said than done at the end of a long day of walking).

We stop for lunch at our dindi's truck. The palkhi stops at pre-appointed places, and the various dindis park their trucks in a pre-appointed order. The line of trucks goes on for kilometres, and yet, year after year, a dindi's truck (or trucks) will somehow occupy the same patch of road on the highway. G. Mauli and the staff of our dindi have reached early in the morning, set up a tent by the side of the road, rested, and cooked for us. After lunch and a brief rest we carry on walking. This afternoon we climb up Diveghat, a winding road where the Warkaris are visible in an endless horde above and ahead, below and behind. Or so I'm told, because the spots with the best views have been cornered by the TV vans.

Most of the Wari's participants are weathered farmers from villages in Maharashtra. But today's leg of the Wari—Pune to Saswad—sees a relatively high urban turnout from Pune. These groups are conspicuous by their sneakers, caps and backpacks, and most strikingly, by the hideous polka-dotted garment called 'sun-coat' that is worn by Pune women to stave off a tan. There's even an 'IT dindi' that does the Pune-abutting legs of the Wari, and who are granted the sort of adoring media coverage that IT professionals receive every time they show the slightest deviance from their supposed nerdiness. *The Times of India*, Pune, reports on 14 June 2012, under the headline *Techies take time off to walk for a cause*, that 'over 150 young IT professionals' walked the first leg from Alandi to Pune with the slogan 'Save the girl child' printed on their caps, and that some of them found the experience 'enlightening' and would walk as far as Saswad. 'We all made professional adjustments to participate,' one of the IT dindi members is quoted as saying, referring to, at most, two days of leave from work.

The farmers have had to make professional adjustments too. This year's Wari is clouded-over by the monsoon having forgotten to make an appearance. Usually farmers sow their crop after the first rains and leave on the Wari. Turnout is relatively low this year because many are waiting for the rains. Others have come on the Wari anyway, having entrusted the sowing to others in the family, but they're anxious. And throughout this Wari the rain will be a tease, with a few brisk showers that promise the monsoon's arrival, followed by days of clear skies to douse hopes.

As we climb up the hill, our group runs into a man they seem to know. I'm still walking with my morning escort

R. Mauli, now joined by his father and aunt who are also part of our dindi. They greet the man warmly and ask him how he is. 'Vitthala, Vitthala,' he responds. We offer him the rajgira slab we're eating, and he says, 'Vitthala, Vitthala,' while signalling through nods and gesticulations that he's already eaten. We take his leave, saying we'll see him later, and he vanishes into the crowd with a parting 'Vitthala, Vitthala.'

The palkhi stops for a rest after the climb. The dindis lounge in clusters on a grassy plain, sipping chai from the stalls that have sprung up there. A helicopter flies in low circles above us. Rumour has it that it's Uddhav Thackeray indulging his fondness for aerial photography. A man stands up and screams at the helicopter as it makes another pass over us: 'Come down! Come down! Take some tea with us!'

It's dark when we reach Saswad. This is the longest leg of the Wari—we've walked around 35 km today by the time we reach our camping place a little outside town. Thanks to the PWD connections of our dindi we're staying at the quarters of the Asst. Divisional Engineer, Saswad. The women will sleep indoors, the men in the yard, and some of the staff in the truck.

The dindi truck is one of the logistical marvels of the Wari. Ours is really an 8-ton mini-truck that's been given a sloping roof of plastic-sheet over bamboo scaffolding. Inside it is modified to create a wide ledge for the dindi's luggage and a long storage box that doubles as a bed. The entrance is barricaded by two drums of water. Inside are food provisions, LPG cylinders and gas-stoves; a trunk for cash and valuables; buckets and mugs; tents, pegs, and tent-poles suspended from loops; a couple of clothes-lines. The truck's driver is a man from Pandharpur named Gnyanoba, but the king of this domain is the supplies manager, Murali Mama, a frail-looking man of around seventy-five with a toothless grin and sinewy arms that can lift surprisingly heavy loads. Then there's the teenager Amol, here as a handyman, but ever-entertaining as a practical joker: he'll urgently shout 'mauli' in a crowd just to see everyone turn; at every place we camp, he'll pretend to be lost and ask people for help in finding the dindi with the largest truck just to see their bewilderment. There are two women who do the cooking and cleaning. Twice a day a tent is hitched against one side of the truck to set up a kitchen from which hot, delightful meals emerge.

The food on the Wari is entirely vegetarian, usually without onion and garlic. Today is ekadashi, so no grains are to be used. If anyone has worked out how to technically observe a fast with minimal sacrifice and even some indulgence, it's the Maharashtrians. Dinner at Saswad illustrates this: there's the seed-based *bhagar* or jungle rice, a dal replacement made from groundnut and tomatoes, potato curry, sabudana khichdi, and a mango chutney that could bring the dead to life. In addition, G. Mauli supervises the serving of food in the traditional manner, assuming that when someone says they've eaten enough, they're only getting started. When we're finally finished, we stagger to our feet and make our way to the yard, where we soon fall asleep.

It's a rest day today, so we have the luxury of waking up as late as 5 a.m. It's still dark, and we go out into the open spaces by the road to join the huddled figures squatting there. Later, I brush my teeth at a water tanker across the road, and bathe in a park next door after fighting a small battle for water from a single pipe around which is a dense knot of women with a bucket-technique so advanced that they must do this every day of their lives. When the entire dindi is bathed and ready, A. Mauli—who works in the PWD at Solapur and is second to none when it comes to devotional punctiliousness— goes around applying a dab of sandal-paste overlaid by a central dot of black tulsi powder on each member's forehead. After tea, it's time for the *Gnyaneshwari parayan.*

R. Mauli, the young engineer in whose company I walked from Pune, has told me that Gnyaneshwar's signal contribution to humanity is a book called the *Gnyaneshwari.* This book, composed when Gnyaneshwar was just sixteen, contains 'all the knowledge in the world.' I ask him what's in it, and he says, 'We can't understand it. It's very high level.' Our dindi has undertaken to read aloud the entire *Gnyaneshwari* during the Wari. Today the group will read for around three hours. G. Mauli instructs me to be present there throughout: 'At least it'll fall on your ears.' He tells me that it's a very powerful book and that miracles have been known to happen while reading it: 'In Pandharpur, illiterates have started reading just by running their fingers along the lines.'

As the group starts reading, I fiddle with my phone and find (miraculously) that there are plenty of resources online about the *Gnyaneshwari,* including an English translation on the Bharatiya Vidya Bhavan website. The

Gnyaneshwari—I read—is a commentary on the Bhagavad Gita written in the Marathi of Gnyaneshwar's time, and is considered a landmark for having liberated the Gita from Sanskrit and made it accessible to the wider public. Gnyaneshwar was born to Brahmin parents who were ostracized and who had ended up taking their lives, and the stories traditionally told about Gnyaneshwar's life illustrate a tension between him and Brahmin orthodoxy (such as the episode in which he proves a point to his Brahmin detractors by making a water-buffalo recite the Vedas). In his wake the Warkari tradition emphasized direct devotion to Vitthala, cutting out ceremonies and priestly middlemen, and earned a large number of followers from across castes. Indeed, at the end of the Wari, the priests at the Pandharpur temple cede the idol to the Warkaris. Instead of interfacing with the lord through arati plates and flames, the Warkari can go right up to the idol and plant his head at Vithoba's feet.

My dindi reads the *Gnyaneshwari* in a rapid singsong. The emphasis is on saying the words rather than understanding them (which is anyway hard for the speaker of today's Marathi). A couple of people in our dindi, notably A. Mauli, even have large parts of the *Gnyaneshwari* committed to memory, which allows them to charge ahead like pious rappers until someone puts in a gasping request to slow down. The rap-like effect is enhanced by the metrical form of the *Gnyaneshwari*—its unit of composition is the *ovi*, which comprises four terse lines of which the first three end in the same vowel sound. It's clear that Gnyaneshwar was a considerably gifted poet—the ovi have a punchy, reassuringly didactic cadence, and the translation I'm reading is full of vivid storytelling and memorably extravagant similes. For instance, when Arjuna wilts on the battlefield, Krishna tells him he should actually be grateful for the opportunity to fight, and likens Arjuna's situation to that of a person who 'while yawning finds that nectar drops have fallen into his mouth'.

As I read, I find it intriguing that the reputedly caste-agnostic Warkari tradition should hold so dear this particular book. Right in the first chapter, verses from the Gita have Arjuna detailing to Krishna the grim consequences of destroying a family: 'With the ruin of the family its ancient customs decline. When these customs perish, immorality overtakes the whole family. When immorality prevails, O Krishna, the women of the family become wanton; with the corruption of women, there arises intermingling of castes. And this mingling of castes leads the family and its destroyers to hell.' Gnyaneshwar's commentary only elaborates the same argument. And later, there are hints that Gnyaneshwar himself might have taken the stratifications of caste for granted. In explaining the verse, 'Better is one's duty, though destitute of merit, than another's duty well performed,' Gnyaneshwar has this analogy to offer: 'Tell me, should a Brahmin, even though poor, partake of sweet dishes which are prepared in the house of a Shudra? Why should a person do such an improper thing?' Could what the book stands for—access to the divine free of arcana and intermediaries—be more important than what it actually says? Within a generation, Gnyaneshwar's most prominent disciple, Namdev, himself a tailor, had collected around him a group of abhang-writing poet-saints that included his maid, a few Brahmins, a gardener, a barber, a potter, a goldsmith, an oilman, a dancing-girl, and a family of untouchables. In later years there were Muslim poet-saints who wrote abhangs in praise of Vithoba.

Regardless of origin, those who give up meat and intoxicants, fast on ekadashi, take the name of Vishnu, and do the Wari can wear the tulsi mala that marks them as a Warkari. This openness has existed at least since the time of Namdev, and is no doubt the source of the caste-busting halo around Gnyaneshwar's legacy. Still, many dindis tended to be organized along caste lines, and Dalit dindis were not allowed to walk as part of the main palkhi procession until the 1970s. The Vithoba temple at Pandharpur did not allow entry to Dalits until 1947 (and that too after a fast-unto-death campaign by the author, teacher and social activist Sane Guruji). The anthropologist Irawati Karve published in 1962 an account of her experience doing the Wari with a dindi composed of Brahmins and Marathas. She describes how, even within the same dindi, the two groups cooked and ate separately. Maybe times have changed: the group I'm with has Brahmins, Marathas, and at least one person from a scheduled caste, and we're all happy to eat together and sleep under the same roof, porch or tent.

Today it's my turn to be untouchable for a while. Here at Saswad each dindi can send two representatives with *naivedya*, an offering of food to the mauli, which is later consumed as prasad. The tradition in our dindi is to send the newest members so that they get an intimate darshan of the padukas. These new members happen to be R. Mauli and me. G. Mauli hands me an inordinately long crimson dhoti and when I emerge from behind the truck after rolling it round my legs, Murali Mama points at me and laughs toothlessly till G. Mauli asks him to cut it out and have some consideration for a guy who's new around here. The dhoti is to be worn folded up between the legs, a skill I have neglected to acquire, so G. Mauli gets busy around me and finally hands me a thick pleat that he tells me to tuck into my underpants to insure against wardrobe malfunction. I set off carrying a large thali-covered thali of food atop which is a steel cup of water with a copper spoon in it. R. Mauli, wearing a simple white dhoti, is walking beside me. We're both barefoot and headed for the mauli's tent 1.5 km away. We cannot be touched by anyone on the way since we're supposed to be in a state of ritual purity. Given how packed Saswad is with Warkaris, it's impossible not to brush against anyone. So we have a security detail—four members of our dindi holding hands around us to create a firewall, and shouting 'mauli' to scatter the crowds ahead of us. Every few steps a Warkari or a resident of Saswad attempts to touch my feet and has to be shooed away by Security. I suppose it's easy to mistake me for a religious personage: crimson dhoti, shawl around the shoulders, bearded visage, forehead marked with sandal paste, hair drawn into a small bun at the back, a less flamboyantly costumed acolyte next to me. And if I weren't a holy man, why would there be this human fence around me? It's all absurd, a charade generated by a system of beliefs for which I have no affection. But the fierce determination with which Security shields me has an inductive effect, and it's not long before I feel it's unquestionably important that I not be touched by anyone. I even catch myself indignantly barking 'mauli' when someone comes too close for comfort, and find that I've become active party to an exclusion I don't even believe in.

The mauli's palkhi is in a dense thicket of tents, and we make our way there along the narrow gaps between tents, stepping over ropes and pegs. My dhoti catches on a peg and it is only G. Mauli's thoroughness that keeps the world from seeing that this maharaj has no clothes. When we reach the mauli's tent the gatekeepers only allow one person from the security detail inside. The two people who were supposed to tell me what to do are outside, so I just stand there with the mauli's padukas in front of me, noticing that they're encased in silver, and that the mauli wore a very small shoe size. One of the priests there does some ceremonial water sprinkling for me after placing the thali on the palkhi and sends me on my way. The three members of the security detail waiting outside are dejected. They'd volunteered so they could get an up-close darshan, but the mauli has willed otherwise. While they're dispirited and off-guard, a villager successfully dives for my feet and we all exchange dismayed glances like a football team that's just let a goal in. I've been warned earlier that if something like this happens we're supposed to return to the dindi, bathe, and repeat the whole exercise. We just pretend it didn't happen.

After dinner, G. Mauli sits me down next to him and describes how he started doing the Wari about twenty years ago. He first went out of curiosity with a couple of friends. A few days into the Wari, he felt so exhausted from the walking that he sat down under a tree and announced that he was going home. Just then a blind man walking in one of the dindis turned his head towards G. Mauli, stared at him for a while through his dark glasses, and walked on. G. Mauli felt inexplicably compelled to follow him, but the blind man proved untraceable. In the meantime G. Mauli's moment of weakness had passed and he made it to Pandharpur. He was a physical wreck by the time he got there though, and had to be supported by two friends when he went for darshan. But the instant he set his forehead to the idol's feet, he felt electrified and was practically gambolling as he left the temple. He decided to become a Warkari: 'I thought, "10 lakh people can't be fools. This guy wrote a book at the age of 16 and people are walking carrying it on their heads even 700 years later! There must be something to it."' He returned to his PWD office a changed man and announced that he would no longer be party to any shady deals. This created a stir in an office where shady deals were the norm, and his nervous colleagues tried to stage an intervention. G. Mauli told them that they could do as they pleased and he wouldn't tell on anyone, but as far as he was concerned it was a straight and narrow life from then on. His leave every year is spent entirely on the Wari, and the mauli appears in his dreams and prods him when it's time to make arrangements. He tells me that I may have come with other ideas in my head, but if I'm here it's because the mauli wants me.

Every other person I meet on the Wari has a story, sometimes a legend. A. Mauli tells me he's been meditating since he was a child and has had Vitthala appear before him a few times. His father only recently told him that many years ago at dusk he once saw A. Mauli levitating during meditation. Even Murali Mama, the supplies manager, came to this dindi eventfully. Almost two decades ago, he was doing the Wari alone, and had one day asked people nearby to look after his belongings while he bathed. When he returned, the strangers were gone, along with everything he had. The dindi had found him clad only in a loincloth, weeping, asking passers-by for money so he could return home. The dindi decided to help him, but on condition that he finished the Wari. So they gave him some of their clothes and took him with them. He's been accompanying the dindi ever since.

It's not the walking that's the hardest part of the Wari; it's the rest of it. We rise at 2.30 a.m. This is because the truck has to leave by 3 a.m. if it is to reach our lunch spot without getting stuck among the other trucks. So we rise at 2.30 a.m., roll up our bedding-cum-bags—squat, stackable plastic packages that unroll into a sleeping-mat with the bundle of clothes acting as a pillow—and hand them to Murali Mama on the truck. If we've been sleeping in a tent, the tent is packed into the truck. Then we visit the fields because the buckets and mugs have to go with the truck. Once the truck is off we can sleep a little longer on plastic sheets in the open, but this is not very comfortable. We will then bathe wherever possible—

at a water tanker, in a canal, at a tap in someone's yard—and set out walking in the morning, carrying a wet towel and any clothes we may have washed. It is not unusual, in the morning, to see men walking with wet underwear on their heads. Much prettier are the nine-yard sarees— bands of colour draped for drying on bushes or between trees, or unfurled on mounds and fields.

From Saswad we walk to Jejuri. The rains make their first appearance on the way and everyone gets out their 'plastics'. The plastic is an indispensable accessory on the Wari—it's a rectangular, person-sized double-layered sheet of plastic that can be used for sitting or sleeping on, and since one of its shorter ends is sewn-up, it can be worn as a poncho in the rain. It sells for Rs 10 or 20, and is made from the bright, uncut packaging material for all sorts of products from across the world. Represented among us are shampoos and detergents, pastries and cured meats. Mine is a brand of coffee called Toulouse, packed in the United States. The person in front of me in the marching dindi shelters under Bakers Complete, 'a balanced doggylicious meal for your adult dog'.

At Jejuri the roads are yellow from the turmeric offered to its resident deity Khandoba. I know of Jejuri from Arun Kolatkar's sequence of poems, and want to explore the town and climb up to the temple, but I don't—my feet register a strong protest at the prospect of more walking.

After Jejuri, I stop walking with the marching dindi. It marches in a self-organizing four- or five-abreast formation, and when the road narrows, or when someone drops out or joins in, there's adroit scampering required to preserve the formation. Any delay means that I find myself in between rows, getting in the relentless way of joyously singing Warkaris, and more than once I am reminded of the story of one of Namdev's disciples—Gora, the potter—who, lost in his singing, trampled his crawling child into clay. There are others in my dindi who for various reasons do not want to march with the palkhi and who, right from day one, have been leaving camp well before the palkhi starts. They become my new companions: W. Mauli (who complains he has short legs and therefore cannot keep up with the marching dindi); Mr and Mrs S. Mauli; Mr and Mrs J. Mauli and their son J. Mauli (Jr). S. Mauli and J. Mauli are both nearing retirement from the PWD; their wives are both large women who are suffering from leg pain, blisters and swollen feet, and prefer to trudge along at their own pace. I walk with some of them, or just up and down beside the marching dindis, enjoying the abhangs without getting in the way.

W. Mauli is sixty-nine, a short man who makes precise mudra-like hand movements when he speaks. This is his eleventh Wari, and when I ask how much longer he plans to keep going, he says, 'As long as the mauli will have me.' With the others I have been talking in Hindi or broken Marathi, but with W. Mauli, who comes from near the border of Karnataka and Maharashtra, I can converse freely in Kannada. Walking with him, I ask what effect the Wari has had on him, and he launches into a story about his alcoholism. He used to be a heavy drinker, bingeing on country liquor for days on end until he steadied himself and reduced his intake to just three quarter-bottles every evening (at which point I can't help but admire his former drinking prowess). But no matter how much he tried, he couldn't stop altogether. When he decided to do the Wari, friends and family warned him that he could end up dead from the effects of withdrawal, and implored him not to go. The night before his first Wari, he drank his regular three quarter-bottles, woke up groggy, started walking, and hasn't touched a drop since. W. Mauli is now a great connoisseur of tea and we stop often to drink 'special chai'—made from scratch for us at added expense because the pre-made chai is prepared to the taste of rural Maharashtra by adding sugar until no more will dissolve (and yet the hapless vendors are berated for their miserliness with sugar).

The chai is served from pushcarts and stalls that line the highway. For the first couple of days I pay no special attention to them, thinking that these carts are from nearby villages. Then, I notice the names of carts and stalls recurring, and soon I'm in a perennial state of déjà vu. I realize that these are actually *accompanying* the Wari for the business opportunity it represents. As also are the stalls that sell *poha*, *bhaji* and other snacks, the kiosks of pineapple juice (so full of artificial colour, flavour and sweetener that it floats ethereally down the gullet leaving behind a chemical clash of aftertastes), the sugarcane juice vendors (who sell the real thing), the trucks selling bottles of water. They come from various places around Maharashtra and their Wari is, if anything, harder than that of the pilgrims—they go ahead and set up their businesses while the walkers rest, and they work when the walkers walk. I soon realize that it's not just sellers of food and drink, but an entire army of service-providers that's accompanying the Wari. There's perhaps no better place in the world for a cobbler to be in, and they're frequently visible sitting just off the road, surrounded by one-sandalled men and women. There are roadside barbers and clothes-pressers. There are—there have to be—vans that sell balms for aching joints and muscles. There are even those who will charge your mobile phones for a price—they hook up car batteries to large power-boards and are always surrounded by a tight circle of squatting men who look like they are recharging themselves as well. There's a truck belonging to an anti-vice organization that is making its point through a loudspeaker, pamphlets and a skull-faced

Getting a shave by the road

scarecrow from which dangle empty liquor bottles and gutkha packets. There's even a sadhu in search of a following: he's bearded and clad in blazing saffron, and he sets himself up ostentatiously at points of maximum visibility—in an attitude of blessing on a ledge overhanging the road, meditating in *vajrasan* at the edge of a field, jumping up and down while leading a group of bemused villagers in forced laughter. J. Mauli (Jr.) names him *Dhongi Baba*, and we're always on the lookout for what he'll come up with next.

At Walhe we're camped on the outskirts in a virtual township of tents and trucks, with craggy hills to one side. Our dindi is tense today—transfer orders are being issued today for PWD officials, and phone lines are restlessly being worked. News arrives in the afternoon that all our dindi members except S. Mauli have managed to maintain status quo or obtain favourable transfers. S. Mauli, with only a few months to go for retirement, has been transferred to an office that everyone agrees is simply unmanageable. After prolonged discussion with the others about what strings can be pulled, S. Mauli takes his fate in his own hands and leaves the Wari to press his petition in Mumbai.

Mrs S. Mauli, a good-humoured woman in her fifties, remains with us. She tells me that the name Walhe derives from Valmiki. There's a temple to Valmiki on a hillock near our camp, and that's where Mrs S. Mauli says the Ramayana was written. I ask her: 'So, since Sita and her twins took refuge with Valmiki, they must have hung out here in Walhe too?' Mrs S. Mauli says, 'No, all that happened near Ayodhya.' And after a pause, she reconciles everything neatly: 'These were divine beings. They could appear and disappear anywhere at will.'

Speaking of divine appearances, the inveterate trickster Amol reports that he did climb up to the Valmiki temple, where he found Dhongi Baba seated in rapt meditation. To pass the time, Amol fell at his feet and mimicked hysterical reverence, following which a few others nearby started taking D.B.'s blessings, and this initiated a chain reaction that soon had people flocking to him. When Amol reached the base of the hill, he'd actually been asked by a group of old men heading up whether he knew where to find the great sage who was rumoured to be on top of the hill. Dhongi Baba may just have found a following, thanks to Amol (or maybe—you never know with Amol—none of this happened and the joke is on us). G. Mauli hears J. Mauli (Jr.) and me laughing at Amol's story and asks us what happened. We tell him, and he bites his tongue and cautions us not to call him Dhongi Baba because we might end up incurring his wrath on the off chance that he's genuine.

In Walhe, the temporary settlement formed by the Wari tents has the atmosphere of a village fair: heaps of sweets, food-stalls, makeshift stages with entertainers, vendors of bangles and trinkets and handbags, Chinese plastic toys, kitchenware. For the villagers on the Wari this is a chance to shop. The board above one of the stalls reads: 'Siddheshwar Ghar Sansar Sale—Anything you buy here is Rs 10'. The Wari is the high point of the year for many of the towns and villages it passes through, but it's followed by a nasty hangover. The Wari leaves in its wake a trail of refuse: plastic cups, plates and bottles.

Charging mobiles by the road

And there's human excrement everywhere. One of the PWD officers in our dindi who works in Pandharpur says it takes months to clean up the town after the Wari.

At Lonand a kind merchant has allowed us to camp in his tin-roofed onion godown (from which the onions have been removed for our comfort). But there's no water in the godown, and the common water-tap some distance away at the village chowk has an endless line at all times of the day and night. Early in the morning, a couple of members from our dindi enterprisingly find a tank of water that doesn't have a crowd around it. It's by the railway tracks behind the godown, and has somehow escaped wider detection. The instant we reach with our buckets, a dozen people materialize with buckets and clothes and vessels. Even as we bathe, an impatient mauli climbs on top of the tank, shifts the concrete slab that covers the tank's opening, and begins dipping his grimy shirt into the water.

It's to be a rest day at Lonand. As at Saswad, we have a marathon *Gnyaneshwari* reading session followed by an offering of food to the mauli (with the opportunity of carrying the plate going to someone else this time). G. Mauli sometimes likes to issue curt rapid-fire instructions even when they're not required—a kind of running commentary in imperative mode. He's doing so while the mauli's plate is being readied, and I hear him say, 'Don't serve salt in the naivedya plate. Remember— salt is never served in the naivedya plate.' I'm intrigued by this, and I ask why. It's the sort of detail behind which there's often a larger principle, or at least a cute story, and I assume from G. Mauli's authoritative tone that he knows. But he doesn't. My question stops him mid-track, and he poses it in turn to Mrs J. Mauli, who ponders for a while and comes up with something about salt coming from the sea, which makes it impure because fish also live in the sea. This seems far-fetched to me and I'm only thinking aloud when I say that the water used for cooking probably came from a river somewhere that also had fish in it, but this causes others to jump into the discussion. One mauli says, 'It's just like that. You don't ask why. It's tradition and you follow it.' J. Mauli (Jr.) chips in: 'It's like asking why two plus two is four.' This last statement comes from a 21-year-old who's studying to become an engineer, and I'm compelled to take it up: I tell him that if it were left to tradition, two plus two could be five or eight or anything at all. Then J. Mauli (Sr.) decides that enough is enough, and that the matter needs to be resolved by someone with authority. He dials a number on his cell-phone and hands it to me saying there's an expert on pooja protocol at the other end who surely knows why. Mine was only a casual question, but it's too late to back out now. I ask the question, receive an answer, and disconnect without argument. I repeat the answer to the five or six people waiting for it: 'Salt is a symbol of our sorrow and we don't want to offer our sorrow to god.' No one looks terribly convinced, but we move on.

It is perhaps this little discussion over salt that leads J. Mauli (Sr.) to later confess to me that he's actually sceptical about some parts of our epics. 'Maybe it's because I don't have enough *shraddha* . . .' he says apologetically. He's hesitant to say it out loud, but he personally thinks there wasn't enough time on the battlefield for Krishna to impart to Arjuna the eighteen chapters of the Bhagavad Gita. He also finds it arbitrary that Draupadi was shared by five brothers, and that all those people looked on while she was disrobed in public. He finds the way Karna was treated unfair overall, and coming to the Ramayana, questions what kind of ideal man Rama was if he couldn't even take care of his wife. (I can see where he's coming from—the J. Maulis are one of those exceptionally happy families, good-naturedly ribbing one another, revelling in each other's presence. On one occasion, the trailing Mrs J. Mauli goes missing for a couple of hours, and Mr J. Mauli begins to weep with regret because he didn't keep her in his sight. It's all okay in the end—Mrs J. Mauli, afflicted by diarrhoea and monstrous blisters on her feet, had flagged a ride to the evening's campsite.)

We're resting at Lonand after an elaborate lunch when G. Mauli decides to do something about the dire water situation. The warehouse next to ours is occupied by a dindi from Kalyan that's large enough for them to have a water-tanker accompanying them. A request for water is bound to be denied, so G. Mauli saunters up to the tanker and fills a bucket of water. His reasoning is that one man in Wari casual-wear—white banian and underpants or folded-up dhoti—looks pretty much like another, so it'll take some time for the other dindi to realize what's going on. G. Mauli's foray turns into a multi-pronged guerrilla effort with more men from our group joining in. The plan works better than expected— in the daring raid we manage to fill nearly all our dindi's vessels and buckets before the tanker is strategically driven away. The next morning we bathe like kings, right at our doorstep. W. Mauli beams at me as we stand by the street in our underwear pouring mugs of cold water over ourselves: 'We were lucky to get that water yesterday.'

At Saswad I was surprised to return to our abode in the evening and find the man who'd say nothing but 'Vitthala, Vitthala' giving a discourse. He's known as Tatya Maharaj, and has been invited to address our group here in Lonand too. He talks about how some people say the Wari is all blind faith, but these people really don't know what they're missing. He attributes this wrong-headedness to the fact that thought (*soch*) has come very far, but feeling (*bhava*) has been left behind. He says the Wari used to be undertaken by Shiva himself, but it became more popular after Gnyaneshwar. (There are discourses all over town, and the one other discourse I go to also goes on at length about the glory of the Wari and how those who mock or ignore it have no idea what they're missing.) But Tatya also touches upon other spiritual matters. He brings up the fact that even a corpse has legs, eyes, mouth, etc., but it does not walk, see or talk. This means that we don't really do anything ourselves, and have to be animated by god. But how can we reach this god? By chanting his name. He whips out his mobile phone, pulls up the calculator and plunges into some serious arithmetic to compute the number of times we need to take the lord's name simply to thank him for each breath of our life. It's an enormous number. 'No guarantee that even if you chant his name these many times you will "get" him. Maybe it's possible across many lives, but you will at least withdraw from the suffering of samsara.'

After the discourse G. Mauli helpfully introduces me to Tatya Maharaj. He's a slight, weary-looking man who's a full-time seeker. He tells me he's from Nagpur, and he first went on the Wari twelve years ago on a lark, but ended up staying in Pandharpur for four months. After he returned to Nagpur he often found himself dreaming about the Chandrabhaga (as the river Bhima is known in Pandharpur). The next year he went on the Wari again, and after completing it decided to make Pandharpur his home. At the moment his spiritual goal is to take Vitthala's name thirteen crore times. He estimates that ten hours of daily chanting for six years should achieve this, and until then he will not indulge in any idle conversation. He's finished four years of chanting, and when I ask him if he feels any different, he smiles blissfully and can't resist asking me that hoary question: 'Can you describe the taste of sugar?' But he does tell me that he finds his mind less '*chanchal*' now.

The word chanchal would just about begin to describe the spring in the sixty-nine-year-old W. Mauli's step as we depart Lonand. He tells me that he's been relieved of a huge burden. He was among the security detail in Saswad when I went with our dindi's offering to the mauli's tent, and he felt jilted when he wasn't allowed in for a close darshan. He tried again yesterday, and was again kept out of the tent. 'I thought mauli was angry with me,' he says. He resolved to stand in the darshan line early this morning, and when he got near the palkhi, the queue was halted for the mauli's padukas to be worshipped and for the palkhi to be decorated. 'I got darshan for one hour,' he tells me triumphantly. 'Maybe mauli wanted this for me and that's why he denied me the other times.' W. Mauli also tells me later that he visits several other well-known shrines in southern and central India. He describes the petitions he has taken to various temples and deities—mostly requests for job appointments, promotions, and postings, first for himself, and then on behalf of his son. The outcomes are sometimes favourable, sometimes not, but with experience he's learnt to see patterns that allow him the satisfaction of occupying a special place in an orchestrated world. The emotional vicissitudes of such a life seem overwhelming to me, but

W. Mauli could reasonably say, given the severity of his past alcoholism, that he might not even be alive if it weren't for his faith.

It's not W. Mauli alone who has had to reckon with problems: the only conversation I have with Amol in which he doesn't make me laugh is one about the scars on his forearms; I mention to J. Mauli (Sr.) how much I'm enjoying walking in the company of his son, and he tells me he's been worried ever since J. Mauli (Jr.) tried to take his own life after a poor examination result a couple of years back; I hear from others in our dindi that Murali Mama had been seriously ill and in hospital a couple of months back, but he's ignored advice to rest and joined the dindi in his usual capacity. In our marching dindi I meet a man whose brother tried to have him killed over an inheritance, so he gave up worldly life in disgust and dedicated himself to the worship of Vitthala. Another man in the marching dindi is so old and has to make such an effort to walk that I'm filled with dread and tenderness whenever I'm around him. The farmers, lakhs of them, are worried sick about the delayed rains. I see a legless woman doing the Wari on one of those hand-powered tricycles; a blind man groping his way forward. From all that I know about its participants, the Wari should be a pageant of misery. But it's not. Those on this road possess a grace, a certitude, even a jauntiness, that never ceases to amaze me. I often stand by the road and watch this multitudinous paradox go by, and once or twice, when there's no one I know around me, I'm overwhelmed to the point of tears.

The palkhi procession is interleaved with events that

keep things lively: at seven places during the Wari there's a *ringan*, where the mauli's horses run through the massed dindis who chant and sway and indulge in light gymnastics; at one place there's the *dhava*, where everyone runs down a hill (reportedly inspired by Tukaram, who began to sprint with joy when he saw the towers of the Pandharpur temple from afar). These events draw large crowds from nearby villages. Even otherwise, the palkhi draws villagers who line its route thickly. Some are content to clap their hands and say 'mauli, mauli' as the palkhi passes; others fling themselves at the palkhi to touch the padukas.

While the main palkhi procession has an undeniable cymbal-clanging grandeur to it, it's the smaller groups I find most moving. These knots, some of men but mostly of women, hurry on towards Pandharpur either in front of or behind the main procession. They aren't part of any dindi—perhaps they cannot afford it—so they walk with their belongings on their head. Many of these groups don't sing abhangs, but keep themselves going with a simple ditty: 'Tukaram Tukaram, Gnyanoba mauli Tukaram.' I see these women sometimes run into others from their villages—there's a thrill of recognition followed by a spontaneous embrace. And if the composite face of Indian womanhood is careworn, here there is much laughter. It is not often that women can take a couple of weeks off from their responsibilities.

Still, even on the Wari, women do a great deal of work. In our dindi, the cooking and cleaning for twenty-odd people is done by two women staff members. Mrs J. Mauli and Mrs S. Mauli wash their families' clothes, and I find out one evening that they do so with a good deal of professional pride. The three of us are washing clothes around a tap—Mrs S. Mauli, Mrs J. Mauli and I. They look at me squelching my clothes on a rock and can barely conceal their amusement—apparently there are glaring deficiencies in my technique. They offer to wash my clothes, but that is out of the question. First, I'm indignant at the suggestion that I can't wash my own clothes, and then, I'm hardly going to hand over my undergarments to these matrons. They coax and cajole, tell me I'm like a son to them, but I stand firm. Mrs S. Mauli then simply reaches over, grabs my partially washed clothes, and proceeds to make quick work of them in the company of Mrs J. Mauli.

My Wari soon turns into a blur. As more palkhis join the procession the crowds grow impossibly dense, to the point that anyone not marching in the main procession is continually sidestepping rather than walking. I take to starting off at three or four in the morning to beat the crowds, and snatch naps on my plastic sheet wherever I can—under trees; in the porticos of shops; in temples; under a truck, where it's surprisingly cool and a world apart from the thousands of feet walking past. One morning at 5 a.m., A. Mauli tosses a small jar of Zandu balm to the stricken Mrs S. Mauli and Mrs J. Mauli as they prepare for a day of walking. As it flies past him, a man with a flowing white beard recognizes it all too well and nods sagely. 'Twenty-two rupees,' he says. 'It used to be twenty.' His face lights up: 'It's the 22nd today! Friday. You need to see dates change on a journey.' But I can't—day melds into night, one day into the other, and all I know is that with every step I'm getting closer to finishing the Wari.

Lonand. Taradgav. Phaltan. Barad. Natepute. Malshiras. Welapur. Bhandishegaon. Wakhri. People come and go. R. Mauli leaves so he can resume going to office; S. Mauli returns after setting right his transfer. A new member joins the dindi, bringing news that people in Pune are talking about building a shrine to the bullock that died while pulling the palkhi. He feels this is pointless: 'Anyway it has attained mukti.'

It's considered a spiritual windfall to die on the Wari. The fortunate are many. A truck with Warkaris overturns along the way killing nine. I run into a government-appointed doctor at a tea shop who tells me that two or three people die on the Wari every day from heart attacks. Many more suffer from respiratory and stomach infections. Ambulances are constantly howling their way through the crowds. There's a tent by the road where people suffering from exhaustion lie on the ground with bags of saline dripping into them. Near the end of the Wari I realize that I haven't seen the old man in our marching dindi for some time now. I look for him every time I pass the group, but I never see him again.

It's only four or five kilometres from Wakhri to Pandharpur. We reach before it's dawn and stop for a cup of tea. The monsoons still haven't arrived. A man is on his haunches beside the tea shop bawling like a child: 'It's not going to rain. It's not going to rain. Do something, Indira Gandhi, do something!'

By the Chandrabhaga river is a shrine to Pundalik, the man who, according to legend, brought Vitthala to

Pandharpur. Pundalik first neglected his parents, then devoted himself to their service with such zeal that when Vitthala visited him, Pundalik, who was massaging his father's legs, only had time to toss a brick over his shoulder for Vitthala to stand on. Vitthala, arms akimbo, is still on that brick, waiting for his devotees to come to him.

There are two lines to enter the temple. One is the *charan-sparsh* line, at the end of which devotees can touch the feet of the idol (whose black basalt rock is dented from centuries of plonked foreheads). This line extends for several kilometres and it can be days before one gets to the idol. The other is the *mukh-darshan* line, only hours long, where one gets a distant glimpse of the idol. This is the line we will wait in.

But first, we bathe in the Chandrabhaga. It's customary for strangers to come up to you and splash water or rub your back as a mark of brotherhood. Partly to avoid this, partly because I long for some solitude, I walk out to the middle of the river, where the water is chest high. After all that walking, my lightness in the water comes as a relief. I float on my back and close my eyes. But not for long—I'm brought back with a start by hoots and splashes. Amol and J. Mauli (Jr.) have sneaked up on me and are celebrating the end of the Wari with a water fight. 'Mauli!' they shout as they direct stinging trails of water at me. What choice does one have in this samsara? I fight back.

Two months after I return from the Wari, there's a death in the family. It's preceded by a sustained emotional pummelling—waiting in dread outside the ICU, jumping every time the phone rings, watching someone I've known all my life fade slowly away. On the thirteenth day after the death the family is supposed to emerge from mourning with a visit to a temple. We go to a Lakshmi temple down the road, one I've passed thousands of times without entering. There I peep into one of the supplementary shrines—it's Panduranga. I feel a rush of affection, as if I've run into an old friend. Now here's a fellow, solid as stone, who'll stand on his brick with his hands on his waist, and wait and wait and wait for you, and that can be no small thing amidst the swirling insubstantialities of life.

EPILOGUE

What is it like to travel in a group? After doing so ten times in a relatively short period, it's the regimented aspect of a conducted tour that stands out most prominently to me: being woken up early in the morning by the door-bell or telephone or by someone shaking me; the inability to dawdle, either in bed or at a place I've taken a liking to. Closely related to this sense of being relentlessly 'conducted' is the feeling of never being alone, taken to new lengths in outings such as the Shodh Yatra or the Wari, in which a week might pass without anyone bolting a door. It's an odd feeling for someone with a concept of privacy to bathe communally, to always be among people. In these cases, the travelling group becomes something of a collective organism.

The travelling unit tends to shape one's experience of the place being visited. I may have been in London, Shillong and Samarkand, but I've only seen those places through the lens of the groups I went with: largely an actual camera lens, the activist's earnest gaze, and a wildly wandering eye, respectively. No museums or parks in London; none of the music or liveliness that I'm told Shillong possesses; only a glance at the history and architectural splendour of Samarkand. To travel with a group is to experience some composite of place and one's fellow travellers. To write about such travel is to write from somewhere in between, a vantage from where both people and place reveal themselves in the other's light.

The occupants of a tour-bus may not be interested in

art or history or architecture, but a couple's first trip together in twenty years of marriage, or a woman visiting a place where she can dress differently and spend time with her husband away from their joint family is significant to them in its own way. Rushing around temples needn't necessarily be about faith or religion: it could serve to reaffirm one's place within a culture and landscape; it can be comforting just to know that there exist shared objects of reverence, even if it is a blank space behind a curtain. The Wari turns out to be more than a pilgrimage, serving for many of its participants as a well-earned break from routine, an occasion for festivity. In Uzbekistan, the fervour with which middle-aged men lapsed into adolescent frolic hints at the rigidity that may be imposed on their routine lives. Tours meant for foreigners, such as those in Kerala or Dharavi, show us being at once pandering and defiant hosts. In villages, people are looking to move to cities to claim their share of a seductive affluence. The children of those who did so a generation or two ago are beginning to look back to villages to see what has been lost in the process. Everywhere the concern is how to hold one's own amidst the tumult.

Too much is made of the difference between the traveller and the tourist. We all set out as a bit of both, and anyone who is alive to contrast, to the simple thrill of moving through places and being among new people, will return touched in some manner by the experience. In my own case I know that my reckoning of music, spirituality and ecology grew richer through some of these tours. More immediately apparent was the change in how I responded to the world around me. A newspaper report detailing caste discrimination in the mid-day meal scheme in Madhya Pradesh meant much more when I could put faces to some of those children and recall their mother's bitterness. After walking through arid villages and among worried farmers, I began to look at rain in a different light. This year, for the first time, I find myself tracking the monsoon's progress.

Things seen in one part of the country are refracted elsewhere—it's the same country after all. As I write this, the news is full of reports of devastation in Uttarakhand following flash-floods and landslides. Thousands have died; thousands more are missing. With environmentalists pointing out that deforestation and unauthorized sand mining have contributed to the severity of the disaster in Uttarakhand, I'm reminded of the delicate balance of the natural world we witnessed in Meghalaya. The touristification of pilgrimage, something evident on the Tamil Nadu tour, has been ongoing in Uttarakhand for a while now. Growing numbers of tourists have led to unauthorized and dangerous river-view guest houses, more roads, a greater requirement for water, power and fuel along with related infrastructure, and all this in an ecologically sensitive area. With large numbers of tourists comes a tourist economy. (Even a decade ago, in Rudraprayag, I was beset by touts for a service I hadn't imagined existed—for a price, they'd fill a bucket of water from the Ganga and deliver it heated to one's guest house for a comfortable *ganga snaan* in the bathroom.) A ruthlessly competitive tourist economy, like the one that has developed in Jaisalmer Fort, may easily contain within it the seed of darker things. The papers report that trapped pilgrims in Uttarakhand were charged extortionate amounts for food, water and even shade; there are dark stories of assault and robbery, of corpses with fingers and earlobes missing along with attached jewellery.

Yet, I wouldn't be surprised if the same people were capable of remarkable kindness at other times. In Jaisalmer Fort, I recall pleasant and quite obviously genuine moments in Raja's company before he cast me out of his guest house. He unburdened himself to me about the death of a friend; there was warmth in his inviting me to a party. But he had a harder side too, and different aspects of the man came to the fore at different times. I encountered this sort of multifacetedness repeatedly. In Uzbekistan, Sharmaji, whose aggression stood out on the dance floor and in the tour bus, was also capable of receiving a call from home and cooing, 'Haan beta, main toys lekar aaonga. Yes, my child, I'll bring toys.' Others on the tour, involved in obviously irreligious activities, suddenly turned pious on a Friday; Rajesh could tell me one day about his interest in spirituality and the arts, and on the next that he believed only in sex and money. On the Wari, a devout pilgrim took a break to fix his unwanted transfer and returned. It seems like the more compartmentalized one's thinking, the easier it is to deal with a complex world: people like the Regional Manager with his Om that dissolves only small brain tumours, or people like the IP lawyer who feels his sacred thread is practical because it presses on a nerve and prevents hydrocele, attempt to reconcile tradition and modernity but end up straddling the two uncomfortably. How much more graceful to be like Mrs S. Mauli, who lives comfortably in today's world while holding conflicting accounts of myth-history to be literally true. It may not be coincidence that so many figures in this myth-history possess multiple heads.

My life ended up being scheduled, for a couple of years, around the tours written about in this book. Looking back, the period itself feels like a giant, spread out conducted tour of my own fashioning, a tour of tours that sampled a vast land and a variety of people and their pursuits. Travel, even—despite Mr Pandey's qualms—travel with a group, offers glimpses of life in different places and conditions, provides intimate access to the lives of others. It is tempting to piece together these fragments from across the tours, to generalize, to generate insights. But those insights that yield themselves easily are obvious, and those that don't are debatable. It may be best to simply invoke that image of multiple heads and let these fragments coexist. After all, it is only the particular that can be said to be true, not the stories we weave from it.

Acknowledgements

Kamini Mahadevan, my editor at Penguin, who helped conceive this book, and then with patience and perspicacity helped bring it to its present form. This is her book as much as it is mine.

Also at Penguin: Ameya Nagarajan for insightful comments and suggestions, Paromita Mohanchandra for making editing painlessly pleasant, Nandini Mehta for the title, Aashim Raj for indulging my whims about the cover and Aman Arora for handling marketing and promotion.

Outlook Traveller magazine, on assignment for which I did two of the tours written about in this book. *OT*'s founding editor Kai Friese has been a great inspiration as a writer and a support as an editor. Amit Dixit unknowingly set this book in motion by sending me on my first conducted tour.

Natarajan Ramamurthy, Sonia Jose, Dnyanada Deshpande, Mathangi Krishnamurthy, Mary Therese Kurkalang, Hormazd Mehta, Samanth Subramanian and Anup Mathew Thomas for reading all or part of the manuscript and offering advice, corrections, reproach and approval.

Anil Ananthaswamy, for advice and encouragement; Smt. Sheela Godbole, Shri Zharkar and Shri Gambhire, for making my Wari possible at such short notice;

Jyothy Karat and Reality Tours and Travel, for permission to use their photographs; Raghu Karnad, for being generous with his time and for his enthusiasm about this book; Vinod Sreedhar, for sharing his insights about travel and travel companies; Samyuktha Varma, for insisting I go to Uzbekistan; Zac O'Yeah, for bringing to my attention the Shodh Yatra and for many beery discussions about the writing life.

Paola Martinez, under whose roof and care much of this book was written.

Madhu, Shruthi and my parents, for being there.

YOU MAY ALSO LIKE

Mother Earth, Sister Seed
Lathika George

A journey through India's farming calendar

In *Mother Earth, Sister Seed*, landscape designer Lathika George looks at India's traditional agricultural communities and the changes—some good, some not—that modernization and urbanization have wrought. Paying tribute to the ancient systems of farming, George talks about the men and women whose livelihoods are derived from the land and the sea. An organic gardener herself, she takes you through the changing seasons of agriculture as she travels around the country, from Rameshwaram in Tamil Nadu and Coorg in Karnataka to the Khasi Hills in Meghalaya and Chamba in Himachal Pradesh, documenting the celebrations, rituals, folklore and recipes associated with each.

Mother Earth, Sister Seed is a lyrical journey dedicated to ways of life that are vanishing. It captures the myriad ways in which the food we eat is produced and brings to life the industrious farmers, fishermen and forest folk behind it.

Non-fiction/PB

The Heart of India
Mark Tully

Stories of depth and eloquence that take us to the very heart of the Indian experience

For more than two decades Mark Tully was the BBC chief of bureau in Delhi, and his name and voice became synonymous with the country he had made his home. For years he sent back dispatches interpreting the subcontinent to the outside world, but the 'truth' of India is remarkably resistant to reportage.

Imbued with his love for the country and informed by his vast experience, Mark Tully has woven together a series of extraordinary stories. All the stories are set in Uttar Pradesh and tell of very different lives. Of a barren wife who visits a holy man and subsequently conceives—but is it a miracle or something more worldly? Of a son's carefully laid plot to take revenge against his father's murderer, with a surprising twist when his case comes to court. Of a daughter, persuaded by her friends to spurn an arranged marriage, whose romance ends in blackmail. Of a man's inability to overcome the conventions of caste and go into business, which leads to his wife breaking purdah and taking control of the family. In these and in other stories, Mark Tully delicately probes the nuances of life in India.

Non-fiction/PB

YOU MAY ALSO LIKE

Following Fish
Samanth Subramanian

'A little jewel of a travelogue'—*Outlook*

In a coastline as long and diverse as India's, fish inhabit the heart of many worlds—food, of course, but also culture, commerce, sport, history and society. Travelling along the coast, Samanth Subramanian tells extraordinary stories about people's relationships with fish—from the art of cooking and eating hilsa in West Bengal to the hunt for the world's fastest fish in Goa, from the history of a Catholic fishing community in Tamil Nadu to the infamous fish cure for asthma in Andhra Pradesh. Full of wit, intelligence and charm, *Following Fish* is a sparkling book and one of the best new non-fiction narratives from India.

Non-fiction/PB

YOU MAY ALSO LIKE

Land of the Seven Rivers
Sanjeev Sanyal

Did ancient India witness the Great Flood? Why did the Buddha give his first sermon at Sarnath? How did the Europeans map India?

Combining scholarship with sparkling wit, Sanjeev Sanyal sets out to explore how India's history was shaped by its geography—answering questions you may never have thought to ask. Moving from geological and genetic origins to present-day Gurgaon, *Land of the Seven Rivers* is riveting, wry and full of surprises.

Non-fiction/PB